To M......

Happy Birtho...

lots of love, Jill xxx

The *Essential*
JOSCELINE DIMBLEBY

The *Essential*

JOSCELINE DIMBLEBY

SIMON & SCHUSTER

LONDON • SYDNEY • NEW YORK • TOKYO • TORONTO

First published in Great Britain by Simon & Schuster Ltd in 1989

Text and recipes © Josceline Dimbleby 1989

This selection © Simon & Schuster Ltd 1989

Cover, title, Introduction and chapter frontispiece photographs © Simon & Schuster Ltd 1989

Other photographs © Sainsbury plc 1978, 1979, 1983, 1984, 1985, 1987, 1988

Simon & Schuster Ltd
West Garden Place
Kendal Street
London W2 2AQ

Simon & Schuster of Australia Pty Ltd
Sydney

British Library Cataloguing-in-Publication Data available.

ISBN 0-671-65315-6

Design and layout: Patrick McLeavey & Partners
Photographs on pages 2, 6/7, 10/11, 34/5, 54/5, 130/1, 146/7 and 206/7: Andrew Whittuck
Food preparation for photography: Allyson Birch
Stylist: Bobby Baker
Other colour photographs: Laurie Evans, John Lee and Bryce Attwell
Typesetting: Goodfellow & Egan, Cambridge
Printed and bound in Spain by Graficas Estella, S. A.

Pictured on the front cover: ; Levantine Lamb Pie (page 90); Saffron and Garlic Mashed Potatoes with Grated Courgettes (page 133); White Lie Bombe (page 153); Christina's Seafood Cradle (page 32).

Pictured on the back cover: Chocolate Rum Marquise (page 183); Intense Chocolate Cake with Redcurrants (page 168); Cranberry Casket filled with Gold (page 151).

Pictured on page 2: Prize Pumpkin (page 97).

Pictured on pages 6/7: Passion-fruit Thrill (page 178); Wrapped Fish Quenelles with Saffron and Vermouth Sauce (page 48); Vegetable Consommé with Shredded Lettuce (page 13).

CONTENTS

Part 1
FIRST COURSES

Soups 12
Pâtés, terrines and dips 17
Vegetables and salads 20
Eggs 28
Fish and shellfish 30

Part 2
LIGHT MEALS

Soups 36
Meat and poultry 37
Vegetables 44
Fish 47
Salads 52

Part 3
MAIN COURSES

Beef 56
Veal 63
Pork 67
Lamb 80
Poultry and game 92
Fish and shellfish 118
Vegetarian 127

Part 4
SIDE DISHES AND
ACCOMPANIMENTS

Vegetables and salads 132
Sauces 141
Dressings 144
Savoury breads 145

Part 5
DESSERTS

Frozen puddings, ice creams
    and sorbets 148
Gâteaux 160
Cheesecakes and jellies 175
Mousses and soufflés 182
Tarts, pies and flans 185
Meringue puddings 197
Fruit salads and fruity puddings 201

Part 6
CAKES, BISCUITS AND
SWEETS

Family and special occasion cakes 208
Bakes and biscuits 216
Mincemeat and sweets 218

INDEX 222

INTRODUCTION

Our kitchen in Damascus was a haven for me. In a busy Diplomatic household, my parents had many duties which couldn't involve a seven-year-old child, so I used to turn to the kitchen, where Joseph the cook and his 'cook's boy' (a beaming forty-five-year-old weighing at least eighteen stone) let me watch and taste as they worked. Outside, on a flat whitewashed roof, fresh apricots were cut in half and put out to dry in the sun. Inside, pomegranates from the garden were pressed through a sieve to produce juice for the evening's drinks. Unleavened bread was made; very thin and floppy, speckled black, with far more flavour than commercial pitta breads we buy now. The smell of freshly ground cumin and chopped mint were predominant. My mother, like her own mother, was a talented and imaginative cook, so when marriage to a Diplomat brought her a fully staffed kitchen and a change of country every three years, she encouraged the cooks to produce their local cuisine instead of the bland international food which can blight embassy life.

Back in England I always stayed with my grandmother and here too my taste buds were tickled at an early age by her excellent cooking. My grandmother really understood what the word delicious should mean. From her I learnt to love puddings; the magic of caramel, the thrill of sharp lemon and egg mixtures, the ecstasy of gooey chocolate and of bananas fried in butter with Barbados sugar and fresh orange juice. Her pièce de résistance was her rice pudding. She made this with brown rice, and cooked it long and slowly so that the result was rich, creamy, nutty and toffee-like, with a zest of lemon to set it off and a dark and wonderful skin. I have never been able to make a rice pudding taste so good. Because she appreciated real flavour my grandmother and I walked for what seemed to me miles to one of the rare health food shops to buy her brown rice, Barbados sugar, crunchy breakfast cereals, nuts, yogurt in little glass pots and my favourite treat – dried bananas.

Eventually I was sent to an English boarding-school where the food was an inevitable let-down. The domestic science classes were so uninspiring that I made no effort at all and my teacher said that I was the worst in the class. I don't know whether she lived to see my cookery books but she would certainly have been astonished that this was the direction her reluctant pupil had taken.

In spite of my enthusiasm for food I didn't do any cooking myself until just before I married. I remember feeling ashamed of the first meal I cooked for my husband – leathery steak and frozen peas – knowing that I could do better. And then a strange thing happened. When friends were coming to meals I would think about what I could cook them so much that I began dreaming about it. But my dreams were not vague, fantastical dreams; they showed practical, real and detailed methods of how things could be made. I began to try out the ideas and methods I had dreamed. To my amazement they worked. This was when I realised that I was lucky enough to be able to sense instinctively what tastes and textures would go well together, and to imagine unusual ways to cook and present them. I am not at all a secretive person, so I always wanted to share the ideas which had sprung from my sleep, and this was what led to my first book and its title *A Taste of Dreams*.

A year or two later, when Sainsbury's gave me the opportunity of writing the first cookery book to be sold in their stores, I found how fulfilling it was to be able to reach such a lot of people, to receive their letters, and discover that having used my recipes they had often found a new and unexpected interest in food. Both I and Sainsbury's were surprised to find that their customers were much more adventurous than we had imagined; they were enthusiastic about my rather unconventional ideas and eager to try out different herbs and spices. Thus it was that in many of my books for Sainsbury's I was able to indulge my penchant for aromatic foods by devising straight-forward recipes which needed no special skill, knowledge, equipment or obscure ingredients, but which nevertheless tasted definitely exotic.

I trained as a singer, not as a cook, but work which revolves around food has fitted in better with family life. In any case, I have always thought that the sensual pleasures of food and music go naturally together. I have never met a musician who was not interested in food.

The most exciting aspect of food for me is the creative one. A new taste or texture can suggest several different possibilities, an unfamiliar dish experienced abroad often shows me that an entirely different approach to certain ingredients can produce some exciting new results. I enjoy not being a purist about food, because if I obey no rules I feel that every conjunction is possible. I am a compulsive experimenter, and find it very difficult to repeat a dish as the urge to try doing it in a new way or with a change of ingredients is always so strong.

Although I have never had cooking lessons, the chemistry of cooking that I have learnt by experiment has also been a fascinating way of revealing new ideas. I enjoy too the different character which emerges in my cooking if I am in a new environment and atmosphere. For some inexplicable reason, which I know is not simply a change of oven, the baking I do while we are at our holiday cottage in Devon is better than at home. My cakes are lighter, my bread rises better and my pastry is more delicate; crisp just for a moment before crumbling in the mouth. Then there is the complete change of cooking abroad. Even though we can now buy such an enormous variety of imported ingredients, cooking with local foods while abroad is often a revelation as everything tastes quite different. Cooking outside produces a unique flavour, and often the most appreciated food of all. In Devon we cook on a rack over a driftwood fire on the beach; appetites are keen as the sea breeze, and pieces of lamb or chicken, marinated beforehand in yogurt and spices, are sublime with the flavour of wood smoke.

Since I began writing recipes I have always tried to use utensils that most kitchens would contain, so that I and my readers are approaching the dish from the same standpoint. In any case I am not at all gadget- or machine-orientated. There are, however, certain things which I would hate to be without. Above all else I must have really sharp knives. The intense pleasure of slicing meat or vegetables with a sharp knife and the terrible frustration of trying to do the same with a blunt one must be one of the most dramatic contrasts in the kitchen. Personally I have never really mastered peeling vegetables thinly with a knife and cannot do without my little swivel-bladed peeler, and one machine I now find indispensible is the food processor. This machine really has at least quartered the preparation time for so many things and made countless dishes possible for busy people, who would never have been able to attempt them in the days when they required labour, patience and often skill. I use my food processor mainly for all kinds and combinations of vegetable purée for which I have a passion. But within seconds I can also make mayonnaise, pastry, fish and meat pâtés, batters, soups and so on. I find the grating blade extremely useful (and a saving on grated knuckles) but unless I want vegetables sliced paper thin and uniform for a particular purpose I prefer to slice them by hand.

The shape and colour of the dishes you use either to cook or to serve food in should be thoughtfully chosen to suit the colour and shape of your recipe. It makes all the difference to the reception your food will have, and the memory it will leave, if its appearance is good. I have always liked earthenware, and its comparatively low price makes it possible to collect several sizes and shapes of dish. Cast iron is expensive but will last for years and has the great advantage that it can be used straight over the heat on top of the stove for sautéeing and boiling, or put into the oven for casseroling and roasting. If someone is prepared to give you a generous present, or if you feel like making an invaluable investment, I urge you to go for a copper pan lined with stainless steel. For years I was too frugal to contemplate splashing out on copper pans. Now that I have a large copper sautée pan and saucepans I wish I had bought them long ago, since they will obviously last at least as long as I do and there is no re-lining to worry about. They conduct the heat evenly and quickly and are a greater pleasure to use than any other kind of pan.

As much as I like creating mystifying flavours, I like presenting food in a beautiful but mystifying way so that someone may exclaim with excited anticipation 'What can this be?' I like my meals to be slightly theatrical, like an enjoyable play with contrasting acts. And I must say that I do enjoy applause at the end; I am afraid that I wouldn't have felt very happy in past eras when it was considered impolite to mention the food at a meal.

I love passing on my ideas to others, but I also want people to enjoy my dishes so much that they begin to have ideas of their own. This book gives you a wide range of my creations, conceived over several years; if after using the book you are inspired to invent even one personal recipe then I shall feel it has succeeded.

Josceline Dimbleby

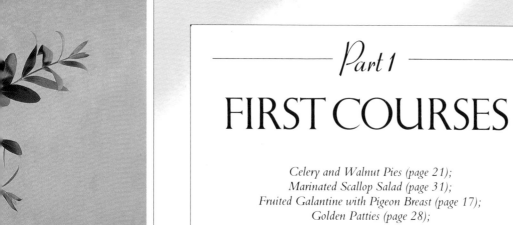

Part 1

FIRST COURSES

Celery and Walnut Pies (page 21);
Marinated Scallop Salad (page 31);
Fruited Galantine with Pigeon Breast (page 17);
Golden Patties (page 28);
Jellied Cream of Spinach and Sorrel Soup (page 16)

COLD SPICED MUSHROOM AND TOMATO SOUP

This cold soup has a Moroccan flavour, being spiced and slightly hot to
the taste. It is very easy to prepare and always seems to stimulate the
appetite. It tastes particularly good as part of a summer meal.

2–3 cloves of garlic, sliced
5 tablespoons olive oil
1 rounded teaspoon paprika
1 teaspoon ground
cinnamon

397 g (14 oz) can of
tomatoes, chopped
juice of 1 small lemon
juice of 1 large orange

250 g (8 oz) large
mushrooms, sliced roughly
1 large, fresh green chilli,
de-seeded under running
water and chopped finely

1 tablespoon tomato purée
600 ml (1 pint) water
6 tablespoons natural yogurt
fresh mint leaves, chopped,
to garnish

Put the sliced garlic in a largish saucepan with the
olive oil. Heat the oil and let the garlic just sizzle over
a medium heat for a minute or so, until beginning to
brown. Add the paprika and cinnamon and stir
around over the heat for a moment. Remove from
the heat and add the tomatoes, lemon and orange
juice, sliced mushrooms and chopped chilli. Finally,
stir the tomato purée into the water and pour into the
pan. Cover, bring to the boil and leave to simmer
gently for 30–40 minutes.

Transfer to a bowl, leave to become cold and chill
in the fridge. Before serving, spoon the soup into
individual bowls and add a large blob of yogurt to
each. Sprinkle the chopped mint leaves on top, as a
garnish.
Serves 6

CHILLED ALMOND AND GARLIC SOUP

Garlic is only really pervasive when it is raw or only briefly cooked;
longer cooking brings out its sweet, mild flavour and smooth consistency.
There are all sorts of garlic soups in Spain, some with almonds in them,
some not, but in my experience they are always served hot. My version,
which is a beautiful creamy white, is chilled instead and I find it extremely
popular. A bright red whirl of paprika, lemon juice and cayenne is
dribbled on top of the white soup.

1 large head of garlic
1 large spanish onion,
chopped roughly

900 ml (1½ pints) milk
125 g (4 oz) ground
almonds

the juice of 1 small lemon
2 teaspoons paprika

3–4 pinches of cayenne
pepper
salt

Separate the garlic cloves from the head and peel
them. Put the garlic cloves and the chopped onion
into a largish saucepan and add 300 ml (½ pint) of the
milk. Bring to the boil, cover the pan and then
simmer very gently for 20–25 minutes until the
onions and garlic are very soft. Pour into a food
processor, add the ground almonds and whizz until
you have a smooth paste. Turn the paste back into the
saucepan and stir in the remaining 600 ml (1 pint)
milk. Season generously with salt. Bring to the boil,
stirring all the time, and simmer, still stirring, for 8–10
minutes. Pour into a bowl and leave to cool, then chill.

This is meant to be a thick soup, but if it is
necessary, you can thin it with a little milk. Then to
serve it, mix the lemon juice with the paprika and
cayenne pepper in a cup with a teaspoon. Spoon the
chilled soup into individual bowls and spoon the
lemon and paprika in a whirl on top of the soup in
each bowl.
Serves 4

VEGETABLE CONSOMMÉ WITH SHREDDED LETTUCE

The lightest possible kind of soup can be useful to have in the house.
Pictured on pages 6/7.

1 large onion	*375 g (12 oz) carrots*	*2 teaspoons caster sugar*	*3–4 tablespoons dry sherry*
500 g (1 lb) tomatoes	*1.5 litres (2½ pints) water*	*2 Little Gem lettuces or 2 lettuce hearts*	*salt and black pepper*

Wash the onion but don't peel it. Then cut it into eight. Cut up the tomatoes and the carrots roughly. Put all the vegetables into a saucepan and pour in the water. Season with salt and black pepper and the caster sugar. Cover the pan, bring it to the boil and simmer it for about 1½ hours.

Line a large sieve with a thin, clean linen teacloth and put it over another saucepan. Pour the soup into the sieve, pushing gently with a wide wooden spoon to get all the liquid through the sieve and the teacloth. Check the soup for seasoning and discard the vegetables. Before re-heating the soup, slice the lettuces across as thinly as you can. Bring the soup to boiling point, add the shredded lettuce, bubble for half a minute only, and then remove from the heat. Stir in the sherry to taste and serve. White bowls look prettiest for this clear, golden soup.
Serves 4–6

WALNUT SOUP

This is an excellent, creamy soup of walnuts and soft, sweet onion.

1 large onion	*1 level tablespoon caster sugar*	*25 g (1 oz) plain flour*	*a handful of finely chopped parsley*
2 tablespoons olive oil		*600 ml (1 pint) good chicken or turkey stock*	*142 ml (5 fl oz) carton of soured cream*
25 g (1 oz) butter	*1 level teaspoon ground mace*	*750 ml (1¼ pints) milk*	*salt and black pepper*
125 g (4 oz) walnut pieces			

Peel the onion, cut it in half and slice it as thinly as possible. Put the olive oil with the butter in a large, heavy saucepan and melt the butter over a medium heat. Add the sliced onion and cook, stirring frequently, for 10 minutes or so until is is softened and slightly browned. Meanwhile, put the walnut pieces in a food processor and grind them finely; don't leave the machine on too long or the nuts will stick together and become oily.

When the onion has softened, remove the pan from the heat and stir in the caster sugar, the ground mace and the ground walnuts. Then stir in the flour. Gradually add the chicken or turkey stock and the milk. Put the saucepan back on the heat and bring it to the boil, stirring frequently. Let it bubble, stirring all the time for 2–3 minutes; then cover the pan and let it simmer very gently for 20 minutes. Adjust the seasoning to taste with black pepper and salt. Before serving, stir the chopped parsley into the soup, and, when it has been ladled out into soup plates, spoon some soured cream on to the soup in each plate.
Serves 6

CHILLED AUBERGINE AND RASPBERRY SOUP

Fruit is often good in soups and this unusual combination works well. The
sweet and sharp raspberries lend themselves well to the rich savoury taste
of aubergine. They also give the soup a pretty pink colour.

*3 aubergines, weighing
about 250–275 g (8–9 oz)
each*

*a little lemon juice or white
wine vinegar
125 g (4 oz) raspberries
fresh or frozen*

*600 ml (1 pint) single
cream
ice cubes*

*salt, sea salt and freshly
ground black pepper
1 tablespoon chopped
chives, to garnish*

Cut the stalks off the aubergines and cut in half
lengthways. Make 3 deep slashes in the flesh of each
half, sprinkle with lemon juice or vinegar and rub well
with salt, rubbing into the slashes too. Leave the
aubergines flesh side down in a colander for ½ – 1
hour to drain away any bitter juices.

Preheat the oven to Gas Mark 4/180°C/350°F.
Rinse the aubergines very well and pat dry. Press the
aubergine halves together again and wrap each aubergine up in foil. Lay them in a roasting pan and cook
in the centre of the oven for ¾ – 1 hour until the flesh
is soft when you stick a knife in it.

Leave until cold; then scoop out the aubergine
flesh and put in a food processor or liquidiser. Add the
raspberries and 450 ml (¾ pint) of the cream and
whizz until smooth. Season with sea salt to taste and
plenty of freshly ground black pepper. Pour the soup
through a sieve to remove any pips, pressing through
with a wooden spoon into a bowl. Chill well in the
fridge. Before serving, pour the soup into individual
soup bowls, add a few ice cubes, dribble on the
remaining cream and sprinkle the top with the
chopped chives.
Serves 6

TWO ONION SOUP

This simple soup, with its slight flavour of orange, makes a more delicate
start to a meal than the traditional onion soups.

*750 g (1½ lb) small to
medium-size onions,
peeled and sliced finely
in rings
4 large cloves of garlic,
sliced*

*4 whole cloves
300 ml (½ pint) orange
juice, from a carton of
unsweetened orange juice*

*1 chicken stock cube, mixed
with 600 ml (1 pint) water
juice of 1 lemon*

*1 bunch of spring onions,
chopped finely, using as
much of the green part as
possible
450 g (15 oz) carton of
natural yogurt
salt and black pepper*

Put the sliced onion, sliced garlic and cloves in a
saucepan with the orange juice and chicken stock.
Bring to the boil, cover the pan and simmer very
gently for ¾ – 1 hour. Add the lemon juice and season
to taste with salt and black pepper. Add the chopped

spring onion to the soup and simmer for another 3–5
minutes. Pour the soup into a hot serving bowl and,
just before serving, stir the yogurt around with a fork
and then mix it, only roughly, into the soup.
Serves 6–8

Chilled Aubergine and Raspberry Soup; Two Onion Soup

JELLIED CREAM OF SPINACH AND SORREL SOUP

Pictured on pages 10/1.

*500 g (1 lb) spinach
a good handful of sorrel
leaves*

*50 g (2 oz) butter
preferably unsalted
25 g (1 oz) plain flour
4 x 425 g (14 oz) can of
consommé*

*450 ml (³/4 pint) milk
juice of 1 lemon
300 ml (½ pint) creamed
smetana*

*salt and black pepper
sprigs of fresh dill, to garnish*

Pull the leaves off the spinach and sorrel and discard the stems. Roughly chop the leaves. Melt the butter in a large heavy saucepan and stir the chopped spinach and sorrel into it. Remove from the heat and stir in the flour. Heat the consommé in another saucepan with the milk and then pour gradually into the spinach saucepan, stirring. Put back on the heat and bring to the boil, stirring all the time. Then put a lid on the pan and simmer gently for about 10 minutes until the spinach is very soft. Remove from the heat and stir in the lemon juice.

Put the mixture (you will probably have to do this in two or more goes) into a food processor and whizz until the spinach is chopped very finely. Mix the soup together again and season to taste with salt and black pepper. Now spoon into individual bowls (glass ones look pretty) and chill in the fridge for at least 1½ hours. When chilled and jellied, spoon a layer of the creamed smetana on top of the soup in each bowl but don't stir it in. Lastly, decorate with feathery pieces of fresh dill, and keep in the fridge until ready to eat.
Serves 8–10

CREAM OF POTATO AND SAFFRON SOUP WITH COURGETTES

This soup can be made even more of a complete meal, and a treat, if you throw in some peeled fresh prawns, mussels or cockles at the last moment.
Pictured on page 27.

*4–6 cardamom pods
125 g (4 oz) butter
750 g (1½ lb) potatoes,
chopped roughly*

*8 large cloves of garlic
50 g (2 oz) plain flour
1.75 litres (3 pints) milk
a generous pinch of saffron
strands*

*4–5 pinches of cayenne
pepper
500–750 g (1–1½ lb)
courgettes cut into small
cubes*

*300 ml (½ pint) creamed
smetana or soured cream
sea salt*

Extract the seeds from the cardamon pods and grind them up in a pestle and mortar. Melt the butter in a large saucepan over a low heat and stir in the ground cardamom seeds. Add the chopped potato and the whole cloves of garlic and turn around to coat with butter. Then stir in the flour. Gradually stir in the milk and add the saffron threads, the cayenne pepper and a sprinkling of sea salt.

Bring to the boil, stirring all the time until the milk has thickened, then cover the pan and leave to simmer very gently for 20–25 minutes, until the potato is very soft. When the potato is cooked, whizz the contents of the saucepan in a food processor until smooth – you will have to do this in two or more goes, depending on the size of your food processor.

Pour the smooth soup back into a saucepan, check for seasoning, bring to the boil, add the cubed courgettes, cover the pan and simmer gently for 4–6 minutes until the courgettes are just cooked but still bright green and slightly crunchy. Then stir in the smetana or soured cream (and the prawns, mussels, etc., if using.) Pour into a pretty soup tureen.
Serves 8–10

CREAMY AUBERGINE PURÉE

This most delicious cold purée from Turkey is deceptively easy to make
and aubergines are plentiful in the shops during the winter. It is very light
in texture and has a distinctive smoky taste. Serve it as a first course with
toast, as a dip at a buffet or simply as a snack.

2 medium-size aubergines
juice of ½ lemon

about 3 tablespoons
sunflower oil

salt and black pepper

a little chopped parsley, to
garnish

Put the aubergines, unpeeled, under a very hot grill, turning them once or twice until the skin is black and beginning to blister. This will probably take 15–25 minutes. Now peel off all the skin. As they will be hot this is easier to do under cold water. Put them in a large sieve and press them down with a wooden spoon or a plate so that as much juice as possible comes out of them. They will now look like old rags, but don't worry, a miraculous transformation is about to take place! Put them into the liquidiser with the lemon juice. Whizz up and add the sunflower oil a little at a time until the mixture is smooth, pale and light. The more you add, the lighter the texture.

Add salt and pepper to taste. Store in a covered plastic dish in the fridge for up to a week, or freeze. To serve, spoon into a bowl and sprinkle on a little chopped parsley.
Serves 6

FRUITED GALANTINE WITH PIGEON BREAST

This galantine is simple to make and looks very pretty when cut in slices.
Pictured on pages 10/1.

1 wood pigeon
250 g (8 oz) turkey livers
59 g (2 oz) unsalted cashew
nuts

50 g (2 oz) soft pitted
prunes, chopped roughly
2 teaspoons chopped
tarragon

3 large cloves of garlic
2 skinned chicken breast
fillets, weighing 250 –
300 g (8–10 oz) in total

oil for greasing
300 g (10 oz) rindless
smoked back bacon rashers
sea salt and black pepper

Using a sharp knife and keeping close to the bone, cut the breasts off the pigeon (keep the carcase for making stock). Skin the breasts and cut them into thin strips. Put these into a bowl with the whole turkey livers. Mix in the cashew nuts and the chopped prunes and tarragon. Peel and slice the garlic and add to the mixture. Season with plenty of black pepper and a sprinkling of sea salt. Put the chicken breast fillets between two sheets of polythene or oiled, grease-proof paper and bash them with a rolling pin until they are thin and spread out. Oil a 500 g (1 lb) loaf tin and line the sides and base with all but two or three of the bacon rashers. Then line the tin once more with the thin pieces of chicken breast, reserving some, with the bacon rashers, for the top. Now spoon the liver and pigeon mixture into the tin and top it with the remaining pieces of chicken breast, followed by the reserved rashers of bacon. Cover with foil. Put a roasting pan half-full of water in the centre of the oven and heat to Gas Mark 3/160°C/325°F. Put the tin in the water for 2 hours.

Lift the foil, pour off the juices into a bowl and strain and reserve them in the fridge. Cover the galantine again with foil and then put a board on top and weigh it down with weights or books. Leave until cold. Dip the tin briefly in hot water and then shake out the galantine on to a board. To keep it in the fridge, wrap it in cling film. Before serving, put the galantine on to a serving plate, melt the juices and brush them all over. Refrigerate until you are ready to eat it.
Serves about 8

NOUVELLE TERRINE

This is typical of the new style of cooking which developed in France and has now become popular in England. I find that this kind of food succeeds best as the first course to a meal because it is always pretty and never too filling. This light terrine has a base of chicken breast which encloses layers of bright green broccoli and prawns (you can of course experiment with other vegetables). Its appearance always impresses people, but if you have a food processor it is deceptively simple to make, and it is most useful at a party since it will feed so many.

For the terrine:
a little oil for greasing
125 g (4 oz) calabrese broccoli, with any thick stalks removed and cut lengthways into small florets

375 g (12 oz) chicken breast fillets, skins removed
250 g (8 oz) curd cheese
6 tablespoons double cream
1 teaspoon cayenne pepper
2 large egg whites (size 1–2)

finely grated rind of ½ orange
125 g (4 oz) peeled prawns, thawed if frozen

For the sauce:
2 large egg yolks (size 1–2)

juice of 1 orange
1 tablespoon tomato purée
1 tablespoon red wine vinegar
250 ml (8 fl oz) milk
1 handful of fresh dill or parsley, chopped finely
salt and black pepper

Preheat the oven to Gas Mark 3/160°C/325°F. To make the terrine, oil a 1 kg (2 lb) loaf tin and line the base with a piece of oiled greaseproof paper. Blanch the broccoli florets in a pan of boiling salted water for 1 minute and drain. Put the chicken breast fillets in a food processor and whizz until finely minced. Add the curd cheese and cream, season well with the cayenne pepper and salt and whizz again. Finally, add the egg whites and whizz until very smooth.

Turn into a bowl and stir in the grated orange rind. Spread about a third of the mixture in the prepared loaf tin and then arrange half the broccoli on top of this, interspersed with about half the prawns. Now spread on half the remaining mixture followed by the rest of the broccoli and prawns and, finally, top with the last of the mixture. Cover the top of the tin with foil. Put a roasting pan half full of water just below the centre of the oven. Place the terrine in the water and cook for 40–45 minutes until firm. Remove from the oven and leave to cool.

Put the egg yolks, orange juice, tomato purée and wine vinegar in a pudding basin and whisk to mix together. Stir in the milk a little at a time. Put the basin over a saucepan half full of simmering water and stir constantly for 5–8 minutes until only very slightly thickened. Remove from the heat and season to taste with salt and black pepper. Leave to cool and then stir in the chopped dill weed or parsley.

Chill both the terrine and the sauce in the fridge. When cold, loosen the sides of the terrine with a knife and turn out on to a board. Using a sharp knife cut into slices each about 2 cm (¾ inch) thick. Spoon the sauce thinly over individual plates and put a slice of the terrine carefully in the centre of each before serving.
Serves 8–10

Pear and Calf's Liver Flower (page 24); Mango Chicken Salad (page 24); Nouvelle Terrine

GLOWING RING

A purée of carrots gives dazzling colour to this light and delicious chilled mousse.

500 g (1 lb) carrots, peeled and cut up roughly
3 teaspoons gelatine
250 g (8 oz) cream cheese

2 tablespoons white wine vinegar
a little oil for greasing
300 ml (½ pint) whipping cream

a few lovage or continental parsley leaves (optional)
2–3 heads of chicory
salt and cayenne pepper

a few slices of carrot, to garnish

Put the chopped carrots in a saucepan with salted water just to cover. Boil until cooked. Remove from the heat, spoon 6 tablespoons of the hot carrot water into a cup, sprinkle the gelatine into this and stir until dissolved. Then drain the carrots and put in a food processor with the dissolved gelatine, cream cheese and wine vinegar. Whizz until completely smooth. Season, more heavily than usual because of the cream to be added later, with salt and cayenne pepper.

Oil a 1.2-litre (2-pint) ring mould tin. When the carrot mixture is cool, whip the cream until thick but not stiff. Fold into the carrot mixture (it looks pretty if you leave it slightly streaky) and then spoon into the ring mould. Chill in the fridge for several hours. Then rub the tin with a cloth wrung out in hot water, loosen the edges with a round-bladed knife and, giving a firm shake, turn out on to a large serving plate.

Arrange the lovage or continental parsley in a circle on top, if used. Take a few whole smaller leaves from the heads of chicory and fan them out round the centre of the ring. Take the remaining chicory leaves and fill the centre of the mould. Garnish with a few slices of carrot and chill in the fridge until ready to eat.
Serves 8–10

BLACK PEARL MUSHROOMS

500 g (1 lb) mushrooms
a bunch of spring onions
3 cloves of garlic

6 tablespoons olive or sunflower oil
coarsely grated rind and juice of 1 lemon

1 tablespoon red wine vinegar
a handful of finely chopped parsley

a pot of Danish lumpfish caviare
a bunch of watercress
salt and black pepper

Slice the mushrooms fairly thinly. Cut the roots off the spring onions and chop the rest into 2.5 cm (1 inch) pieces using as much of the green part as possible. Peel the garlic cloves and slice them across very thinly.

Put the oil into a large, deep frying-pan over a medium heat, add the sliced garlic and stir it around for a minute or so; add the sliced spring onions and the grated lemon rind and stir for a minute more. Next add the lemon juice, the wine vinegar and the sliced mushrooms to the pan. Stir for a minute or two until the mushrooms are just beginning to soften. Remove the pan from the heat, add plenty of black pepper and stir in the chopped parsley. Turn the mixture into a bowl and when it has cooled, stir in the Danish lumpfish caviare; check for seasoning and add a little salt only if necessary. Keep in the bowl, covered, in the fridge.

When ready to eat, spoon the mixture on to a serving plate and pick the leaves off the watercress stems to use in bunches as a border.
Serves 6

CELERY AND WALNUT PIES

These little pies should be served hot but they can be made ahead and
re-heated. Serve them, if you like, as a first course; I make a cold sauce to
accompany them from a can of chopped tomatoes, seasoned with a real
bite of cayenne pepper and a little lemon juice; or serve them as
something to nibble with drinks. The pies have a flaky, cheesy pastry
which is quickly made.
Pictured on pages 10/1.

For the filling:
2 celery hearts, weighing about 375–425 g (12–14 oz) in total
3 large cloves of garlic
50 g (2 oz) butter
1 teaspoon dill seeds

1 tablespoon plain flour
250 ml (8 fl oz) milk
2 rounded teaspoons whole-grain mustard
18 walnut halves
3–4 good pinches of cayenne pepper
salt

For the pastry:
250 g (8 oz) plain flour, plus extra for rolling
½–1 teaspoon salt
about 175 g (6 oz) frozen butter

50 g (2 oz) mature Cheddar cheese, grated coarsely
6–7 tablespoons cold water
milk

Make the filling first. Chop the celery hearts into small
pieces. Peel and chop the garlic finely. Melt the butter
in a largish frying-pan, add the celery and cook it over
a gentle heat, stirring now and then, for 10–15
minutes, until soft. Then add the chopped garlic and
the dill seeds and continue cooking for another 5
minutes. Remove the pan from the heat and stir in
the flour. Then gradually stir in the milk. Put the pan
back on the heat and let it bubble, stirring all the time,
for about 3 minutes, until thickened. Stir in the
mustard. Season to taste with salt and the cayenne
pepper. Turn into a bowl, cover with a piece of
greaseproof paper and leave on one side to cool.

Now make the pastry. Sift the flour and salt into
a bowl. Holding the block of frozen butter in a cloth
at one end, grate it coarsely, mixing it into the flour
a bit at a time with a fork. Then fork in the grated
cheese. Finally mix in the cold water with a fork until
the dough begins to stick together. Gently press it

together into a ball and leave it in the fridge for 30
minutes or more. Roll out just under three-quarters
of the dough on a floured surface to about 3 mm
(⅛-inch) thick. Cut out 18 rounds with a 7.5 cm
(3-inch) diameter pastry cutter and line the tins. Pile
a heaped tablespoon of the filling in each round and
then place a half-walnut on top of the filling. Roll out
the remaining dough and, using a 6.5 cm (2½-inch)
cutter, cut out another 18 rounds to top the pies. Put
the tops on and press the edges to seal. Cut a slit in
the top of each pie for the steam to escape.

Heat the oven to Gas Mark 7/220°C/425°F.
Brush the tops of the pies with milk. Cook them in
the centre of the oven for 15–20 minutes until golden
brown. After removing them from the oven leave the
pies to rest in the tins for 8–10 minutes before gently
easing them out with a knife and transferring them to
a cooling rack, or a plate.
Makes 18 little pies

AVOCADO ORANGES

Don't make this more than two hours in advance.

2 medium-size oranges
1 tablespoon white wine
vinegar

3 tablespoons olive oil
1 teaspoon Dijon mustard
1 large ripe avocado

1 handful of parsley,
chopped finely
4 small pinches of cayenne
pepper

salt and black pepper
lettuce leaves, to garnish

Cut the oranges in half crossways. Using a small sharp knife, carefully cut and scoop out the orange flesh and juices into a bowl, discarding the seeds and pith. Put the vinegar, olive oil and mustard in a jam jar with a lid and season well with salt and black pepper. Put the lid on the jar and shake up to mix; then add the orange flesh. Cut the avocado in half and scoop out the flesh with a teaspoon. Put these scoops in a bowl with the orange flesh and dressing. Add the chopped parsley and mix well. Leave in a cool place.

Just before serving, place the scooped-out orange halves on individual plates. Spoon in and pile up the orange mixture in each half and sprinkle a small pinch of cayenne pepper on the top of each. Add one or two lettuce leaves to each plate, to garnish.
Serves 4

GLOSSY-TOP AVOCADO GÂTEAU

This decorative vegetable first course has a pale green avocado base and a glistening top of carrot and cucumber slices set in lemon aspic. Serve with hot crusty bread. Make sure that you eat this dish the same day it is made.

125 g (4 oz) carrots,
scraped and sliced very
thinly in rounds
300 ml (1/2 pint) salted
water
2 teaspoons gelatine

juice of 1 lemon
125 g (4 oz) piece of
cucumber, peeled and sliced
as thinly as possible in
rounds

1 large avocado
3 teaspoons white
wine vinegar
375 g (12 oz) curd cheese
cayenne pepper

salt and black pepper
extra gratings of carrot to
garnish

Put the sliced carrot rounds in a saucepan with the salted water, cover the pan and bring to the boil. Simmer for about 5 minutes or until the carrots have softened. Using a slotted spoon, remove the carrots and put aside on a plate. Sprinkle the gelatine into the pan of water and stir over the heat until dissolved. Remove from the heat and stir in the lemon juice. Season to taste with salt and cayenne pepper.

Pour a little of the pan juices through a strainer into the bottom of a 1.2- litre (2-pint) soufflé dish. Lay in some rounds of carrot backed by larger rounds of cucumber in a neat pattern. Lay the remaining cucumber on top of this, followed by the rest of the carrots. Strain in the remaining pan juices. Cool and then chill in the fridge until set.

Cut the avocado in half, scoop the flesh out into a bowl, sprinkle with the wine vinegar, add the curd cheese and mash together very thoroughly until smoothly mixed (or simply whizz together in a food processor). Season to taste with salt and black pepper. Spoon the mixture on top of the set, jellied vegetables and spread level. Chill well.

Shortly before serving, loosen the sides with a round-bladed knife, turn the dish upside-down on to a serving plate and rub the bottom with a hot cloth. Give a shake to turn out, sprinkle the extra gratings of carrot around the base and chill again.
Serves 6

Glossy-top Avocado Gâteau; Avocado Oranges

PEAR AND CALF'S LIVER FLOWER

Pictured on page 19.

For the calf's liver:
3 teaspoons ground coriander
3 teaspoons paprika
4 good pinches of cayenne
pepper

2 tablespoons caster sugar
2 tablespoons olive oil
1 teaspoon water
250 g (8 oz) thick pieces
of calves' liver
salt

For the spinach
mayonnaise:
375 g (12 oz) spinach
150 ml (¼ pint) olive oil
juice of 1 lemon
1 teaspoon caster sugar

For the pears:
2 large ripe pears
a little lemon juice
a sprig of mint or other
fresh herb, to garnish

Heat the grill to its highest. Prepare the liver: put the coriander, paprika, cayenne, caster sugar and a sprinkling of salt in a small bowl. Stir in the olive oil and water. Put the pieces of liver into this sauce to coat. Lay the liver on the grill and spoon over any extra sauce. Grill very close to the heat for 2–3 minutes on each side, depending on thickness – the insides should still be pink. Transfer the liver on to a plate to cool.

Now make the 'mayonnaise'. Pull the stalks off the spinach and plunge the leaves into boiling salted water. Boil for 2–4 minutes until just soft. Turn into a colander, rinse through with cold water to cool and then drain very thoroughly, pressing out the liquid by wringing the bundle of spinach in your hands until as dry as possible. Put in a food processor or liquidiser and whizz until fine. Then add the olive oil very gradually, whizzing all the time. Whizz in the lemon juice and the caster sugar. Lastly, season to taste with salt and black pepper. Spread the spinach mixture over a fairly large round serving plate.

Peel the pears, halve them lengthways, slice thinly lengthways and smear with lemon juice to stop them discolouring. Arrange about half the slices round the edge of the spinach, like separate petals. Then, using a sharp knife, slice the liver finely. Arrange these slices overlapping each other in a starburst a little further in from the pear slices. Arrange the remaining pear slices like a full flower in the centre of the dish and place a sprig of mint or other herb in the middle, if you wish.
Serves 6

MANGO CHICKEN SALAD

Pictured on page 19.

500 g (1 lb) skinless
chicken breast fillets
white wine vinegar

500 g (1 lb) can of sliced
mangoes
4–6 good pinches of
cayenne pepper

40 g (1½ oz) plain cashew
nuts
1 clove of garlic, peeled

2 heaped tablespoons
mayonnaise or soured cream
salt and black pepper
2 – 3 heads of chicory

Using a sharp knife, cut the chicken fillets into 2.5 cm (1-inch) pieces. Lay them all over the bottom of a shallow pan or dish and pour in just enough wine vinegar to cover. Leave for ½ –1 hour until the chicken has become pale. Then steam the chicken pieces, either in a steamer or in a large sieve over boiling water in a big covered pan, for 5–6 minutes.

Strain the juices from the mangoes into a mixing bowl, add a generous seasoning of salt, black pepper and the cayenne pepper and then stir in the hot chicken pieces. Leave until cold. Meanwhile, toss the cashew nuts round over a fairly high heat in a dry pan until just golden-brown. Leave on one side.

When the chicken is cold, strain the mango juice into a food processor through a sieve and add the sliced mango and peeled garlic. Whizz together until smooth and then whizz in the mayonnaise or soured cream. Spoon into the bowl and mix with the chicken.

Shortly before serving, arrange the chicory leaves to fan out round a fairly flat serving dish; then spoon the mango chicken mixture into the centre and scatter the toasted cashew nuts on top.
Serves 6

AVOCADO AND WATERCRESS SURPRISE

8 medium-size to large eggs
(size 2–3)
a little oil for greasing
juice of 1 lemon

1 teaspoon white
wine vinegar
1 tablespoon water
3 teaspoons gelatine

2 large or 3 medium-size
avocados
1 bunch of watercress, with
the stalks removed
3 Petit Suisse cheese

1 teaspoon caster sugar
a little single cream
(optional)
radicchio lettuce leaves
salt and black pepper

Poach the eggs in oiled poachers over gently simmering water for 4–6 minutes until the whites have just set, and they are still soft inside. Turn them out on to a plate and leave on one side to cool.

Put the lemon juice, wine vinegar and water in a saucepan. Sprinkle in the gelatine, put over a medium heat and stir until the gelatine has dissolved into the liquid. Remove from the heat.

Cut open the avocados and scoop out the flesh. Put in a food processor, pour in the hot gelatine liquid and then add one third of the watercress leaves and the Petit Suisse cheeses. Whizz until very smooth.

Add the caster sugar and season to taste with salt and black pepper. If the mixture seems rather stiff, add a little single cream if you like. Turn the mixture into a bowl and leave for a short time to cool.

Lay one or two radicchio leaves on individual plates. Put a poached egg in the centre of each plate, near the end of the radicchio. When the avocado mixture is cold (thick but not set), spoon heaped tablespoons of the mixture over the poached eggs, covering them completely. Arrange the remaining watercress leaves around the edge. Cool, then serve.
Serves 8

EASTERN PROMISE

2 tablespoons white
wine vinegar
1 large or 2 medium
aubergines weighing about
500 g (1 lb)
6 tablespoons extra-virgin
olive oil

2 large cloves of garlic,
chopped finely
2 teaspoons paprika
2 teaspoons cinnamon
3 tablespoons lemon juice
25 g (1 oz) sultanas

500 – 625 g (1–1¼ lb)
courgettes, cubed
4 pinches of cayenne pepper
a handful of fresh dill,
chopped

40–50 g (1½–2 oz) pine
kernels
about 16 large cup-shaped
radicchio leaves
sea salt

Put the wine vinegar into a saucepan of water and bring to the boil. Meanwhile slice the unpeeled aubergines across into 1 cm (½-inch) slices and then cut into 1–1.5 cm (½–¾-inch) cubes. Add to the saucepan, cover and bring to the boil; then simmer for 10 minutes until the aubergine pieces are soft. Drain in a colander and then on absorbent paper.

Put 3 tablespoons of the olive oil in a large, deep frying pan, preferably one which has a lid. Put the open pan over a high heat and add the aubergine.

Fry, stirring now and then, for about 5 minutes. Then add the chopped garlic and stir for half a minute. Next add the paprika and cinnamon and stir around for another 2 minutes. Now add the remaining 3 tablespoons of olive oil, the lemon juice, the sultanas

and the cubes of courgettes. Season with sea salt and the cayenne pepper. Stir round to mix the ingredients, cover the pan with a lid or foil and put back on the heat for 3–4 minutes, stirring once or twice, just until the courgettes are bright green. Then remove from the heat, add the chopped dill and spread the mixture on to a large plate to cool quickly.

Put the frying pan back over a high heat and empty in the pine kernels. Toss about for a minute or two until browned. Then add to the cooling vegetable mixture and leave until cold, but don't refrigerate. Before serving, arrange large cup-shaped radicchio leaves on individual plates, and spoon the vegetable mixture on to the leaves.
Serves 8

VEGETABLES IN A LIGHT CRUST

I first made this as a main course for supper when we had two vegetarian guests. At a large dinner party it can be made as an extra dish for vegetarians, or you can serve it as a first course. Non-vegetarians will never complain if it is served instead of meat or fish because it tastes so good. Leeks, bulb fennel and grilled red peppers are combined in a thick, creamy cheese sauce with lots of fresh dill added to it. This mixture is put into a puff pastry crust which has been ingeniously cooked upside down over a cake tin so that it is absolutely crisp. As a main course I serve this with a bowl of new potatoes and a tomato salad.

1 large red pepper
1 large bulb of fennel
500 g (1 lb) leeks, trimmed
125 g (4 oz) butter, plus extra for greasing

75 g (3 oz) plain flour
600 ml (1 pint) milk
125 g (4 oz) mature Cheddar cheese or Vegetarian Cheddar, grated coarsely

¼ of a whole nutmeg, grated
250 g (8 oz) packet of puff pastry
1 egg yolk

1 bunch fresh dill, chopped
salt and black pepper

Cut the red pepper in half lengthways and discard the seeds and stems. Then put it skin upwards under a very hot grill until thoroughly blackened in patches. Cool slightly, then peel off the charred skin and cut into short thin strips. Cut the base and stalks off the fennel, reserving any feathery pieces to mix with the dill later. Slice the fennel into 2.5–4 cm (1–1½-inch) lengths. Slice the trimmed leeks across in 5 mm (¼-inch) rings.

Now melt the butter in a fairly large, heavy saucepan over a medium heat. Add the sliced fennel and leeks and stir over the heat for about 10 minutes until softened. Then remove from the heat and stir in the flour. Gradually stir in the milk, return to the heat and bring to the boil, stirring often. Then simmer, stirring constantly for 2–3 minutes until thickened. Add the grated cheese and stir until melted. Then sprinkle in the grated nutmeg and season to taste with salt and black pepper. Add the grilled pepper pieces.

Butter a large baking sheet. Put a 15 cm (6-inch) diameter deep cake tin upside-down on the sheet and smear very generously with butter all over. Roll out the puff pastry in a roughly circular shape measuring about 30 cm (12 inches) so that it is big enough all over to cover the cake tin and touch the baking sheet. Lay the pastry over the tin and press lightly in folds against the side of the tin with the overlapping edges at the bottom spread out on the baking sheet. Prick the pastry lightly all over with a fork. If there is time, leave for 20–30 minutes in a cool place.

Heat the oven to Gas Mark 7/220°C/425°F. Brush the pastry all over with the egg yolk and put the baking sheet on the centre shelf of the oven for about 20 minutes until the pastry is a rich brown. Remove from the oven and leave for a few minutes to cool slightly. If necessary, very carefully loosen the sides between the pastry and the cake tin with a round-bladed knife. Gently ease the cake tin up out of the pastry case and put the case into a large, round but shallow serving bowl.

Reheat the filling mixture, stir in the chopped dill, spoon the mixture slowly and gently into the pastry case and serve at once.

Serves 4 as a main course, 6 as a first course

Vegetables in a Light Crust; Cream of Potato and Saffron Soup with Courgettes (page 16)

SPRINGTIME EGGS

A variation of French *'Oeufs en Gelée'*, these glossy little cocottes look
pretty with their mixture of green and orange.

6 eggs
250–500 g (8 oz – 1 lb)
spring greens, according to
the size of the cocotte
dishes

25 g (1 oz) piece of carrot,
peeled and shredded very
finely
450 ml (3/4 pint) water

2 tablespoons white
wine vinegar
2 teaspoons caster sugar
1 teaspoon ground coriander

2 teaspoons gelatine
salt and black pepper

Using a poacher, soft poach the eggs (4–5 minutes)
and leave on one side. Tear only the leaf part off the
spring greens, and discard the stems. Plunge into a pan
of salted, boiling water for just 2–3 minutes. Drain
well, pressing out all the liquid. Divide the greens
between 6 cocotte dishes and, using your fingers,
press firmly right up the sides of the dish to line all
round. Then pop the poached eggs into the centres –
in this way they will be encircled by the greens.

Put the carrot shreds in a pan with the water, wine
vinegar, caster sugar and ground coriander and season
with salt and black pepper. Now cover the pan and
boil gently for 5 minutes. Remove the pan from the
heat, sprinkle in the gelatine and stir around for a
minute or two to dissolve. Then spoon the carrot and
the liquid evenly into the filled cocotte dishes. Cool
and then chill in the fridge before serving.
Serves 6

GOLDEN PATTIES

These always prove a bit of a mystery, because no-one can quite identify
the ingredients. I invented them as a hot first course, and they can also be
handed round as a snack with drinks. The patties are like little mousseline
omelettes, but the lovely flavour is produced by a combination of eggs,
grated carrot, cheese, nutmeg and rosemary. Sometimes I put anchovy
fillets on the tops, sometimes not – they are good both ways,
so it is up to you.
Pictured on pages 10/1.

125 g (4 oz) butter, plus
extra for greasing
4 large eggs (size 1–2),
separated
3 tablespoons milk
175 g (6 oz) carrots, grated
75 g (3 oz) mature
Cheddar cheese, grated

1/4 – 1/2 whole nutmeg,
grated
leaves of 1 good sprig of
fresh rosemary, chopped
finely
50 g (2 oz) fresh brown
breadcrumbs

50 g (1 3/4 oz) can of
anchovy fillets
sea salt and black pepper
watercress, to garnish

For the sauce:
225 g (7 oz) carton of
Greek yogurt or 250 g
(8 oz) fromage frais
sea salt and black pepper

Generously butter two trays of 12 patty or bun tins.
Whisk the butter in the bowl of an electric mixer until
soft. Then whisk in the yolks of the eggs and continue
to whisk until pale. Gradually whisk in the milk (it
does not matter if the mixture curdles). Then stir in
the grated carrots, cheese, nutmeg and the chopped

rosemary. Season with plenty of black pepper and a
sprinkling of crushed sea salt. Stir in the breadcrumbs.
Heat the oven to Gas Mark 5/190°C/375°F.
Now whisk the egg whites until they stand in soft
peaks and fold into the mixture a little at a time, using
a metal spoon. Spoon the mixture into the patty or

bun tins, (they should be almost full up). Tear off pieces of anchovy and put a piece on top of each pile of mixture. Put one tray on the centre shelf of the oven and bake for 15–17 minutes until golden brown.

Remove from the oven and put in the second tray to cook. Carefully lever out the cooked patties with a round-bladed knife and arrange them on a serving plate. Repeat with the second tray when they are cooked. If you are eating soon, simply keep the patties warm in a low oven. If eating much later, put the cold patties on a baking tray, and re-heat them briefly in a low to medium oven.

For the sauce, simply put the yogurt or fromage frais into a mixing bowl, season with salt and black pepper and spoon into a serving bowl. Serve the sauce cold with the hot patties. If liked, garnish the serving plate of patties with small sprigs of watercress.
Serves 6

TEA LEAF EGGS

This is a Chinese idea which one can vary with different flavourings. It is easy to do and the appearance of the brown marbled eggs always intrigues people. The eggs are boiled for a long time with aromatic tea leaves and other flavourings, which all permeate and colour the flesh of the eggs. They can also make an unusual and tasty addition to a picnic.

6 large eggs (size 1–2)
1 large onion, unpeeled but cut into quarters
1 orange, unpeeled but cut into quarters

5 cm (2-inch) piece of fresh ginger, unpeeled but chopped roughly
1 teaspoon whole cloves
5 teaspoons Earl Grey tea

1 tablespoon soft dark brown sugar
4 teaspoons salt
1 teaspoons cayenne pepper

To serve:
5 tablespoons salad oil
2 tablespoons white wine vinegar
1 medium-size curly endive
salt and black pepper

Simply put all the ingredients (except those for serving) in a saucepan. Cover with water and put a lid on the pan. Bring up to the boil and then simmer gently. After about 20 minutes knock each egg so that the shell cracks. Continue simmering for 2½ –3 hours, checking every so often to see that the water isn't boiling away too much. Leave the eggs to cool in the pan.

To prepare for serving, arrange a bed of the curly endive on a pretty serving plate or on individual plates. Peel the eggs, cut in half lengthways and arrange yolk side down on the leaves so that their speckly marbling shows. Just before serving, mix the oil, vinegar and seasoning together and spoon over the eggs and curly endive.
Serves 6

STUFFED SMOKED SALMON PARCELS

Serving smoked salmon on its own as a first course is an easy but expensive way out. These parcels, with a filling of fennel purée, curd cheese and skinned broad beans are a good way of stretching the smoked salmon, but also show that you have been more imaginative, and have taken time and trouble over the dish – an effort which will please and flatter your guest. These quantities can be multiplied if there are more than two of you.

1 small bulb of fennel, cut up roughly	*50 g (2 oz) curd cheese*	*75 g (3 oz) smoked salmon, sliced thinly*	*salt and cayenne pepper*
½ tablespoon lemon juice	*40 g (1½ oz) frozen broad beans*		*lettuce leaves*

Chop the feathery green fennel leaves finely and reserve. Boil or steam the fennel for about 10 minutes until completely soft. Drain and leave until cold (or rinse with cold water to cool). Pat dry.

Then put in a food processor with the lemon juice and the curd cheese and whizz until smoothly mixed. Season to taste with salt and cayenne pepper and then turn into a mixing bowl. Put the broad beans into a bowl, cover them with boiling water, then drain and pop the green insides of the beans out of their skins into the bowl of fennel mixture.

When all the beans are popped, stir them into the mixture. Add the fennel fronds. Cut the smoked salmon into squares – roughly 7 x 7 cm (3 x 3 inch). Spoon some of the stuffing mixture into the centre of each square and then bring up the four corners together to make parcels. Cover the parcels loosely with cling film and chill in the fridge. To serve, arrange the parcels on a bed of lettuce leaves.
Serves 2

SMOKED OYSTER SURPRISES

You can serve these stuffed pork meatballs at a supper for six, accompanied by vegetables or simply by bread and salad, but I like them best as a snack if friends come over for a drink, in which case they would serve about ten people. If you want to make them ahead, they also taste good eaten cold.

625 g (1¼ lb) lean pork mince	*2.5 cm (1-inch) piece of fresh ginger*	*2 rounded teaspoons whole-grain mustard*	*1 tablespoon sunflower oil*
1 large clove of garlic		*105 g (3 ½ oz) can of smoked oysters*	*salt and black pepper*

Put the minced pork into a bowl. Peel the garlic and ginger, chop them together finely and then mix them into the pork, with the mustard, a sprinkling of salt and a generous grinding of black pepper. Drain the oysters, reserving the oil. Take up small handfuls of the pork mixture and flatten them out into circles like little hamburgers. Place a smoked oyster in the centre and wrap the meat up round the oyster to enclose it. Form into a ball. Continue like this until the meat is used up and then smear the oil from the oyster can over the meatballs. Heat the sunflower oil in a large frying-pan over a medium heat. Fry the meatballs for about 15 minutes, turning them gently.
Serves 6–10

SUBLIME SCALLOPS IN THEIR SHELLS

8 large fresh scallops with
shells
lemon juice
8 small florets of calabrese
broccoli

300 ml (1/2 pint) dry
white wine
1 rounded teaspoon caster
sugar
a pinch of saffron strands

2 teaspoons gelatine
somewhat less than 300 ml
(1/2 pint) creamed smetana
salt

2–3 pinches of cayenne
pepper

Cut the orange coral from the scallops and keep whole. Slice the white part of the scallops across thinly. Put the slices and the coral close together in a shallow dish and cover with lemon juice. Leave on one side while you prepare the rest of the ingredients.

Cut the broccoli florets into small sprigs, cutting off any stems. Steam or boil the broccoli for a few seconds only, just until bright green. Then rinse with cold water to cool, and leave on one side. Put the white wine in a saucepan, and bring to the boil. Remove from the heat and stir in the caster sugar, the saffron strands, salt and cayenne pepper to taste. Add the gelatine and stir until completely dissolved.

Put the scallops into a sieve to drain off the lemon and then rinse them with cold water. Put a heaped dessertspoon of creamed smetana into the centre of each scallop shell. Place the corals of the scallops on top of the smetana, and arrange the scallop slices all around. Dot the sprigs of broccoli amongst the slices, with some making a border around the edge of the shells. Then put the shells onto patty tins to keep them level, and slowly spoon the wine and saffron mixture into each shell. Leave until the aspic is cold, then carefully transfer, on the patty tins, to the fridge and leave until set.
Serves 8

MARINATED SCALLOP SALAD

Make sure the ones you buy are very fresh. The benefit of marinating rather than cooking them is that they don't shrink, so that you seem to have more of them, and they have a smoother, softer texture. In fact the scallops don't taste raw: the lemon juice, in effect, lightly 'cooks' them.
Pictured on pages 10/1.

6 large fresh scallops
juice of 3 large lemons
500 g (1 lb) tomatoes

extra-virgin olive oil
a good sprig of fresh dill,
chopped finely or 4
teaspoons dried dill

3 large avocados
salt and black pepper

sprigs of fresh dill, to garnish

Slice the white part of the scallops into 3 – 4 slices and the orange part into 2. Put the scallops in a bowl and pour over the lemon juice – there must be enough to cover the scallops. Sprinkle with black pepper, cover the bowl and leave in the fridge for half an hour, or more if convenient. Pour boiling water over the tomatoes in a bowl, leave for a moment, then peel them and cut across in thin round slices.

Pour the lemon juice from the scallops into a jam jar and then add about double the amount of olive oil, and season; shake vigorously or whisk with a fork to make a vinaigrette dressing. Mix the chopped dill

with the scallops. Shortly before you want to eat, cut the avocados in half, remove the stones, peel off the skin carefully and slice across thinly in half-moon slices. Arrange the avocado slices alternately with the tomato slices on a large, shallow, circular serving dish, leaving a space in the middle for scallops. Spoon the scallops on to the space, overlapping the avocados and tomatoes slightly. Lastly, spoon the vinaigrette dressing over the whole dish and garnish with sprigs of fresh dill. Serve as soon as possible, with crusty bread, if you like.
Serves 6

LITTLE MUSSEL PIES

For the pastry:
250 g (8 oz) plain flour
1 teaspoon turmeric
150 g (5 oz) butter, cut into small pieces
cold water

For the filling:
50 g (2 oz) stoned green olives, chopped very finely
2 cloves of garlic, chopped very finely
2 tablespoons tomato purée

150 ml (5 fl oz) double cream
3–4 pinches of cayenne pepper
150 g (5 oz) can of natural Danish mussels, drained

1 handful of parsley, chopped finely
salt
small lettuce leaves, shredded, to garnish

To make the pastry, sift the flour and turmeric into a bowl. Rub the butter into the flour with your fingertips until the mixture resembles breadcrumbs. Add just enough cold water to make the dough begin to stick together, mixing it in with a fork. Form into a ball, wrap in cling film and leave in the fridge for half an hour or more. Preheat the oven, to Gas Mark 6/200°C/400°F.

Mix the chopped olives and garlic together in a bowl with the tomato purée and cream, seasoning with the cayenne pepper and a very little salt. Stir in the mussels and chopped parsley.

Roll out the pastry to about 3 mm (⅛ inch) thick and cut out circles with a 7.5 cm (3-inch) fluted cutter. Line tartlet or patty tins with the pastry – there will be some left over. Spoon some filling into each pastry lining – there will also be some filling left over. Cook the pies just above the centre of the oven for about 20 minutes until the pastry and tops are lightly browned. Leave the pies in the tins for a few minutes and then gently ease out with the edge of a knife.

Roll out the remaining pastry and line as many tins as it will make, putting some filling in each. Cook as before. Arrange the pies on a flat ovenproof serving dish or plate so that you can warm them up gently before you are ready to eat them. Garnish the dish with shredded lettuce leaves.
Serves 8

CHRISTINA'S SEAFOOD CRADLE

My friend Christina is the best natural cook I know and she made this delectable dish to inspire me. At times when fresh mussels and scallops are plentiful it is a delight.
Pictured on the front cover.

For the pastry crust:
250 g (8 oz) strong plain flour
1 teaspoon salt
150 g (5 oz) butter
2 tablespoons water

For the filling:
300 ml (½ pint) water
1 glass of white wine
1.75 kg (4 lb) mussels, washed and scrubbed

1 clove of garlic, chopped finely
a generous 25 g (1 oz) cornflour

4 scallops, cut into halves
1 tablespoon lemon juice
1 large handful of parsley, chopped finely
salt and black pepper

Sift the flour and salt into a bowl. Melt the butter gently in the water in a small saucepan and then add to the flour, a little at a time, stirring with a wooden spoon to form a soft dough. Press the warm dough evenly over the bottom and up the sides of a 19–20 cm (7½–8-inch) deep, loose-based cake tin. The top edge will probably be uneven, but this is as it should be. Refrigerate the lined tin for at least 30 minutes. Preheat the oven to Gas Mark 6/200°C/400°F.

Loosely crumple up pieces of foil and fill the pastry-lined tin with them. Bake the pastry for 20–25 minutes until it is golden-brown round the edge. Take out of the oven, remove the foil and put the pastry back in the oven for another 5 minutes. Take out and leave to cool a little in the tin, and turn the oven down to Gas Mark 1/140°C/275°F. When fairly cool, push the pastry case up carefully out of the cake tin and put it, still on the base for safety, on to an earthenware serving plate. Put back in the very low oven to keep warm while you prepare the filling.

Put the water and wine in a large saucepan and bring to the boil. Add the mussels, cover the pan and boil for 3–5 minutes until all the mussels have opened (discard any which do not). Strain the liquid into another saucepan. Now take the mussels from their shells and put aside in a bowl. Put the liquid back on the stove, adding the chopped garlic. Cover the pan and boil gently for about 5 minutes; then remove the liquid from the heat. Mix the cornflour with 3 table-spoons water until smooth and stir into the liquid with a wooden spoon. Bring to the boil and simmer, stirring for 2–3 minutes until thickened. Season to taste with salt and black pepper.

Add the halved scallops, cover the pan and bubble for about a minute, just until they look opaque. Remove from the heat and add the lemon juice followed by the mussels and chopped parsley. Leave for about 5 minutes before spooning slowly into the warm pastry case. Serve.

Serves 6–8

SAFFRON SEA CAKES

Once in a while it is lovely to have a crispy-fried hot first course and these little crab and fish cakes are irresistible. If you use groundnut oil for the frying it won't smell, and you can make the cakes in advance of your meal and keep them hot in a low oven. It is important to start preparing this dish well beforehand, to allow the fish mixture to get properly cold.

75 g (3 oz) butter
2 cloves of garlic, chopped finely
50 g (2 oz) plain flour, sifted, plus extra for flouring
300 ml (½ pint) milk

1 packet of powdered saffron
250 g (8 oz) cod fillets, skinned and cut into fairly small pieces
200–250 g (7–8 oz) crab meat, fresh or canned

1 handful of parsley, chopped finely
about 5 tablespoons breadcrumbs
groundnut oil for frying

salt and black pepper
whole sprigs of parsley and lemon slices, to garnish

Melt the butter in a saucepan and add the chopped garlic. Remove from the heat and stir in the sifted flour. Gradually stir in the milk and sprinkle in the saffron. Put back on the heat and bring to the boil, stirring all the time with a wooden spoon. Bubble, still stirring, for about 2 minutes. Add the pieces of cod, reduce the heat and bubble gently, still stirring, for 3–4 minutes only. Remove the pan from the heat and add the crab meat. Season well with salt and black pepper and stir in the chopped parsley. Turn the mixture into a shallow dish or roasting pan and leave until cold; then chill thoroughly in the fridge.

Put the breadcrumbs in a bowl and flour your hands. Take up small amounts of the mixture and lightly roll each into a round shape, roughly the size of a ping-pong ball. Dip the cakes in the breadcrumbs. Heat deep groundnut oil in a heavy saucepan or a deep frying pan and fry the cakes, only 3 or 4 at a time, over a high heat for a short time until rich golden-brown. Take out with a slotted spatula and drain on kitchen paper towelling. When all the cakes are cooked, keep warm in a low oven. Before serving, garnish with the parsley sprigs and lemon slices.

Serves 6–8

Part 2
LIGHT MEALS

Leek and Parsnip Soup (page 36); Chinese Hedgehogs (page 41);
Exotic Ravioli (page 42); Pear and Pork Parcels (page 41);
Yellow Pepper Tart (page 45)

LEEK AND PARSNIP SOUP

There is no need to wonder where the inspiration for this soup came
from: it is, of course, a version of one of France's most famous soups,
Vichyssoise. I have had many different versions of it in France, ranging
from a thick, steaming-hot, homely mixture to something chilled and
delicate with a satin-smooth texture. This recipe, in which I use parsnips
instead of potatoes for their lovely sweet taste, veers towards the homely,
being a good family soup to have for lunch with crusty bread.
Pictured on pages 34/5.

75 g (3 oz) butter	500 g (1 lb) leeks, trimmed	450 ml (3/4 pint) milk	2 good tablespoons chopped
250 g (8 oz) parsnips,	and sliced roughly	1 tablespoon lemon juice	chives
peeled and chopped	600 ml (1 pint) chicken	150 ml (5 fl oz) single	salt and black pepper
	stock	cream	

Heat the butter in a large, heavy-based saucepan over
a medium heat. Add the chopped vegetables and stir
them around in the butter for about 5 minutes. Then
add the chicken stock, cover the saucepan and simmer
the contents gently for 15–20 minutes.

Pour the soup into a food processor or liquidiser
and whizz it until smooth. Pour the purée back into
the saucepan and stir in the milk. Season to taste with
salt and black pepper. Reheat the soup gently and
then stir in the lemon juice. Just before serving roughly mix in the cream and the chopped chives.
Serves 4

CLEAR CHICKEN BALL AND WATERCRESS SOUP

This is a really pretty looking soup and it is simple to make. Glowing
white balls of chicken breast, flavoured with lemon and tarragon, float
amongst watercress leaves in a clear lemony consommé. You can serve
the soup either as a first course or for a light summer lunch accompanied
by bread and cheese.

275 g (9 oz) skinned	finely grated rind and juice	a bunch of watercress	300 ml (1/2 pint) water
chicken breast fillets	of 1 lemon	2 x 13 oz (400 g) can of	salt and black pepper
2 teaspoons finely chopped	1 egg white	beef consommé	
tarragon			

Either mince or chop the chicken breast fillets finely
in a food processor. Put in a bowl and add the
chopped tarragon and lemon rind. Season well with
salt and black pepper and then beat in the egg white
thoroughly with a wooden spoon. Using wet hands
form the mixture into small balls. Pick just the leaves
off the watercress stems and keep on one side. Empty
the consommé into a saucepan and add the water.
Strain in the lemon juice through a fine sieve and
bring to a rapid boil. Then drop in the chicken balls
and boil for 4–5 minutes. Add the watercress leaves
to the soup, remove from the heat after a second or
two and serve.
Serves 6

EGYPTIAN PIZZA

Since the Egyptian cook who I watched making what looked like a kind
of layered pizza worked so swiftly and spoke no English I could not be
sure of how he did it; but for these I have used a Chinese pancake method
and have recreated the Egyptian flavour from memory. Served with a
green salad it makes a good supper dish. If you want a more fiery taste
scatter on a finely chopped green chilli as well.

For the dough:
375 g (12 oz) plain flour,
plus extra for rolling
½ teaspoon salt
300 ml (½ pint) boiling
water

For the filling:
groundnut oil
250 g (8 oz) lean ground
beef
1 teaspoon ground cinnamon

4–6 pinches of cayenne
pepper
1 tablespoon tomato purée
40 g (1½ oz) butter
1 egg

125 g (4 oz) small onions
(red ones if available),
chopped small
a large handful of parsley,
chopped roughly
sea salt

To make the dough, sift the flour and salt into a bowl
and gradually pour in the boiling water, stirring with
a wooden spoon until the mixture sticks together.
Then gather it up and knead it with the palms of your
hands on a flat surface for a few minutes until the
dough is smooth and elastic. Cover it with cling film
and leave it for 30 minutes or more but do not chill.
Meanwhile, heat 1 tablespoon of groundnut oil in a
frying pan over a high heat. Add the ground beef and
stir it around, digging with a spoon to break it up. Add
the ground cinnamon and the cayenne pepper and stir
the beef for 4 –5 minutes until browned. Then stir in
the tomato purée, and remove the pan from the heat.

Melt the butter in a saucepan and put it on one
side. Break the egg into a bowl and whisk it lightly
with a fork. Now roll the ball of dough out on a
floured surface into a large circular shape 45 –50 cm
(18–20 inches) in diameter. Brush it all over with the

melted butter and then evenly scatter on the cooked
meat, the chopped onion and the parsley, and sprinkle
it lightly with sea salt. Pour the egg roughly over the
centre and roll up the pancake, making a long, flattish
roll. Now carefully fold over the roll into a spiral to
form a sort of wheel. Using plenty of flour, roll out
the circle into a large pancake 25–28 cm (10 –11
inches) in diameter and 1–2 cm (½–¾-inch) thick.
If you have a very big frying pan roll the pancake
slightly wider.

Heat a film of groundnut oil in a large frying pan
over a medium heat. Carefully transfer the pancake
to the pan and fry it for a few minutes until it is rich
brown underneath. The easiest way to turn it is with
a wide spatula and an oven glove, literally lifting it up
and over. Fry the other side and then turn it on to a
serving plate and serve at once.
Serves 4–5

MY MOTHER'S STEAK TARTARE

I much prefer this version to the usual recipe. Developed years ago by my
mother, it incorporates mayonnaise instead of egg yolks into the raw beef.
Use fresh, not frozen, beef for this recipe. Serve it as a first course or as
part of a cold meal accompanied by rather thickly cut wholemeal bread.

*8 tablespoons mayonnaise
(a good commercial kind
will do)*

*1 large onion, chopped finely
a good handful of parsley,
chopped finely*

*2–3 teaspoons capers,
chopped finely
lettuce leaves*

*500 g (1 lb) fresh ground
beef*

Mix the mayonnaise with the onion, parsley and
capers. Arrange the lettuce leaves on four individual
serving plates. Shortly before you eat mix the beef
with the mayonnaise mixture and spoon into a pile
on top of the lettuce leaves.
Serves 4

WELLINGTON PIES

These are little open-topped cold pies – suitable for a picnic or a cold
meal. They are made with lean beef which is cooked so that it is still pink
in the centre. Amidst the meat is a surprise smoked oyster, which imparts
a lovely, smoky flavour to the whole pie. The crisp, tasty pastry is made
with olive oil.

*For the pastry:
175 g (6 oz) plain flour
1/2 teaspoon salt
4 tablespoons olive oil
2 tablespoons water*

*For the meat mixture:
500 g (1 lb) lean beef mince
a bunch of spring onions,
chopped finely, using as
much of the green part as
possible*

*1 teaspoon green peppercorns
105 g (3 1/2 oz) can of
smoked oysters, drained
salt and black pepper*

Oil 8 deep patty tins. To make the pastry, sift the flour
with the salt into a bowl. Heat the oil and the water
in a saucepan until beginning to bubble; then add the
hot liquid to the flour gradually, stirring in with a
wooden spoon. Press the warm dough into a ball and
then divide into 8 pieces. Press a piece of dough with
your fingers into each patty tin to line, bringing the
dough up above the edge of the tins. Put in the fridge
for a short time and preheat the oven to Gas Mark
6/200°C/400°F.

When the pastry is cold and firm, put the tins just
above the centre of the oven and cook for 15 minutes
or until golden brown. Remove from the oven and
leave on one side while you prepare the filling, turning the oven up to Gas Mark 8/230°C/450°F.

Put the minced beef in a bowl. Add the chopped
spring onions and green peppercorns; then season
with salt and a little black pepper. Mix thoroughly
together with a wooden spoon. Put a heaped teaspoon of the mince mixture into each lined patty tin
and then lay the smoked oysters on top, dividing them
evenly between the pies. Spoon the remaining mince
on top of the oysters to enclose them, heaping the
mince up and over them. Cook the pies towards the
top of the oven for 10–15 minutes until just browned
on top. Leave to cool in the tins and when cold ease
the pies out with a spatula. Serve cold but not chilled.
Serves 4 or 8

KIDNEY AND BACON DUMPLINGS

A bowl of soured cream to spoon over the kidneys when you cut into the
pastry is nice.

375 g (12 oz) parsnips	2 teaspoons baking powder	12 thin rashers of rindless	1 egg yolk
12 skinned lamb's kidneys	½ teaspoon salt	bacon	salt and black pepper
375 g (12 oz) plain flour	175 g (6 oz) butter		

Peel the parsnips and steam or boil until soft. Then purée in a food processor, adding a little salt, and leave until cold.

Cut the kidneys almost in half, and, with kitchen scissors, snip out the white core piece.

Sift the flour, baking powder and salt into a mixing bowl and add a generous sprinkling of black pepper. Cut the butter into the bowl and crumble it into the flour with your fingertips until it looks like coarse breadcrumbs. Add the cold parsnip purée and with floured hands work it into the mixture, kneading slightly until you have a smooth dough.

Roll the dough out thinly and evenly on a well-floured surface. Cut out a square of pastry approximately 10 x 10 cm (4 x 4 inches). Roll a rasher of bacon around one of the kidneys and place it in the centre of the square of pastry. Dampen the edges and bring the pastry up around the kidney, pressing the edges to seal it in completely. Continue with the rest of the kidneys, re-rolling the pastry as necessary.

Grease a large shallow ovenproof dish and lay the pastry-wrapped kidneys, join side down, in the dish. If there is time refrigerate until ready to cook.

Heat the oven to Gas Mark 6/200°C/400°F. Brush the pastry parcels with egg yolk and cook in the centre of the oven for 25–30 minutes until rich golden brown.
Serves 6

CRUNCHY STUFFED MEATBALLS

124 g (4 oz) cracked wheat or couscous	4 tablespoons mango chutney	a small handful of parsley, chopped	groundnut oil for deep-frying
500 g (1 lb) lean beef mince	a handful of mint leaves, chopped	1 large egg (size 1–2)	salt and black pepper
1 large clove of garlic, chopped finely			

Put the cracked wheat or couscous in a bowl, cover with plenty of cold water and leave to soak. Put the minced beef in a bowl. Mix in the chopped garlic and season well with salt and black pepper. Put the chutney in another small bowl and mix in the chopped mint and parsley leaves. Take up enough mince to form into a ball the size of a ping-pong ball and then flatten it in the palm of your hand so that it looks like a small hamburger. Put a blob (a scant teaspoon) of chutney in the centre and then very gently bring up the sides of the meat to enclose it, patting lightly into a ball again. Continue like this until all the mince is used up.

Drain the cracked wheat through a sieve and press out the moisture with a wooden spoon. Whisk the egg lightly in a bowl. One at a time, dip the meatballs in the egg and then in the cracked wheat, lightly patting it on to coat thickly.

Heat fairly deep oil in a large frying pan to a very high heat. Put in the meatballs and fry, turning carefully only once, for 2–3 minutes on each side until light golden brown. Lift out with a slotted spoon and drain on kitchen paper towelling. If possible, eat at once; otherwise keep the meatballs warm in a very low oven for a short time until ready to eat.
Serves 4

TOMATOES STUFFED WITH PORK AND CHEESE

Some recipes for stuffed tomatoes give a rather stodgy filling, including breadcrumbs or rice. This is not one of them. These stuffed tomatoes can be served hot or cold, either as a first course or as the main course of a light meal accompanied by rice and a green salad. They really are luscious!

4 very large (Marmande) tomatoes
just over 2 tablespoons olive oil

2 cloves of garlic, chopped finely
a sprig of rosemary, chopped finely
1 tablespoon caster sugar

250 g (8 oz) pork mince
50 g (2 oz) Gruyère, Emmenthal or Jarlsberg cheese, grated

5–6 fresh basil leaves, chopped roughly (optional)
salt and black pepper

Slice off the tops of the tomatoes and reserve. Scoop out all the seeds and most of the flesh and chop the flesh into small pieces. Salt the insides of the empty tomatoes and lay them upside-down in a colander to drain away the liquid. Preheat the oven to Gas Mark 4/180°C/350°F.

In a large frying pan heat 1 tablespoon of the olive oil and add the chopped tomato, garlic and rosemary. Bubble over a high heat, stirring all the time, for 4–5 minutes, until the sauce is reduced and fairly thick. Stir in the caster sugar and bubble for a minute more. Remove from the heat and season well with salt and black pepper. Spoon the sauce into a bowl and put on one side.

Heat another tablespoon of oil in the frying pan. Season the pork with salt and pepper and fry over a high heat, stirring and breaking up with a wooden spoon for about 5 minutes, until well browned and separated. Stir the fried meat into the tomato sauce. Then add the grated cheese and the basil, if used.

Rinse the salt from the tomato shells and dry with kitchen paper towelling. Place the tomato shells in an open ovenproof dish. Spoon the meat mixture into the tomatoes and then replace the cut-off tops of the tomatoes. Brush the tomatoes all over with a little olive oil and cook in the centre of the oven for 20–30 minutes, until the tomatoes are soft.

Serves 4

PEAR AND PORK PARCELS

Pictured on pages 34/5.

250 g (8 oz) pork mince
1 large clove of garlic, peeled and chopped finely

2.5 cm (1-inch) piece of fresh ginger, peeled and chopped finely
1 tablespoon sunflower or groundnut oil

1 tablespoon soy sauce
2 large firm dessert pears
a little lemon juice

250 g (8 oz) very thin rashers of rindless streaky bacon
salt and black pepper
lettuce leaves, to serve

Preheat the oven to Gas Mark 4/180°C/350°F. Put the minced pork in a bowl and mix in the chopped garlic and ginger. Season with salt and black pepper. Heat the oil in a frying pan to a high heat. Add the pork and stir around for 5 – 6 minutes until cooked and slightly browned. Then add the soy sauce and stir around for a minute more. Remove from the heat.

Peel the pears, cut in half lengthways and rub all over with a little lemon juice to prevent discoloration. Carefully cut out the cores to make a proper hollow in each pear half. Now, on a flat surface, divide the bacon rashers into four. Lay out one pile of bacon flat so that the rashers slightly overlap. Lay a pear half in the centre. Spoon a quarter of the cooked mince mixture into the hollow of the pear – don't worry if a little tumbles over the sides on to the bacon. Carefully bring the bacon up to enclose the pear and mince and then lay in a roasting pan. Repeat for the other piles of bacon and pear halves.

Cook in the centre of the oven for 20–25 minutes. Arrange a bed of lettuce leaves on a serving plate, put on the bacon parcels, spoon any pan juices over them and serve.
Serves 4

CHINESE HEDGEHOGS

The Chinese have the most ingenious ideas with food and this is one of them which I have slightly adapted. A mixture of pork and water chestnuts is formed into balls, studded with rice and then steamed so that everything cooks together. Serve with soy sauce.
Pictured on pages 34/5.

200 – 250 g (7–8 oz) pudding rice
500 g (1 lb) pork mince
2 cloves of garlic

2.5 cm (1-inch) piece of fresh ginger
227 g (8 oz) can of water chestnuts

50 g (1¼ oz) can of anchovies
2–3 pinches of chilli powder
3–4 tablespoons cornflour

salt
a few spring onions, the top halves sliced thinly, to garnish

Put the rice in a sieve and rinse thoroughly with cold water; then put in a bowl of salted cold water and leave to soak for an hour or more.

Meanwhile put the minced pork in a bowl. Peel the garlic and ginger and chop them both finely. Drain the cans of water chestnuts and anchovies and chop them both finely, too. Add all four ingredients to the minced pork and mix thoroughly. Season with a little salt and the chilli powder. Form the mixture into balls the size of large marbles.

After soaking, drain the rice thoroughly in a sieve and put in a mixing bowl. Put the cornflour in another bowl and dip the balls in the cornflour to coat them completely. Then, with wet hands, dip the balls in the rice, patting it on to cover the balls closely. Lay the balls slightly apart in a large steamer or in two layers in a smaller steamer. Cover and steam for 30 minutes. Gently transfer the balls from the steamer to a warmed serving plate and garnish.
Serves 5–6

EXOTIC RAVIOLI

Here is a real mixture of cultures; this heartening dish of home-made
ravioli is not as Italian as it looks. The spicy chicken stuffing of the egg
pasta 'pillows' owes something to North Africa, India and Indonesia. But
this should not really seem incongruous since forms of pasta have been
eaten in the East for centuries and it is only a European habit to assume
that it must always be Italian. Ravioli can easily be made at home without
a machine. The 'pillows' are bigger and more untidy in shape than the
commercial types but I think they taste far better.
Pictured on pages 34/5.

For the filling:
2 tablespoons groundnut oil
*1 medium-size onion (a red
one if possible), chopped
finely*
1 teaspoon ground cinnamon
1 teaspoon ground cumin
1 teaspoon paprika
1/2 teaspoon cayenne pepper
*175 g (6 oz) skinless
chicken breast, chopped very
small*
grated rind of a small lemon
*1 level tablespoon peanut
butter*
salt to taste

For the dough:
*250 g (8 oz) strong plain
flour, plus extra for
kneading*
1/2 teaspoon salt
2 large eggs (size 1–2)
1 tablespoon milk

For the sauce:
2 teaspoons cornflour

2 tablespoons milk
250 g (8 oz) natural yogurt
*1 level teaspoon black onion
seeds*
1/4 teaspoon cayenne pepper
*a small handful of roughly
chopped fresh coriander or
mint leaves*
salt

Heat the oil in a large frying pan. Add the chopped
onion and stir it over a fairly high heat for a few
minutes until softened. Turn down the heat a little
and add the ground spices including the cayenne
pepper. Stir, and then add the chopped chicken. Toss
it around until it is sealed and add the grated lemon
rind, the peanut butter and salt to taste. Stir and cook
for another minute or two. Remove from the heat
and leave to cool.

Meanwhile, make the pasta dough. Put the flour,
salt, eggs and milk into a food processor and whizz
until the mixture has stuck together into a dough.
Then knead with both hands on a smooth surface,
stretching the dough and pushing it back with the
palms of your hands for about 10 minutes until it is
smooth and elastic. Cover it in cling film and leave it
to rest for about 15 minutes. Roll out the dough very
thinly on a floured surface into a large rectangle. Cut
it in half and spoon little piles of chicken mixture on
one half of the pasta about 4 cm (1½ inches) apart.

Brush between the piles with a wet pastry brush to
moisten the pasta. Lay the second sheet of pasta on
top and then, using a fluted pastry cutter or a knife,
cut between the piles of filling to make your ravioli.
Make sure the edges of the ravioli are firmly sealed,
by pressing them together.

Put a large saucepan of salted water on to boil,
and, meanwhile, start to prepare the sauce. Mix the
cornflour in a cup with the milk and pour into a small
saucepan. Add the yogurt and onion seed and season
with salt and cayenne pepper. Leave on one side.
When the water is boiling, drop in the ravioli, cover
the pan and boil for 12 minutes. Meanwhile, bring
the sauce to the boil, stirring with a wooden spoon,
and then bubble it gently, still stirring, for 2–3
minutes. Cover the pan and leave it until the ravioli
is ready. Then drain the ravioli and pile them in a
heated serving dish. Pour over the yogurt sauce,
sprinkle with the chopped herb leaves, and serve.
Serves 4–5

GRILLED CHICKEN STRIPS, INDIAN-STYLE

625–750 g (1¼–1½ lb) chicken or turkey breast, boneless and skinless

For the marinade:
2.5 cm(1-inch) piece of fresh ginger, peeled and chopped roughly

1 small onion, sliced roughly
6–8 cloves of garlic, peeled
3 teaspoons ground coriander
2 teaspoons ground cumin
2 teaspoons ground cinnamon

1 teaspoon ground cardamom
½ teaspoon ground cloves
½ teaspoon cayenne pepper
3 tablespoons red wine vinegar

3 tablespoons sunflower oil
1 tablespoon tomato purée
1 rounded teaspoon salt

Slice the chicken breast into thin strips, about 1 cm (½ inch) wide, and put in a bowl. Then simply put all the marinade ingredients into a liquidiser and whizz to a smooth paste. Mix the marinade very thoroughly with the chicken strips, cover the bowl and leave in a cool place or in the fridge for 4 hours or more (overnight if convenient).

Set the grill to the highest heat. Spread the chicken pieces on a baking sheet (you may have to cook them in two batches) and grill for 8–10 minutes on each side, until almost black in patches.
Serves 4

PORK, ONIONS AND MUSHROOMS IN CRISPY BATTER

I have arrived at this dish, which everyone seems to love, by a devious route. It is both Chinese and Japanese in idea but the batter made with beer, which is what makes it so light and crispy, is something I had at a friend's house in Turkey. (Try the batter also with pieces of fish, mussels or prawns and other raw vegetables – it is mouthwatering!) Serve a simple salad with this – I don't think it needs anything else.

375 g (12 oz) belly of pork rashers
1 tablespoon soy sauce
2–3 pinches of cayenne pepper

2 small onions, sliced finely in rings
75 g (3 oz) mushrooms, sliced

For the batter:
125 g (4 oz) self-raising flour
1 teaspoon salt
1 small egg

150 ml (¼ pint) beer (any kind)
oil for deep-frying

Cut the skin off the pork rashers, cut them into approximately 2.5 cm (1-inch) squares and put into a steamer or sieve suspended over boiling water in a covered saucepan. Steam for 10–15 minutes, until the pork is cooked.

Put the pork in a bowl and stir in the soy sauce and cayenne pepper. Leave to cool a little. Then add the sliced onions and mushrooms.

To make the batter sift the flour and salt into a bowl, mix in the egg and gradually add the beer. Beat until smooth (or simply whizz all the ingredients up in a liquidiser or food processor). Leave the batter for 20 minutes or so.

Heat the oil in a large, deep pan until smoking. Empty the batter into the bowl of pork and vegetables and stir to coat thoroughly. Fry over a high heat in batches until golden brown, separating the pieces as much as possible and draining on absorbent kitchen paper. Pile on a plate and serve immediately.
Serves 4–5

TURKISH PASTIES

In Turkey, you can find all sorts of 'börek' which are like tiny pasties made with crisp, paper-thin filo pastry. Some are filled with white cheese, some with meat, some with spinach. They are usually eaten as a snack or as an appetiser before a meal. These spiced leek and potato pasties are a little more substantial and can be eaten for lunch with a salad, or taken on a picnic, wrapped up to keep them warm. The pastry is a Turkish one made with yogurt and melted butter, quite a different type from filo but light and tasty.

For the filling:
300 g (10 oz) leeks
175 g (6 oz) potatoes
1 tablespoon olive oil
15 g (½ oz) butter
1 clove of garlic, chopped finely

2 teaspoons ground coriander
2 pinches of cayenne pepper
salt

For the pastry:
125 g (4 oz) butter, plus extra for greasing
1 tablespoon olive oil
1 small egg (size 5–6)
150 g (5 oz) carton of natural yogurt

300 g (10 oz) plain flour, plus extra for kneading
¼ teaspoon bicarbonate of soda
1 teaspoon salt
1 egg yolk, beaten

Make the filling first. Wash the leeks and slice them across in thin rounds as far up the stalk as possible. Then chop the slices in half. Peel the potatoes and cut them into a very small cubes. Heat the oil and butter in a largish frying pan over a medium heat. Add the potatoes and cook stirring round now and then, for 5 –7 minutes until the potatoes are just tender. Then stir in the chopped garlic, the coriander and the chopped leeks. Cook, stirring often, for 2–3 minutes, just until the leeks have softened. Season well with salt and the cayenne pepper, remove from the heat and leave until cold. Preheat the oven to Gas Mark 6/200°C/400°F.

Melt the butter in a saucepan over a gentle heat and leave on one side. Put the olive oil and egg into a mixing bowl and whisk them lightly together. Stir in the yogurt. Using a wooden spoon stir the melted butter into the yogurt and egg mixture, a little at a time. Sift the flour with the bicarbonate of soda and the salt and then gradually stir it into the yogurt and butter mixture. Then knead the rather soft dough with your hands on a floured surface for a few minutes. Roll the dough to a thickness of 5 mm (¼ inch), and, using a glass or sundae dish 10 cm (4 inches) in diameter, cut out circles from the pastry. On to one side of each circle pile about 2 teaspoons of filling; then fold over the other side to form semi-circular pasties and press the edges to seal them. Re-roll the pastry as necessary until the filling is used up. Lightly grease a large baking sheet, lay the pasties on it and brush them with beaten egg yolk. Cook just above the centre of the oven for about 20 minutes until golden brown.
Serves 4–5

YELLOW PEPPER TART

This shallow tart is inspired by the *Pissaladière* of Provence but it has quite
a different filling: sweet yellow peppers bound with an egg and saffron
cream. You can, of course, make the tart with peppers of any colour, but
there are moments of the year when the shops seem to be full of beautiful
yellow ones, which I always think taste particularly mild and sweet. I
usually include one red pepper as well, because it looks so pretty speckled
in the rich yellow. The semolina gives the pastry a crisp and light texture.
I often serve the tart with a green salad for a light lunch but it also makes a
good hot first course, in which case it would serve up to eight people.
You can also serve it cold.
Pictured on pages 34/5.

150 ml (1/4 pint) milk	*125 g (4 oz) butter*	*1 red pepper, de-seeded*	*2 egg yolks*
2 pinches of saffron or 1	*1 tablespoon water*	*and chopped fairly small*	*1 large egg (size 1–2)*
packet of powdered saffron	*2 tablespoons olive oil*	*2 cloves of garlic, peeled*	*2 teaspoons caster sugar*
125 g (4 oz) semolina	*750 g (1 1/2 lb) yellow*	*and chopped finely*	*salt and black pepper*
125 g (4 oz) plain flour	*peppers, de-seeded and*		
	chopped fairly small		

Preheat the oven to Gas Mark 7/220°C/425°F. Bring
the milk to the boil and pour it on to the saffron in a
bowl. Stir, and leave on one side. Put the semolina
and flour into a bowl and mix them. Gently melt the
butter, with the water, in a saucepan; then pour the
liquid on to the flour, mixing it in with a wooden
spoon. Take bits of the dough and press them evenly
round the sides and over the bottom of a 25 cm
(10-inch) loose-based fluted aluminium flan tin, and
then refrigerate the flan case.

   Heat the olive oil over a medium heat and add the
chopped peppers and garlic. Cook, stirring frequently, for 10–15 minutes or until the peppers are soft and
then leave on one side to cool slightly. Whisk the egg
yolks and the egg together in a mixing bowl, and then
whisk in the saffron milk and season with salt and
black pepper. Stir in the cooled pepper and garlic and
then pour the mixture into the chilled pastry case.
Level the surface and sprinkle it with the caster sugar.
Cook the tart towards the top of the oven for about
25 minutes until it is just set in the middle and speckles
of black have appeared on the peppers.

   Push the tart carefully up out of the tin and on to
a serving plate. As the pastry is very crumbly, however, you will probably want to keep it on the tin base.
You can keep the tart warm in a low oven or re-heat
it later.
Serves 6

EGG AND VEGETABLE CURRY

Eggs take extremely well to spices and I always find this dish useful for my
vegetarian mother-in-law because it is substantial enough to make a main
meal, accompanied by a bowl of basmati rice. The cucumber adds a
refreshing texture.

2 medium-size aubergines
2.5 cm (1-inch) piece of
fresh ginger
3–4 cloves of garlic
2 tablespoons oil

2 teaspoons ground coriander
1 teaspoon ground cinnamon
1/2 teaspoon turmeric

1 teaspoon ground cumin
1/2 teaspoon cayenne pepper
1 large green pepper, sliced
1 small cucumber, sliced in
2.5 cm (1-inch) thick
chunks

1 tablespoon lemon juice
397 g (14 oz) can of
tomatoes
salt
6 eggs
chopped coriander leaves or
parsley, to garnish

Cut the aubergines into 5 cm (2-inch) slices, rub all
over with salt and leave in a colander for half an hour
(to drain away any bitter juices). Peel the ginger and
garlic and chop finely together. Preheat the oven to
Gas Mark 3/160°C/325°F.

Heat the oil in a flame-proof casserole, add the
chopped ginger and garlic and the dry spices and fry
for a minute or two. Rinse the salt off the aubergines,
dry them and add to the casserole with the other
vegetables, the lemon juice and the tomatoes. Season
with salt. Bring to the boil on top of the stove and
then put in the oven for about half an hour.

Meanwhile, boil the eggs semi-hard, shell them
and cut them in half. When the curry is cooked add
them and put the dish back in the oven for another 5
minutes. Before serving sprinkle with chopped coriander leaves or parsley.
Serves 4–5

ONION TART WITH OLIVE PASTRY

All over France you will find different versions of Tarte à l'Oignon and
almost all are delicious. I much prefer a pure onion tart to any other
combination. For my personal version I use pastry made with olive oil,
which is something I tried when I had brought back some oil from
Provence. It is particularly good for tart crusts because it can be baked
blind, keeps its shape well and retains its crispness, while adding a subtle,
southern flavour of olives to the pastry. With a green salad this makes
an excellent light lunch.

For the pastry:
175 g (6 oz) plain flour
1 teaspoon salt
5 tablespoons extra-virgin
olive oil

1 tablespoon water
2 cloves of garlic, crushed

For the filling:
3 tablespoons extra-virgin
olive oil

750 g (1 1/2 lb) french or
spanish red onions, sliced
very thinly
25 g (1 oz) black olives,
stoned and chopped finely

250 ml (8 fl oz) double
cream
1 egg
2 egg yolks
salt and black pepper

Preheat the oven to Gas Mark 7/220°C/425°F. To
make the pastry, sift the flour and salt into a bowl. Put
the olive oil and water into a saucepan and add the
crushed garlic. Heat for a minute or two until just
beginning to bubble. Add the hot liquid gradually to
the flour, stirring it in with a wooden spoon. Using
your fingers, press pieces of the crumbly dough firmly
against the sides of a 24 cm (9 1/2-inch) fluted, loose-

based aluminium flan tin. Then press the remaining dough evenly over the base of the tin. Refrigerate the pastry case while you make the filling.

Heat the olive oil in a large frying pan over a gentle heat. Add the sliced onions and cook slowly, stirring around often, until completely soft but not browned at all. Stir in the chopped olives and remove from the heat.

Cook the unfilled pastry case in the centre of the oven for 10–15 minutes. Then remove from the oven and turn down the heat to Gas Mark 5/190°C/375°F. In a mixing bowl, finish the filling. Whisk the cream well with the egg and egg yolks and season with salt and black pepper. Stir the cooked onions into the cream and pour the mixture into the pastry case. Put it back in the centre of the oven for 25–35 minutes until the centre of the filling is only just set.

Serves 6

STUFFED SARDINES

The smell of sardines grilling, the most common method of cooking them, is powerful; appetising yet pervasive. The taste is delicious. Now that it is easier to buy large fresh sardines in this country there is another way to cook them: stuffing them and baking in the oven, which minimises the smell and makes a refreshing change.

1 tablespoon olive oil, plus a little extra
2 cloves of garlic, chopped finely
375 g (12 oz) chicory, sliced thinly

about 8 large lettuce leaves, chopped small
grated rind of 1 small orange
2 teaspoons caster sugar

8 fresh sardines, about 20–25 cm (8–10 inches) long
25 g (1 oz) fresh breadcrumbs

25 g (1 oz) grated cheese
salt and black pepper

Preheat the oven to Gas Mark 9/240°C/475°F. Heat the olive oil in a largish frying pan over a medium heat. Add the chopped garlic, stir for a moment and then add the sliced chicory. Stir around with a wooden spoon for 4–5 minutes until the vegetables are softened. Stir in the chopped lettuce and then add the orange rind and the caster sugar and fry for a moment more. Remove the pan from the heat, season to taste and leave it to cool.

Meanwhile, wash the sardines, rubbing off any scales with your fingers. Carefully cut open the abdomen from below the head to the tail. If they are not already cleaned, remove the innards with your fingers under running water and pinch off the heads. Pull back the flesh of the fish away from the bones and gently pull out the backbone, breaking it off above the tail. Take each fillet and spoon some of the cool filling on to the flesh side. Fold the fish lightly together – the filling will be bursting out – and very carefully put them in a large gratin dish. If there is any filling left over, spoon it evenly into the fish to fill them even more. Mix the breadcrumbs and cheese together in a bowl and scatter them over the fish. Dribble a little olive oil over the top. Put the dish towards the top of the oven and bake for 15 minutes.

Serves 4–5

FILLETS OF PLAICE WITH TROPICAL STUFFING

Pictured on page 51.

2 large, slightly unripe bananas
juice of 1 lemon
2.5–4 cm (1–1½ inch) piece of fresh ginger, peeled and chopped very finely

2 cloves of garlic, chopped finely
2–3 pinches of cayenne pepper
a little oil
6 small plaice fillets, with the skins removed

For the sauce:
½ teaspoon turmeric
300 ml (½ pint) soured cream
1–2 pinches of cayenne pepper

1 small handful of fresh coriander, chopped finely
salt
whole coriander leaves, to garnish

Preheat the oven to Gas Mark 6/200°C/400°F. Peel the bananas and cut them into small pieces. Put in a bowl and mix with the lemon juice. Stir in the chopped ginger and garlic. Season with salt and the cayenne pepper.

Lightly oil a shallow ovenproof dish or pan. Lay the fillets in the dish one at a time, skin side upwards, and spoon some of the banana mixture on to each. Bring the plaice up either side of the mixture. When all the fillets are rolled up around the fillings and arranged in the dish, spoon a little oil over each fillet and cover the dish with foil. Cook in the centre of the oven for 20 minutes. Remove from the oven and leave until cold.

Transfer the rolls with a slotted spoon on to a serving plate. To make the sauce, mix in a small bowl the turmeric with the soured cream and season to taste with salt and the cayenne pepper. Stir in the chopped coriander leaves. Spoon the sauce over each stuffed plaice, decorate the dish with the whole coriander leaves and chill in the fridge before serving.
Serves 6

WRAPPED FISH QUENELLES WITH SAFFRON AND VERMOUTH SAUCE

Pictured on pages 6/7.

425 g (14 oz) smoked cod or haddock fillets
2 large egg whites (size 1–2)
1 tablespoon chopped fresh fennel leaves

3–4 pinches of chilli powder
4 white, skinned plaice fillets (about 375 g / 12 oz)
a little olive oil
1 tablespoon cornflour

275 ml (9 fl oz) milk
10 –15 strands of saffron
2 large egg yolks (size 1–2)
2 tablespoons dry Vermouth
salt

a few leaves of continental parsley or other decorative herb, to garnish

Preheat the oven to Gas Mark 6/200°C/400°F. Skin the smoked cod or haddock if necessary and either mince or chop finely in a food processor. Put in a bowl and mix in the egg whites with a wooden spoon. Add the fennel leaves and 2–3 pinches of the chilli powder. Lay out the plaice fillets skin side down. Divide the minced fish mixture into four and pat into fat sausage shapes. Lay one of these on each plaice and roll up loosely. Place in an ovenproof dish, join side downwards, and brush all over with olive oil. Cook the fish rolls in the open dish just above the centre of the oven for 20 minutes.

Meanwhile, make the sauce. Put the cornflour with 2 tablespoons of the milk in a saucepan and mix until smooth. Stir in the remaining milk and add the saffron. Bring to the boil, stirring all the time, and bubble, still stirring, for 3 minutes. Then remove from the heat and stir in the egg yolks. Add the Vermouth and season to taste with salt and a pinch or two of chilli powder. Just before serving pour the sauce over the fish and decorate.
Serves 4

FISH ROLLS WITH SPANISH SAUCE

For the rolls:
125 g (4 oz) peeled
prawns, chopped roughly
50 g (2 oz) flaked almonds
1 large clove of garlic,
crushed
6 small fillets of plaice

cooking oil
salt and black pepper

For the sauce:
500 g (1 lb) tomatoes,
dipped in boiling water and
skinned

about 3 tablespoons olive or
sunflower oil
juice of 1 orange
1 tablespoon dried oregano
1 large clove of garlic,
crushed
salt and black pepper

chopped fresh parsley or
chives (or, best of all, fresh
basil), to garnish
salt and black pepper

Preheat the oven to Gas Mark 6/200°C/400°F.

Mix the prawns, almonds and the crushed garlic with salt and pepper in a bowl. Lay out the fillets of plaice and spoon some of the mixture on to each one. Roll the fillets over the stuffing, secure with a wooden toothpick (don't worry if a little stuffing tumbles out at either end) and arrange in a shallow, oiled, fireproof dish.

Brush the stuffed fillets with oil. Cover the dish with foil and bake in the centre of the oven for 20 minutes. Take out, drain off and reserve any juices, and leave to cool.

Meanwhile, cut the peeled tomatoes into small pieces and put them in a frying pan with the reserved fish juices, olive oil, orange juice, oregano, crushed garlic and salt and black pepper to taste. Cook very gently, stirring often until the tomatoes have gone mushy and the mixture has become a thick sauce. Cool in the pan and then stir again.

Carefully transfer the fish rolls to a serving dish, remove the toothpicks and scrape off the skin. Spoon the sauce over the fish and sprinkle with the parsley, chives or basil. Chill in the fridge before serving.
Serves 6

SMOKED FISH AND FENNEL IN OLIVE OIL

2 large bulbs of fennel cut in
thin slices lengthways
8 tablespoons extra-virgin
olive oil

2 teaspoons dried green
peppercorns, crushed

4 large cloves of garlic
chopped in very thin slices

300–375 g (10–12 oz)
smoked haddock or cod fillet
juice of 1 lemon
sea salt and black pepper

Reserve the feathery green leaves of the fennel. Put 6 tablespoons of the olive oil into a large, deep pan.

Put the open pan over a medium heat, add the crushed green peppercorns and a sprinkling of black pepper. Then add the fennel slices and the garlic and turn around to coat with oil. Now put a lid on the pan and leave over a low heat for 10–12 minutes.

Meanwhile, skin the smoked fish and slice it very thinly across. Arrange over the bottom of a shallow serving dish. When the fennel is soft, add the lemon juice and salt to taste. Remove from the heat while bubbling and spoon the mixture on top of the fish slices. Cover tightly with a piece of foil or a lid and leave until cold.

Before serving, roughly chop the feathery fennel leaves, scatter them on top of the dish and dribble over the remaining 2 tablespoons of olive oil.
Serves 6

MOUSSELINE FOR CAPTAIN BEALE

I made this when I came back from visiting a remarkable man who lives on the remote and beautiful Andaman Islands far south in the Bay of Bengal. My recipe has a delicate and sophisticated touch to it, which makes it a suitable dinner party piece, but the spices are exactly those which the boys on Captain Beale's boat used when cooking the fish caught as we glided along between the islands. The tropical fish was strong and meaty, just right for the spices, which is why I have used kipper for my mousseline – it seems to catch the same character.

10 whole cardamom pods
5 cloves
1 teaspoon turmeric
1/2 teaspoon cayenne pepper
2 small green chillies,
de-seeded under running
water

2 cloves of garlic, peeled
50 g (2 oz) butter
250 g (8 oz) kipper fillets,
skins removed and chopped
finely
juice of 1 lemon

1 tablespoon tomato purée
2 rounded teaspoons
gelatine
4 large eggs (size 1–2),
separated

450 g (15 oz) carton of
natural yogurt
salt (optional)
fresh coriander or mint
leaves, to garnish

Put the whole cardamom pods and cloves in a coffee grinder and grind finely. Sift through a sieve (so that any cardamom husks are discarded) into a small bowl and mix with the turmeric and cayenne. Chop the chilli flesh up finely with the garlic.

Melt the butter in a saucepan, add the mixed spices and stir round for a moment over the heat. Add the chopped chilli and garlic and stir over a gentle heat for a minute. Next, stir in the chopped kipper, lemon juice and tomato purée. Cover the pan and cook over a very gentle heat for 10 minutes. Meanwhile, sprinkle the gelatine into 4 tablespoons of barely boiling water and stir until dissolved. Add this liquid to the fish mixture, remove the pan from the heat and stir in the egg yolks with a wooden spoon. Return the pan to a very low heat and stir constantly for 3–4 minutes without allowing to bubble.

Remove from the heat. Taste the fish mixture now, taking into account that it is to be slightly diluted with the whisked egg whites. (The kipper should provide enough salt but add more if you have to.) Turn the mixture into a large bowl and leave to cool. When just cool but not setting, whisk the egg whites until they stand in soft peaks and fold gently into the fish mixture, a third at a time, using a large metal spoon. Oil a bread tin or rectangular dish of about 600 ml (1 pint) capacity, turn the fish mixture into it and spread level. Chill well in the fridge.

Shortly before serving dip the tin briefly in hot water and, giving it a shake, turn the mousseline out on to a board. Spread a thin layer of yogurt over individual plates, cut thickish slices of the mousseline and lay them in the centre of the yogurt. Decorate around the edges with a few fresh coriander or mint leaves.

Serves 6–8

Fillets of Plaice with Tropical Stuffing (page 48); Mousseline for Captain Beale

PRAWN PASTA

This is a simple dish of pasta and prawns with a sauce which combines
some of my favourite Italian tastes: good olive oil, cooked fennel, garlic,
and nutmeg. Even frozen prawns are enlivened by it, and fresh ones make
a real treat, or you can use any other seafood.

1 large bulb of fennel	375 g (12 oz) pasta shells	250 g (8 oz) peeled	grated parmesan cheese, to
6 tablespoons virgin olive oil	1/4 – 1/2 nutmeg	prawns, thawed if frozen	serve (optional)
4 cloves of garlic, cut into		salt and black pepper	
slivers			

Chop the fennel into small pieces, reserving any leafy
bits. Put 3 tablespoons of the olive oil in a frying pan.
Heat over a medium heat and add the chopped fennel. Fry gently for about 10 minutes, and then add the
sliced garlic and cook for another 2–3 minutes.
Remove from the heat and keep on one side. Bring
a pan of salted water to the boil and add the pasta
shells. While the pasta is cooking – it will take 12–15
minutes, depending on whether it is the fresh kind or

not – grate the nutmeg into the frying pan of fennel
and garlic. Add the remaining 3 tablespoons of olive
oil and the prawns and season with a little salt and
plenty of black pepper. Stir in any reserved fennel
leaves. When the pasta has cooked, drain it and empty
it into a heated serving bowl. If necessary, very gently
re-heat the contents of the frying pan, and then turn
it into the pasta, mixing well. Serve immediately.
Serves 4

COLD DUCK WITH TUNA CREAM SAUCE AND SPRING ONIONS

This makes a duck go much farther than usual and is a very popular, yet
out-of-the-ordinary, dish.

1.75–2.25 kg (4–5 lb)	For the sauce:	5 tablespoons single cream	a small bunch of spring
duck	198 g (7 oz) can of tuna	a bunch of parsley	onions, to garnish
oil	juice of 1/2 lemon	salt and black pepper	
salt			

Heat the oven to Gas Mark 6/200°C/400°F. Rub the
duck with oil and salt and put it on a rack in a roasting
pan on its side. Roast for about 30 minutes, then for
a further 30 minutes on the other side and then for 30
minutes more on its back. Allow it to cool.

To make the sauce, put the tuna (including the
oil from the can), lemon juice and cream in a food
processor or liquidiser and whizz until smooth. Season to taste with salt and black pepper. Add the parsley
and whizz until finely chopped.

When the duck is quite cold (it will cut best if it
has been chilled in the fridge first) carve very thinly
and arrange on a serving dish. Arrange the larger
pieces of meat neatly round the edges and pile any
smaller bits in the centre. Before serving, spoon the
sauce over the pile in the centre so that it oozes down
on the larger pieces of meat. Then cut the spring
onions into small pieces, using as much of the green
stalk as possible, and sprinkle them all over the dish.
Serves 6–8

SOFT ROE SALAD

This can be one of the main dishes at a cold lunch, accompanied by other salads. As a child I had a passion for soft herring roes, which pleased my mother as she felt they were so nutritious. I am still intrigued by their smooth consistency and subtle taste.

250 g (8 oz) soft herring roes, fresh or canned
½ cucumber, weighing 250–300 g (8–10 oz)

125 g (4 oz) button mushrooms
6 tablespoons natural yogurt

3 tablespoons mayonnaise (a good commercial kind will do)

salt and black pepper chopped parsley or mint, to garnish

Steam the soft roes over boiling water in a steamer or a sieve suspended in a closed pan for 5–7 minutes until cooked. Allow to become cold and then cut into small pieces. Peel the cucumber and cut into smallish chunks. Without removing the stalks slice the mushrooms thinly downwards, retaining the mushroom shape.

Arrange the roe, cucumber and mushrooms in a fairly shallow serving dish. In a bowl, mix the yogurt and mayonnaise and season well with salt and black pepper. Spoon this mixture all over the salad and garnish with chopped parsley.
Serves 4

RED KIDNEY BEAN SALAD WITH STREAKY PORK

Bean salads are always popular, and extremely useful when you have to feed a lot of people and as a more substantial salad during the winter. You can use white haricot beans as an alternative for this recipe.

250 g (8 oz) red kidney beans
250 –300 g (8–10 oz) belly of pork

salt
1 tablespoon oil

1 onion, chopped finely
a bunch of parsley, chopped finely

French Dressing with Mustard and Garlic (page 144) with ½ –1 extra clove of garlic (crushed) added, to taste

Soak the kidney beans in water for 8 hours or overnight. Then boil them in unsalted water until soft but not mushy – the time this takes depends on the age of the beans, but boil for at least 15 minutes. Drain and cool.

Cut off the rind and slice the pork into small dice, and rub all over lightly with salt. Heat the oil in a

frying pan and fry the pork over a medium to high heat, turning until crisp. Remove with a slotted spoon and cool on a piece of absorbent paper.

Put the beans in a salad bowl and mix with the chopped onion and parsley. Scatter the pork on top. Dress with the French Dressing.
Serves 6–8

Part 3

MAIN COURSES

Pheasants in Saffron Sauce (page 114);
Anglo-chinese Pie (page 78);
Marinated Shoulder of Lamb Stuffed with Swiss Chard, with a Tomato,
Brandy and Cream Sauce (page 89);
Pumpkin and Goat's Cheese Lasagne with Yogurt and Cardamom
(page 128)

OXTAIL CASSEROLE WITH PRUNES

I think that the rich flavour of oxtail goes best with a sweetish flavour, and
prunes give the dish a dark, glossy appearance and an almost sumptuous
character. However, if you object to prunes, substitute tomatoes and use
300 ml (½ pint) stout instead of the stock.

1 kg (2 lb) oxtail
a little fat for frying
2–3 onions, sliced

grated rind and juice of 1
orange
5–6 whole cloves

450 ml (¾ pint)
well-seasoned beef stock

250 g (8 oz) prunes,
soaked overnight and then
stoned

Preheat the oven to Gas Mark 8–9/230–240°C/450–
475°F. Fry the oxtail in a little fat until browned all
over. Transfer to a casserole dish.

Fry the onions in the remaining fat until brown.
Add them to the casserole, together with the grated
orange rind and juice, cloves and stock. Cover and
put in the oven for 20 minutes, until bubbling. Turn
the oven down to Gas Mark 1/140°C/275°F, add the
prunes and continue cooking for another 2½–3½
hours or until the meat is falling from the bones. Pour
off any excess fat and check for seasoning.
Serves 6

BEEF AND MUSHROOM PIE WITH CHEESY SUET CRUST

Pies look beautiful and everyone seems to like them. This is a tasty pie
with a double cheesy crust.

For the filling:
500 g (1 lb) beef mince
a little cooking fat or oil
1–2 cloves of garlic,
chopped finely

1 tablespoon tomato purée
1–2 teaspoons paprika
125 g (4 oz) mushrooms,
sliced
salt and black pepper

For the crust:
175 g (6 oz) plain flour
1 teaspoon baking powder
¼ teaspoon salt

50 g (2 oz) fresh white
breadcrumbs
50 g (2 oz) cheese, grated
125 g (4 oz) shredded suet

Season the mince with salt and black pepper. Melt a
little fat in a pan and fry the mince for about 3–4
minutes over a strong heat, stirring with a wooden
spoon. Add the garlic, tomato purée and paprika.
Remove from the heat and stir in the mushrooms.
Check for seasoning and let the mixture cool.

To make the pastry, sift the flour, baking powder
and salt into a bowl and stir in the breadcrumbs,
cheese and suet. Add enough cold water to form a stiff
dough.

Preheat the oven to Gas Mark 6/200°C/400°F.

Grease a 23–25-cm (9–10-inch) flat pie plate. Divide
the pastry in half and roll on a floured board. Shape
into two circles big enough for the pie plate. Line the
plate with one circle and spoon in the meat filling.
Dampen the edges and cover with the other circle.
Trim the edges and roll out the trimmings to cut out
decorations for the top. Brush with milk and bake in
the centre of the oven for 25–30 minutes.

A green vegetable or green salad is all that is
needed to accompany this pie.
Serves 4–6

BEEF AND BEAN HOTPOT

There is something wonderful about the smooth thickness that soaked
dried beans give when they are cooked in a stew.

*250–375 g (8–12 oz)
dried beans (red kidney,
haricot or butter beans)
500 –750 g (1–1½ lb)
stewing beef*

*250 g (8 oz) smoked
streaky bacon, with the rind
cut off
a little cooking fat or oil
2 onions, peeled and sliced*

*1 tablespoon plain flour
300 ml (½ pint) can of
beer or equivalent amount
of good stock
4–6 cooking tomatoes,
chopped roughly*

*½–1 teaspoon ground
nutmeg
2 cloves of garlic, crushed
a sprinkling of
Worcestershire sauce
(optional)
salt and black pepper*

Soak the beans in cold water for 8 hours, or overnight.
Then boil them in unsalted water until just soft.

If you are using the oven rather than the top of
the stove, preheat it to Gas Mark 1/140°C/275°F.
Chop the beef into cubes. Cut the bacon in pieces.

Melt enough fat or oil to cover completely the
base of a large, heavy saucepan or iron casserole dish.
Toss the beef, bacon, beans and onions in the flour,
add to the pan and cook gently for 2–3 minutes. Add
the beer and just enough water to cover the ingredients and stir in the tomatoes, nutmeg and garlic.
Sprinkle with salt, plenty of black pepper and the
Worcestershire sauce, if used.

Bring to the boil and simmer very gently, either
on top of the stove or in the oven for 2½–3½ hours.
Serves 5–6

BEEF AND MUSHROOM RISSOLES IN FRESH TOMATO SAUCE

*500 g (1 lb) beef mince
1 medium-size onion,
grated
a handful of parsley,
chopped finely*

*1 egg, beaten
125 g (4 oz) mushrooms,
chopped small
1 tablespoon olive oil
salt and black pepper*

*For the sauce:
500 (1 lb) tomatoes
50 g (2 oz) butter or
margarine
1 medium-size onion,
sliced finely in rings*

*2 cloves of garlic, chopped
finely
salt and black pepper
chopped parsley, to garnish*

Put the beef in a bowl and knead it with your hands
for a few minutes until it is soft and pasty. Add the
onion, parsley and egg. Mix with a wooden spoon,
mix in the mushrooms and season well with salt and
black pepper. Form into balls each the size of a
ping-pong ball.

Heat the olive oil in a large frying pan and fry the
balls over a high heat for a few minutes, just to brown
them, turning carefully once or twice. Turn off the
heat.

To make the sauce, put the tomatoes in a bowl,
pour boiling water over and leave them for half a
minute. Then drain and skin them and chop up small.
Heat the butter or margarine in a large, heavy saucepan and add the tomatoes, onion and garlic. Cover
the pan and simmer gently for 5–10 minutes, until
both the onions and tomatoes are soft; then season to
taste with salt and black pepper.

Spoon the rissoles into the saucepan together with
any frying pan juices. Cover the pan and simmer
gently for 20 minutes. Turn into a serving dish and
sprinkle with plenty of chopped parsley before serving.
Serves 4–5

SPICY BEEF AND GUINNESS PIE

A golden pie which looks and tastes extra-special. It can be prepared well beforehand and will only need putting into the oven to bake. If you have an aversion to prunes don't be put off – they disintegrate in the stout and produce the most delicious, rich, dark sauce. The juniper berries are optional but can be found in most delicatessens and will add tantalisingly to the flavour. Allspice is best ground from whole berries but you can also buy it ground (just to muddle you it is sometimes known as Pimento or Jamaica pepper). If you can't find allspice use more nutmeg and two more cloves. For the top you can use packet puff pastry if you like but the easy flaky pastry is very little trouble and beautifully crisp. Make your pastry first or while the pie filling is cooking.

For the easy flaky pastry:
250 g (8 oz) plain flour
a good pinch of salt
175 g (6 oz) from a block
of frozen butter or
margarine
6 tablespoons very cold
water – preferably chilled in
the fridge
1 egg yolk, to glaze

For the pie filling:
1 teaspoon whole
allspice berries
6 cloves
1 teaspoon juniper berries
(optional)
1 tablespoon oil
¼–½ whole nutmeg,
grated

2–3 large cloves of garlic,
chopped finely
1 kg (2 lb) lean stewing
beef, chopped in cubes
300 ml (½ pint) bottle
Guinness or other stout
250 g (8 oz) large prunes,
soaked in water overnight

500 g (1 lb) carrots, cleaned
and sliced
salt and black pepper
2 teaspoons arrowroot

To make the pastry, sift the flour and salt into a bowl. Put a grater into the bowl on top of the flour. Hold the frozen butter or margarine in its wrapping and coarsely grate off 175 g (6 oz) (three-quarters of the block). With a palette knife mix the fat into the flour until crumbly. Now add the water gradually, mixing again with the knife and then gather the dough up with your hands into a ball. Wrap in foil or cling film and put in the fridge for at least an hour.

Preheat the oven to Gas Mark 1/140°C/275°F. Crush the allspice and cloves together in a pestle and mortar or in a coffee grinder, add the juniper berries and crush roughly. Heat the oil in the bottom of an iron casserole. Put the crushed spices together with the grated nutmeg and chopped garlic into the hot oil and stir over the heat for ½ minute. Add the beef and just seal all over for 2–3 minutes over a high heat. Stir in the stout and ½ cup of water. Remove the stones from the soaked prunes and add. Bring to the boil and then cover the dish and cook in the oven for an hour. (Make the pastry now if you haven't already.) Then add the carrots and continue cooking for a further 1–1½ hours until the meat is tender. Season to taste with salt and black pepper. Blend the arrowroot with a spot of water and stir in. Bubble for a minute or two on top of the stove. Then pour into a 1.5-litre (2½-pint) pie dish and leave until cold.

When the filling is cold, roll out the pastry on a floured surface to roughly the size and shape of the pie dish. Moisten the edge of the dish and lay the pastry on top. Cut round the edges and press down lightly. Roll out the trimmings and use to make a pattern. Cover the pastry loosely with cling film or foil and put the complete dish in the fridge until the next day, or in the freezer (if the freezer, remember to defrost before baking).

To bake, preheat the oven to Gas Mark 7/ 220°C/425°F. Brush the pastry all over with egg yolk and cook in the centre of the oven for about 20 minutes until a rich golden brown. Serve with a green salad.
Serves 6–8

Spicy Beef and Guinness Pie

BRAISED BEEF IN WALNUT, CHILLI AND CHOCOLATE SAUCE

Chocolate is used in savoury dishes in South America, Spain and even in
Italy. It must have originated from a chocolate drink found in Mexico in
the 16th century, which was unsweetened.

*75 g (3 oz) walnut pieces,
ground finely
1 medium-large onion,
chopped roughly
3 – 4 green chillies,
de-seeded and chopped
roughly*

*1 large clove of garlic,
chopped roughly
25 g (1 oz) raisins
4 – 5 cloves
1 rounded tablespoon cocoa
powder*

*397 g (14 oz) can of
tomatoes
3 tablespoons sunflower oil
1 teaspoon ground
cinnamon
600 ml (1 pint) beef stock*

*750 g (1 ½ lb) lean
braising beef, cubed
a bunch of spring onions,
chopped, using as much of
the green part as possible
salt*

Preheat the oven to Gas Mark 2/150°C/300°F. Put
the first eight ingredients in a food processor. Whizz
thoroughly until as smooth as possible. Now heat 2
tablespoons of the sunflower oil in a large iron or
other flameproof casserole over a medium heat. Add
the cinnamon and stir, and then add the mixture from
the food processor and let it bubble, stirring constantly, for 5 minutes. Now stir in the stock, remove the
pan from the heat and add salt to taste. Heat the
remaining tablespoon of sunflower oil in a large frying
pan to a very high heat. Add the beef and fry it until
sealed and browned all over. Add to the sauce in the
casserole, together with any pan juices. Put the casserole back on the heat and bring it to bubbling; then
cover the dish and cook in the preheated oven for
2½ – 3 hours until the meat is tender. Before serving,
stir in the chopped spring onions.
Serves 4–5

KATE'S PIE

*a little oil for frying
2 cloves of garlic, chopped
finely
½ – 1 teaspoon
chilli powder*

*500 g (1 lb) beef mince
1 tablespoon tomato purée
175 g (6 oz) frozen
sweetcorn*

*4 hard-boiled eggs, peeled
and chopped roughly
50 g (2 oz) butter
25 g (1 oz) plain flour
600 ml (1 pint) milk*

*a large handful of parsley,
chopped
250 g (8 oz) puff pastry,
thawed if frozen
egg yolk or milk for glazing
salt*

Melt a little oil in a large frying pan over a medium
heat. Add the chopped garlic and chilli powder and
stir; then add the minced beef. Dig around with a
wooden spoon until the beef has separated and
cooked and any liquid has evaporated. Stir in the
tomato purée, remove from the heat and add salt to
taste. Add the sweetcorn and chopped eggs. Turn into
a 2-litre (3-pint) pie or fairly shallow ovenproof dish
and pat level. Preheat the oven to Gas Mark
7/220°C/425°F.

Now melt the butter in a saucepan. Remove from
the heat and stir in the flour. Stir in the milk and put
back on the heat. Bring up to the boil, stirring, and
then bubble, still stirring, for 2–3 minutes. Remove
from the heat, add the chopped parsley and season.
Pour over the mince in the dish and leave to cool.

Roll out the pastry to a size big enough to cover
the pie dish. Moisten the edges of the dish, lay the
pastry on top and cut the edges off. Use the trimmings
to cut out decorations. Pierce two holes in the pastry
to allow steam to escape and brush the pie with egg
yolk or milk. Cook the pie just above the centre of
the oven for 20 –25 minutes.
Serves 6

BOXING NIGHT BEEF

This rich and glossy casserole of beef and mushrooms cooked in a dark
chestnut sauce doesn't have to be served on Boxing night.

2 large onions
4 tablespoons olive oil
1.1 kg (2½ lb) lean
braising steak, cubed
3 bay leaves

450 g (15 oz) can of
unsweetened chestnut purée
1 level tablespoon black
treacle
2 teaspoons paprika

450 ml (¾ pint) beef stock
375 g (12 oz)
medium-size mushrooms,
halved

5 rounded tablespoons
fromage frais or Greek
yogurt
4 teaspoons whole-grain
mustard
salt and black pepper

Peel the onions, cut in half and slice thinly. Heat 3 tablespoons of the olive oil in a large frying-pan over a low to medium heat. Add the onions and cook, stirring around often until softened and slightly browned at the edges. Remove the pan from the heat and, using a slotted spoon, transfer the onions to a plate on one side. Sprinkle the beef lightly all over with salt. Heat the remaining tablespoon of olive oil in the frying-pan over a high heat. Add the pieces of meat (you will probably have to do this in several batches, adding a little more oil if necessary) and turn around to brown on all sides. Then remove them with a slotted spoon and put them in a flameproof casserole. Add the onions and bay leaves. Spoon the chestnut purée into a food processor with the black treacle, the paprika, plenty of black pepper and the beef stock. Whizz until smooth and then pour it over the beef and onions. Heat the oven to Gas Mark 2/150°C/300°F. Cover the casserole and bring the sauce to bubbling on top of the stove; then cook just below the centre of the oven for 2 hours.

Add the mushrooms, and return to the oven, turning down the heat to Gas Mark 1/140°C/275°F. Continue cooking for another hour or so until the beef is very tender. Meanwhile, put the fromage frais or yogurt into a bowl and stir in the mustard. Before serving the casserole spoon the fromage frais or yogurt on top of it; it will mix in roughly as you serve it out to your guests.
Serves 6

BARBECUE MEATBALLS WITH SURPRISE CENTRE

If possible buy extra-lean minced beef, which is chopped more finely than
usual and sticks together better. Also, if available, use dark red onions.

1 kg (2 lb) lean beef mince
2 small onions, chopped
finely

2 teaspoons dill seed
1 large egg (size 1–2),
whisked

cayenne pepper
2 small avocados

olive oil
sea salt and black pepper

Put the minced beef into a mixing bowl, mix in the chopped onion and dill seed and the whisked egg and season well with crushed sea salt, black pepper and 3 – 4 good pinches of cayenne pepper. Cut the avocados in half, then peel them and cut up into 12 pieces each. Now divide the beef mixture into 24 parts.

Using moist hands, take up one of these parts, flatten it on the palm of your hand, put a piece of avocado in the centre and then bring the meat up and round, pressing it together to enclose the avocado. Continue like this with the pieces of meat and avocado until you have 24 meatballs. Smear them with olive oil. For these meatballs you should wait until your barbecue is really hot as they should be cooked for about 2– 4 minutes on each side.
Serves 8–12

MEAT LOAF WITH BLUE CHEESE FILLING

This is a personal variation of the American type of meat loaf – a meal
which is easy to make and popular with the whole family.

500 g (1 lb) beef mince
75 g (3 oz) mushrooms,
chopped finely
50 g (2 oz) fresh
breadcrumbs
125 g (4 oz) streaky bacon,
chopped finely

1 clove of garlic, chopped
finely
1 small onion, peeled and
chopped finely
1 teaspoon oregano or thyme
3 tablespoons tomato
ketchup

1 large egg (size 1–2)
beaten
salt and black pepper

For the filling:
125 g (4 oz) Danish Blue
cheese

1 tablespoon single cream or
top of the milk
1 egg, beaten
a good pinch of chilli powder
3 tablespoons tomato
ketchup
a few sprigs of parsley, to
garnish

Preheat the oven to Gas Mark 4/180°C/350°F. In a
bowl mix all the ingredients (except those for the
filling) together thoroughly and season well with salt
and pepper. Grease a 1 kg (2 lb) loaf tin.

Spoon half the mixture into the loaf tin. Crumble
the cheese in a small bowl, mix well with the cream
or top of the milk and beaten egg and add the chilli
powder. Spread this on the layer of meat in the tin.
Spoon the remaining meat mixture evenly on top.

Bake in the centre of the oven for 1 hour and then
remove from the oven.

Turn up the oven to Gas Mark 9/240°C/475°F.
Loosen the sides of the loaf with a knife and turn it
out very gently on to an ovenproof serving dish.
Smear the loaf all over with the tomato ketchup and
put back into the oven, cooking for 10 –15 minutes.
Serve garnished with sprigs of parsley.
Serves 4–5

INDIAN-SPICED MEATBALLS STUFFED WITH CURD CHEESE

These aromatic meatballs have a soft filling of curd cheese. They make a
good summer meal when arranged on a bed of fresh mint leaves and
served with a salad and bread.

500 g (1 lb) ground beef
2 teaspoons coriander seeds
8 pods of cardamom
6 –8 cloves

3–4 pinches of chilli powder
3–4 cloves of garlic,
chopped finely

1 egg, beaten
125 g (4 oz) curd cheese
1 tablespoon of oil
salt

chopped mint leaves or
parsley, to garnish

Put the ground beef in a bowl and mash with a large
wooden spoon until pasty. Grind the coriander seeds,
the cardamom seeds (discarding the pods) and the
cloves in a coffee grinder or pestle and mortar. Add
to the beef with the chilli powder and garlic and
season with salt. Thoroughly mix in the beaten egg.

With wet hands, form the mixture into small balls,
the size of ping-pong balls, and then flatten them out

into circles on an oiled surface. Put a teaspoon of curd
cheese on each circle and carefully bring the meat up
round to encase the cheese completely.

Heat the oil in a large frying pan. Fry the meatballs
over a medium heat for about 5–7 minutes on each
side, until brown. Transfer to a serving dish and
sprinkle with the mint or parsley.
Serves 4–5

OSSI BUCHI WITH GREEN LEMON SAUCE

The Italian dish Ossi Buchi, knuckle of veal with marrow bone, is traditionally cooked in a rich tomato sauce. This way of cooking it is different and refreshing – good with new potatoes and baby carrots.

6 large pieces of veal knuckle with marrow bone
a little olive oil

25 g (1 oz) fresh white breadcrumbs
1 large onion, peeled and chopped roughly

2 teaspoons caster sugar
2–3 cloves of garlic, peeled
juice of 1 lemon
300 ml (½ pint) water

375 g (12 oz) spinach
150 –300 ml (¼ –½ pint) double or single cream
salt and black pepper

Fry the veal pieces in a little oil over a high heat quickly on both sides, just to brown a little and seal. Transfer with a slotted spatula to a flameproof casserole dish. Preheat the oven to Gas Mark 3/160°C/325°F.

Put the breadcrumbs, chopped onion, sugar, garlic, lemon juice and water in a food processor with a sprinkling of salt and pepper and whizz until as smooth as possible. Pour this mixture over the veal.

Bring to bubbling on top of the stove, cover and cook in the oven for 1¾–2 hours, or until the meat seems very tender.

Wash the spinach well, take off the stalks and plunge into boiling, salted water for just a minute or two until limp. Drain well and chop up as finely as possible. Stir the chopped spinach into the veal, pour the cream on top in a whirl and serve at once.
Serves 6

VEAL AND TUNA CROQUETTES WITH CREAMY CAPER SAUCE

The Italians are familiar with the combination of veal and tuna in a delicious dish called Vitello Tonnato – slices of cold veal in a tuna and mayonnaise sauce. These hot croquettes are extremely simple to make and, I think, equally tasty.

375 g (12 oz) veal mince
198 g (7 oz) can of tuna
1–2 cloves of garlic, crushed
a sprig of rosemary leaves, chopped finely

1 large egg (size 1–2), beaten
1 teaspoon green peppercorns (optional)

25 g (1 oz) butter
284 ml (½ pint) carton of single cream

2 rounded teaspoons capers, crushed roughly
salt and black pepper
a little parsley, to garnish

Put the veal, the tuna with its juices and the crushed garlic and chopped rosemary in a mixing bowl and season with salt and black pepper. Pound very thoroughly and mix together well with a large wooden spoon. Then mix in the beaten egg and the green peppercorns, if used. With wet hands, form the mixture into small, short sausage shapes.

Heat the butter in a large frying pan and cook the croquettes over a medium heat for about 5 minutes on each side, turning carefully, until golden brown. Remove them with a slotted spoon and put in a heated serving dish.

Pour off the fat from the pan, pour in the cream and heat to just bubbling. Stir in the crushed capers, season with salt and pepper and allow the cream just to bubble for 30 seconds. Then pour the sauce over the croquettes, and garnish with a little parsley.
Serves 4

ROLLED AND STUFFED VEAL ESCALOPES

Veal escalopes can be rather dry and dull. Not so in this recipe. Thinly
beaten out, they are rolled round a delicious cheesy purée of celeriac,
which has a thin layer of tomato on one side and spinach on the other.
I serve this dish with a bowl of flat egg noodles, well buttered and
peppered, and either a crisp green vegetable or a salad.

250 g (8 oz) spinach
500–625 g (1–1¼ lb)
celeriac
2–3 tablespoons white
wine vinegar

50 g (2 oz) butter
75 g (3 oz) cheese, chopped
roughly
1 rounded teaspoon ground
coriander

1 large egg (size 1–2),
whisked
4 veal escalopes,
375–425 g (12–14 oz)
total weight

1 large clove of garlic,
crushed
tomato purée
olive oil
salt and black pepper

Wash the spinach well and take the stalks off. Bring a
large pan of salted water to the boil. Plunge in the
spinach leaves and boil for just a minute until limp.
Drain well and then chop up finely.

Peel the celeriac, cut it up roughly and put it
immediately in a saucepan of salted water to which
you have added the wine vinegar (this is to stop the
celeriac discolouring). Cover and boil until soft. Then
put it in a food processor with the butter, the cheese,
the coriander and the whisked egg. Whizz until
smooth. Season well with salt and plenty of black
pepper and leave to cool slightly.

Put the veal escalopes between two sheets of oiled
greaseproof paper and bash out with a rolling pin or

heavy object until the meat is as thin as you can get.
Preheat the oven to Gas Mark 9/240°C/475°F.

Smear the crushed garlic on one side of each veal
escalope. Then spread each one all over with tomato
purée, fairly thinly. Next spread on a thick layer of
the slightly cooled celeriac purée and scatter the
chopped spinach evenly on top. Roll the escalopes up
loosely and lightly over the filling and place them, join
side down, in a lightly oiled, shallow ovenproof dish.

Generously smear the rolls with more olive oil
and cook at the very top of the oven for 15 minutes.
(If you are not ready to eat, the rolls can be kept warm
for a bit in a very low oven.)
Serves 4

VEAL ROULADE WITH WALNUT AND TOMATO SAUCE

A minced mixture is stuffed with soft onions, and the accompanying sauce
is mouth-watering.

1 tablespoon olive oil, plus
extra for greasing
375 g (12 oz) onions,
chopped fairly small
2 large cloves of garlic,
chopped finely

2 teaspoons caster sugar
500 g (1 lb) lean veal mince
8–10 sage leaves, chopped
finely
1 rounded teaspoon ground
coriander

parmesan cheese, finely
grated
salt and black pepper

For the sauce:
125 g (4 oz) mushrooms,
chopped roughly

50 g (2 oz) walnut pieces,
chopped fairly small
1 tablespoon olive oil
397g (14 oz) can of
chopped tomatoes
2 tablespoons natural yogurt
salt and black pepper

Heat the oil in a frying pan, add the chopped onions
and stir over a medium heat until soft. Then add the
chopped garlic and stir for another minute. Add the
sugar and season with salt and black pepper. Leave on
one side to cool.

Put the minced veal in a bowl, and stir in the
chopped sage leaves and coriander. Season well with
salt and pepper. Lay out a sheet of oiled greaseproof
paper and press the meat out firmly on it in a 18 x 25
cm (7 x 10 inch) rectangular shape, about 5 mm

(¼ inch) thick, pressing out any cracks that form. Spoon on the cooled onion mixture and pat down evenly all over the meat, stopping a little short of the edges. Roll up very gently with your hands from the short end like a Swiss roll and lay carefully in a roasting tin. Sprinkle with a little finely grated parmesan.

Heat the oven to Gas Mark 4/180°C/350°F and put the roulade in the centre. When the roulade has been cooking for 20 minutes, remove from the oven, baste, and then spoon the chopped mushrooms and walnuts into the pan round the roulade. Dribble the olive oil onto the mushrooms and nuts and return to the oven for another 20 minutes.

Carefully take out the roll with a spatula and put on to a warmed serving plate in a low oven. Empty the chopped tomatoes into the roasting pan with the mushrooms and chopped nuts and heat to boiling, stirring, on top of the stove. Season to taste with salt and black pepper, and very roughly stir in the yogurt. Pour into a sauce bowl to serve with the roulade. If you like, garnish the roll with sage leaves.
Serves 4

SPINACH NOODLES WITH VEAL AND SWEETBREAD SAUCE

This recipe is for a rich and creamy sauce with a sophisticated flavour which goes particularly well with the green spinach-flavoured noodles. However, it can equally well be a sauce for other types of pasta. If you can obtain fresh basil it is the best herb of all for pasta, but dill or tarragon will do very well. Serve simply with a green salad and a bowl of grated parmesan cheese to sprinkle over the noodles.

250 g (8 oz) sweetbreads
25 g (1 oz) butter or margarine
175 g (6 oz) veal mince

4 – 5 tomatoes, chopped small
125 g (4 oz) small mushrooms, sliced finely downwards

a generous sprinkling of chopped fresh basil, dill or tarragon leaves
1 – 2 pinches of chilli powder

284 ml (½ pint) carton of single cream
275 g (9 oz) flat green (spinach-flavoured) noodles
salt

Soak the sweetbreads in a bowl of cold water, changing the water two or three times until they are clear of all traces of blood. Then drain and cut up fairly small. Prepare and set out the remaining ingredients.

Melt the butter or margarine in a large frying pan. Fry the veal mince over a fairly hight heat, stirring for about a minute, just to seal. Add the chopped tomatoes and stir for another 2–3 minutes. Then reduce the heat to low and add the chopped sweetbreads. Cook just until the sweetbreads look pale and then stir in the sliced mushrooms and chopped herbs.

Season with the chilli powder and salt. Finally, add the single cream and bubble in the pan for a minute. Check for seasoning and add more chilli powder and salt if necessary. Take the pan off the heat and leave on one side.

Put the noddles in a large open pan of boiling salted water and cook for 8 –12 minutes, until just soft. Drain and rinse with hot water and put in a warm serving bowl. Reheat the sauce in the frying pan, mix with the noodles and serve.
Serves 4 – 5

ITALIAN MOUSSAKA

There are certain ingredients which seem to represent the food of a country more than any others. Tomatoes, mozzarella cheese and veal could only mean Italy and aubergines always remind me of Turkey, where they feature on every menu. Here is a different kind of moussaka made with veal; it has a topping of baked tomatoes capped with grilled mozzarella cheese. A good family dish. Garnish with a sprig of basil.

*2 large aubergines
750−875 g (1½−1¾ lb)
juice of 1 lemon
500 g (1 lb) veal mince*

*2 large cloves of garlic,
chopped finely
1 tablespoon finely chopped
rosemary*

*3 tablespoons olive oil
1 tablespoon soy sauce
1 medium-size onion,
chopped*

*500−625 g (1−1¼ lb)
medium-size firm tomatoes
2 teaspoons caster sugar
1 mozzarella cheese
salt and black pepper*

Peel the aubergines, slice thinly across and put in a bowl. Sprinkle generously with half of the lemon juice and rub with salt. Turn into a colander and leave in the sink for half an hour to drain away the bitter juices. Meanwhile, put the minced veal in a bowl, add the chopped garlic and rosemary and season with plenty of black pepper.

Heat 1 tablespoon of the olive oil in a large frying pan to a high heat. Add the minced veal and dig around with a wooden spoon for about 5 minutes until any liquid has evaporated. Add the remaining lemon juice and the soy sauce. Stir around and then remove from the heat. Empty the mince into a bowl and keep on one side. Put another tablespoon of the olive oil in the pan and turn the heat down to medium. Add the chopped onion and cook, stirring around a bit, until soft. Add the onion to the mince. Now put the tomatoes in a bowl and pour boiling water over them. Leave for a moment and then drain, peel and halve the tomatoes.

Preheat the oven to Gas Mark 4/180°C/350°F. Rinse the aubergines very thoroughly to wash away the salt. Drain and pat dry with kitchen paper towelling. Put half the sliced aubergines on the bottom of a 1.75-litre (3-pint) ovenproof dish and sprinkle with black pepper. Then spoon in the mince mixture, spread level, lay on the remaining aubergines and sprinkle with black pepper again. Finally arrange the tomato halves, cut-side down, in neat circles to cover the aubergines. Brush the tomatoes with the remaining oil and sprinkle evenly with the caster sugar.

Cook in the centre of the oven for 1½ hours. Just before serving slice the mozzarella cheese across thinly and place the slices on top of the tomatoes. Grill for 2−3 minutes just to melt the cheese.
Serves 6

MINCED PORK WITH APPLES AND SPINACH

This is a quickly made recipe with a mild and unusual flavour. It is a good supper dish and goes well with rice or mashed potatoes.

50 g (2 oz) butter or margarine
375 g (12 oz) pork mince
1 heaped teaspoon ground coriander

2 medium-size cooking apples, peeled, quartered, cored and sliced
250 g (8 oz) finely chopped spinach, fresh or thawed from frozen

1 teaspoon finely grated orange rind
1 tablespoon caster sugar
1 tablespoon wine vinegar

150 ml (5 fl oz) soured cream
salt and black pepper

Heat 25 g (1 oz) of the butter or margarine in a large frying pan or saucepan. Add the pork and stir and break it up with a wooden spoon over a moderate heat to separate and seal. Add the coriander and season well with salt and black pepper. Then add the remaining butter or margarine, sliced apples, chopped spinach, grated orange rind, caster sugar and vinegar. Season again with salt and pepper.

Cover the pan and cook gently for about 5 minutes. Uncover, very roughly stir in the soured cream and transfer to a warm serving dish.
Serves 4

PIGLET PIE

Children adore this pie. It has a delicious crust of potato pastry (a good way to use up leftover boiled potato) and is filled with a tasty mixture of pork, tomatoes and sweetcorn, flavoured with mustard and coriander. A perfect family meal. Serve it with carrots or a green vegetable.

1 tablespoon sunflower oil
375 g (12 oz) pork mince
2 teaspoons ground coriander (optional)
2 teaspoons French mustard

3–4 tomatoes, chopped fairly small
250 g (8 oz) frozen sweetcorn, boiled until tender

salt and black pepper

For the pastry:
125 g (4 oz) plain flour
1 teaspoon baking powder

a pinch of salt
125 g (4 oz) butter or margarine
175 g (6 oz) cold mashed potato
a little milk for glazing

Heat the oil in a large frying pan. Season the pork with salt and black pepper and fry it, stirring and breaking it up with a wooden spoon over a fairly high heat, until sealed. Stir in the coriander, mustard and chopped tomatoes and cook more gently, still stirring, for a further 5 minutes. Stir in the cooked sweetcorn and spoon the mixture into a 1.2–1.5-litre (2–2½ pint) plate or pie dish and leave to cool. Preheat the oven to Gas Mark 5/190°C/375°F.

To make the potato pastry sift the flour, baking powder and salt into a bowl. Rub in the butter or margarine until the mixture resembles breadcrumbs.

Then work in the mashed potato with your hands and knead slightly until you have a smooth dough.

Gather the pastry into a ball and roll out on a floured board into a piece a little larger than the dish. Lay it over the dish and cut off the excess carefully; press this on to the side of the rim all round. Dampen this pastry rim, lay the pastry lid over it and press down to seal. Trim the edges and make cuts round the edges of the pastry with the back of a knife.

Brush the pie with milk and cook in the centre of the oven for 25 –35 minutes, until golden all over.
Serves 4–5

STEAMED PORK PUDDING WITH RED PEPPER AND GREEN PEPPERCORNS

I find the flavour of this pudding quite delicious. The red peppers are grilled beforehand to add a smoky taste. It is a good change from meat loaf and just as easy to make. Serve it with boiled potatoes to mop up the tasty juices and a green vegetable, such as crisply cooked cabbage.

2 large red peppers
500 g (1 lb) pork mince
2 large eggs (size 1–2), beaten

2 tablespoons tomato purée
1 rounded teaspoon whole green peppercorns

2–3 pinches of chilli powder
a little butter for greasing

150 ml (5 fl oz) soured cream
salt

Cut the peppers lengthways into four and remove the seeds. Lay the pieces skin side up under a hot grill for about 10 minutes, until the skins are completely blackened and blistered. Then, under cold water, peel off the skins. Chop up as finely as possible.

In a bowl, mix the pork thoroughly with the chopped peppers, beaten eggs, tomato purée and green peppercorns. Season well with salt and the chilli powder.

Generously butter a 1.2-litre (2-pint) pudding basin. Spoon in the meat mixture and smooth the top. Cover the basin with foil and secure with string, also tying on a string handle. Put the basin in a saucepan with enough hot water to come half-way up. Cover the pan and let the water simmer gently for 1 hour (checking occasionally to see that the water is not boiling away).

Remove the basin from the pan and leave to sit for 5 minutes or so. Then turn out on to a round plate – a fairly large one, as the pudding will be surrounded by delicious juices. Just before serving stir the soured cream with a teaspoon until smooth and spoon over the top of the pudding.
Serves 4–5

ROLLED PORK AND POTATO PIE

This is a good family dish, equally popular with adults and children. It is made swiss roll fashion, with garlic-flavoured mashed potato encasing a tasty minced pork mixture and then baked until crispy golden. Serve with a green vegetable or simply a salad.

750 g (1½ lb) potatoes
75 g (3 oz) butter or margarine, plus a little extra

3 –4 cloves of garlic, chopped finely
1 egg, beaten
500 g (1 lb) pork mince

1 large green pepper, chopped finely
50 –75 g (2–3 oz) smoked rindless bacon, chopped finely

2 teaspoons French mustard
a little plain flour
salt and black pepper
sprigs of parsley, to garnish

Preheat the oven to Gas Mark 4/180°C/350°F. Peel and boil the potatoes. Drain and then mash them smoothly with the butter or margarine. Season with salt and black pepper. Incorporate the garlic and the beaten egg, using a wooden spoon.

Put the pork in a bowl and add the green pepper and bacon. Stir in the mustard and season very well with salt and pepper.

Sprinkle a sheet of greaseproof paper or kitchen foil generously with flour. Spoon the potato on to the paper and, with floured hands, pat out into an oblong about the size of a swiss roll tin. Spread the meat mixture evenly on top. With the help of the grease-proof paper or foil, roll up the pie from the short end like a swiss roll and then slip it carefully off the paper or foil on to a well-greased rectangular ovenproof dish. Criss-cross the top of the roll with a fork and dot all over with the extra butter or margarine.

Cook in the centre of the oven for 1–1¼ hours until the roll is a rich golden brown. Serve surrounded by sprigs of parsley.

Serves 6

STUFFED PORK RISSOLES WITH APRICOT AND ONION SAUCE

When fresh apricots first appear in the shops they are usually too hard and rather too tasteless to eat raw. However, when cooked they come to life and it's useful to know of savoury ways to use them as well as sweet. Pork is famous for going well with sweet and sharp flavours and so in these rissoles the apricots are used for the soft stuffing as well as the creamy sauce.

25 g (1 oz) butter
750 g (1½ lb) fresh apricots, halved, stoned and chopped roughly
2 large cloves of garlic, chopped finely

2 teaspoons caster sugar
750 g (1½ lb) pork mince
2 rounded tablespoons chopped fresh marjoram
3 teaspoons ground coriander

a little oil for greasing
a little plain flour
2 tablespoons olive oil
1 large onion, peeled and chopped roughly
250 ml (8 fl oz) water

1 tablespoon lemon juice
150 ml (5 fl oz) double cream
salt and black pepper
lettuce leaves, to garnish

Heat the butter in a frying pan over a medium heat, add half the chopped apricots and the garlic and stir around over a medium to low heat for about 5 minutes until soft and mushy. Then stir in the caster sugar, turn on to a plate and leave to cool while you prepare the rissole mixture. Preheat the oven to Gas Mark 4/180°C/350°F.

Put the minced pork in a bowl, add the chopped marjoram and ground coriander and season well with salt and black pepper. Divide the mince into four parts and form into large balls. Press the balls out like large, rather flat hamburgers on an oiled surface. Divide the cooked apricots into four parts and spoon each on to the centre of one 'hamburger'. Then carefully draw up the sides to enclose the apricots and pat gently into a ball again. Roll the balls in a little flour and place in a roasting pan. Cook in the centre of the oven for ¾–1 hour until lightly browned.

Meanwhile, start the sauce. Put the olive oil in a heavy saucepan over a gentle heat, add the chopped onion and stir around until softened and translucent. Then add the water, the rest of the chopped apricots and the lemon juice. Cover the pan and continue cooking over a low heat for at least 30 minutes until the apricots have become soft and rather mushy. Then remove from the heat and leave on one side.

When the rissoles are ready, pour the pan juices into the saucepan of onions and apricots. (If necessary keep the rissoles warm in a very low oven.) Add the cream to the onion and apricot mixture and season to taste with salt and plenty of black pepper. Before serving, reheat the sauce just up to boiling point. Arrange lettuce leaves all round a heated serving dish, carefully pour the sauce into it and place the rissoles on top.

Serves 4

ROMAN COBBLER

In our family this recipe is more popular than shepherd's pie, which is saying a lot, and it is not much more trouble to make.

For the topping:
¼ whole nutmeg, grated
600 ml (1 pint) milk
125 g (4 oz) fine semolina
75 g (3 oz) grated cheese
25 g (1 oz) butter or margarine

1 egg, lightly whisked
salt and black pepper

For the filling:
625 – 750 g (1¼–1½ lb) boneless pork shoulder steaks

25 g (1 oz) butter or margarine, plus a little more
1 tablespoon oil
2–3 cloves of garlic, chopped finely
a small handful of fresh sage leaves, chopped finely, or 1 teaspoon dried sage

125 g (4 oz) mushrooms, sliced
a sprinkling of grated parmesan cheese
salt and black pepper

Make the topping at least 2 hours in advance, as follows. Add the nutmeg to the milk in a saucepan, together with salt and black pepper. Stir in the semolina. Bring the milk to the boil and simmer gently for 3 – 4 minutes until very thick, stirring all the time. Remove from the heat and add the grated cheese, butter and whisked egg. Return to a low heat and stir for a minute more. Oil a large Swiss roll tin or a roasting pan. Spread the mixture evenly over the bottom of the tin. Cover with a cloth and leave to get completely cold – in the fridge if possible.

Using a sharp knife, cut the pork into very small pieces and season with salt and pepper. Melt the butter or margarine and the oil in a large frying pan. Stir the pork pieces and chopped garlic over a medium heat for about 5 minutes, until cooked. Add the sage and mushrooms and cook for a further minute or two, stirring the mixture.

Transfer the meat and mushrooms with a slotted spoon into a shallow, ovenproof dish. Bubble the remaining liquid in the pan over a strong heat for a moment or so, until reduced and slightly thickened, and pour over the meat.

Set the grill on medium heat. Cut the cooled topping mixture into fingers (about 5 x 2.5 cm, 2 x 1 inch) and arrange in an overlapping pattern all over the meat. Dot with butter, sprinkle generously with grated parmesan and put under the grill until a rich, golden brown.
Serves 4–5

SPINACH STUFFED WITH PORK, CHEESE AND MUSHROOMS

500 g (1 lb) fresh pork or beef mince
50 – 125 g (2–4 oz) mushrooms, chopped

2–3 cloves of garlic, chopped finely
2 rounded teaspoons paprika

125 g (4 oz) grated cheese
1 teaspoon sugar
500 g (1 lb) spinach

a little butter or margarine
salt and black pepper

Preheat the oven to Gas Mark 6/200°C/400°F.

In a bowl mix together the pork, mushrooms, garlic, paprika, 75 g (3 oz) of the grated cheese, the sugar and plenty of salt and black pepper.

Butter a fairly shallow ovenproof dish. Wash the spinach and take the stalks off. Lay about half the spinach leaves on the bottom and up the sides of the dish. Spoon the pork mixture and cover with the remaining spinach. Sprinkle the rest of the grated cheese on top and dot with butter. Cover tightly with buttered foil or a lid and bake below the centre of the oven for ¾–1 hour. If you like, sprinkle on a little extra grated cheese before serving.
Serves 6

Roman Cobbler

WHOLE ORANGE PORK AND MUSHROOM CASSEROLE

A purée of whole boiled oranges forms the basis of the sauce in this lightly
spiced dish. A wonderfully intense smell of fresh oranges fills the house as
it cooks. Serve with egg noodles or rice and a green vegetable.

2 oranges
1–2 fresh green chillies
3 cloves of garlic
1 large red pepper
*2 tablespoons white wine
vinegar*

2–3 tablespoons honey
2 pinches of cayenne pepper
25 g (1 oz) butter
*2 tablespoons sunflower or
groundnut oil*

*750 g (1½ lb) stewing
pork, cut in cubes*
*2 teaspoons ground
coriander*
*250 g (8 oz) mushrooms,
sliced*

salt
*300 ml (½ pint) soured
cream or natural yogurt,
to serve*

First boil the whole, washed oranges in a covered
saucepan of water for 2 hours (or for 30 minutes in a
pressure cooker).

Meanwhile, under running water, cut open the
green chillies and discard the seeds. Peel the garlic and
chop finely together with the chillies. Cut the pepper
in half and then quarters, discarding the seeds, and
slice across fairly thinly.

When the oranges are ready, cool a little under
cold water until easier to handle and then cut open
and pick out the pips. Put in a food processor with
the vinegar, the honey and the cayenne pepper and
whizz until smooth. Then whizz in 4 tablespoons
water and season to taste with salt. Preheat the oven

to Gas Mark 4/180°C/350°F.

On top of the stove heat the butter with the oil in
a flameproof casserole. Over a high heat add the pork
and stir round to seal all over. Then stir in the chopped
garlic and chillies and ground coriander. Stir around
for a minute and then add the orange purée and the
sliced red pepper.

Cover the dish and cook in the centre of the oven
for 30 minutes; then turn down the oven to Gas Mark
1/140°C/275°F for another hour. After this add the
sliced mushrooms and cook for 10–15 minutes more.
Before serving, spoon the soured cream roughly over
the top.
Serves 4

GINGER PORK STEAKS WITH CHINESE NOODLES

This is a convenient supper dish because it makes a complete meal. It's
popular, especially for the slices of hot avocado amongst the noodles. If
you want, you can make it more Chinese by slicing the pork up thinly
and cooking it more quickly – but I think the meat is more succulent
cooked in large pieces.

6 pork shoulder steaks
2 cloves of garlic, crushed
*2 tablespoons sunflower or
groundnut oil*

*2.5 cm (1-inch) piece of
fresh ginger*
150 ml (¼ pint) dry sherry

150 ml (¼ pint) water
625 g (1¼ lb) carrots
2 large avocados

*375 g (12 oz) Chinese egg
noodles*
soy sauce
salt and black pepper

Rub the steaks with the crushed garlic and season
with salt and black pepper. Heat the oil in a large
frying pan, put in the steaks over a high heat and seal
for 2–4 minutes on each side until browned. Then
turn the heat down very low. Peel the ginger and slice
across finely. Lay the slices on top of the steaks. Pour

over the sherry and water, cover the pan tightly with
foil and continue cooking for 30–45 minutes until
the meat feels tender when pierced with a knife.

Meanwhile, peel the carrots and slice across as
finely as possible; this is easier with a food processor.

Towards the end of the cooking bring a large pan

of salted water to the boil. While the water is coming to the boil cut the avocado in half, peel it and cut across in thin slices. Put the noodles in the boiling water and then add the sliced carrots and avocado. Turn off the heat, cover the pan and leave for 6 minutes until the noodles are soft. Drain the noodles and vegetables and put in a large warmed serving dish.

Sprinkle generously with soy sauce.

Transfer the pork steaks with a slotted spatula on to the noodles. Finally, sprinkle a little more soy sauce into the pan juices and boil them up over a fierce heat for a few minutes until reduced and syrupy. Pour this sauce over the meat and serve.

Serves 4

PORK RISSOLES STUFFED WITH FENNEL

In this unusual dish the minced pork is subtly flavoured with orange rind and fennel or dill leaves, and there is a lovely surprise as you bite into a tender centre of bulb fennel. The rissoles are served under a brilliant carrot sauce flavoured with orange juice. The result is extremely good. Serve with new or mashed potatoes and a green salad.

250 – 500 g (8 oz – 1 lb) bulb of fennel	*finely grated rind of 1 orange*	*1 large egg (size 1–2), beaten*	*For the sauce:*
750 g (1½ lb) pork mince	*1 good tablespoon chopped fennel or dill leaves*	*salt and black pepper*	*400 g (13 oz) carrots*
125 g (4 oz) fresh white breadcrumbs			*450 ml (¾ pint) water*
			1 chicken stock cube
			juice of 1 orange
			salt and black pepper

Preheat the oven to Gas Mark 4/180°C/350°F. Cut any long stalks off the fennel bulbs, reserving the leaves for garnish later. Slice the bulbs into 1 cm (½-inch) strips. Steam or boil for a few minutes until tender and rinse with cold water to cool.

Mix the pork mince with all the other rissole ingredients in a bowl and season well with salt and black pepper. Divide the cooked fennel into eight equal piles. Then, with wet hands, divide the meat mixture also into eight equal piles. Still with wet hands, press one pile of meat out flat on a wet board. Lay one pile of fennel on top. Bring the meat up round the fennel and form with your hands into a large, fairly round shape, completely encasing the vegetable. Repeat with the other piles.

Lay the rissoles in a roasting pan and cover with foil. Cook the rissoles in the centre of the oven for 1 hour, removing the foil for the last 20 minutes to brown them a little.

While the rissoles are cooking make the carrot sauce. Peel a 25 g (1 oz) piece of carrot, cut it into the thinnest possible little strips and leave on one side. Bring the water to the boil in a saucepan, add the chicken stock cube and stir to dissolve. Peel and cut up the remaining carrots, add to the stock, cover the pan and simmer until soft. Add the orange juice and leave to cool a little.

When the rissoles have cooked pour the juices off into a saucepan and boil fiercely for 3 – 4 minutes, until reduced to a thick, syrupy sauce. Transfer the rissoles to a serving plate and spoon the syrupy sauce over them. Keep warm in a low oven while you finish the carrot sauce.

Whizz the carrots and their stock in a food processor or liquidiser until smooth. Then pour into a saucepan, add the reserved carrot strips, reheat and bubble for 1 minute. Check for seasoning and then pour the sauce over the rissoles. Sprinkle with the fennel leaves.

Serves 6–8

PORK ROLLS STUFFED WITH ARTICHOKE, WITH MUSHROOM AND MUSTARD SAUCE

Remember to drink some water while you are eating these
artichoke-stuffed rolls; even city tap water will taste like a mountain
spring! This is good accompanied by buttered
egg noodles and broccoli.

3 large globe artichokes
1 tablespoon lemon juice
1 clove of garlic, peeled and
chopped roughly

8–10 black olives, stoned
4 thinly cut pork escalopes
weighing about
375–500 g (12 oz – 1 lb)

olive oil
caster sugar
300 ml (½ pint) milk
25 g (1 oz) butter
2 tablespoons cornflour

4 tablespoons whole-grain
mustard
125 g (4 oz) button
mushrooms, halved
salt and black pepper

Preheat the oven to Gas Mark 4/180°C/350°F. Break the stems off the artichokes and boil them in salted water for 45 minutes or until the leaves come off easily. Put them into a sink of cold water to cool and after a few minutes twist out the centre leaves, revealing the hairy choke. Scrape out the choke and discard it. Remove them from the water, and, on a board, scrape the flesh off the remaining big leaves and put it in a food processor, adding lastly the delicious bottom of the artichoke. Add the lemon juice, the chopped garlic and the stoned olives and whizz to a purée. Season to taste with salt and black pepper and spread the paste on to the pork escalopes. Then roll the escalopes up gently and loosely like little swiss rolls and lay them in an open ovenproof dish, join-side down. Smear the rolls with olive oil, sprinkle them lightly with a little caster sugar and bake the dish in the centre of the oven for 1 hour.

Meanwhile, put the milk into a measuring jug. When the pork has cooled, pour the juices off into the measuring jug, with the milk. Put the rolls in a very low oven to keep warm. Melt the butter in a saucepan, remove from the heat and add the cornflour. Stir with a wooden spoon until smooth. Then stir in the milk and juices and the whole-grain mustard. Put the pan back on the heat, bring the sauce to the boil and let it bubble for 2–3 minutes. Add the button mushrooms and bubble it for another minute. Season to taste and spoon over the rolls.
Serves 4

MY BUBBLE AND SQUEAK

This dish can only be said to be vaguely related to Bubble and Squeak. To
transform it into an even more 'grown-up' dish stir 300 ml (½ pint)
soured cream in at the last moment.

500 g (1 lb) potatoes,
scrubbed and cut into
1–2.5 cm (½ –1-inch)
pieces

1 tablespoon olive oil
2 cloves of garlic, chopped
finely

1 teaspoon caraway seeds
½ teaspoon dill seeds
300 g (10 oz) pork mince

the top half of 1 chinese
cabbage, sliced thinly
salt and black pepper

Steam or boil the potato pieces until cooked. Heat the olive oil in a large frying pan to a medium heat, add the chopped garlic and the caraway and dill seeds and stir around. Add the minced pork and dig around for 5 minutes or so until cooked and separated. Then add the sliced chinese cabbage and stir for a minute or two until limp. Lastly, add the cooked potatoes and stir for another minute or so to heat them. Season before transferring to a heated serving dish.
Serves 4–5

Pork Rolls Stuffed with Artichoke, with Mushroom and Mustard Sauce

VEAL-STUFFED PORK ROLLS WITH LEMON AND PARSLEY SAUCE

These tender little rolls are quite delicious. The pork fillet is flattened until very thin and then wrapped around a stuffing of minced veal and tomato flavoured with coriander and garlic. It is a dish which is equally suitable for a family meal or a dinner party.

1 tablespoon olive oil
1 medium-size onion, chopped
2–3 cloves of garlic, chopped finely

2 rounded teaspoons ground coriander
375 g (12 oz) veal or lamb mince
2 medium-size tomatoes, skinned and chopped small

4–6 pinches of chilli powder, or to taste
375 g (12 oz) pork fillet
1 egg, beaten
300 ml (1/2 pint) water

juice of 1 lemon
2 teaspoons cornflour
a handful of parsley, chopped finely
salt and black pepper

Heat the oil in a large frying pan and fry the onion gently, until soft. Then add the garlic and coriander and stir for half a minute. Increase the heat, add the mince and fry, stirring and breaking up with a wooden spoon, until cooked. Lower the heat again and add the tomatoes. Cook, stirring, until the tomatoes are soft and the mixture dry. Season with salt and the chilli powder. Put to one side and preheat the oven to Gas Mark 4/180°C/350°F.

Cut the pork fillet across into 1 cm (1/2-inch) slices. Lay the slices, well spaced out, on a large sheet of oiled greaseproof paper. Cover with another sheet of oiled paper. Beat out evenly with a rolling pin, not too hard or the meat will break up, until the pieces are thin and 2–3 times their original size.

Mix the beaten egg into the mince mixture and then spoon the mixture across the middle of each thin piece of pork. Roll the meat up round the mince filling and place the rolls in a roasting pan, join side down. Press any mince that falls out back into the rolls. Pour the water into the pan and cover with foil. Cook in the centre of the oven for 45 minutes.

Using a slotted spoon or fish slice, transfer the rolls, when cooked, to a serving dish. Strain the juices into a saucepan and add the lemon juice. Mix the cornflour with 2 tablespoons water until smooth and then stir into the stock and lemon juice. Bring to the boil, stirring, and allow to bubble, still stirring, for 2–3 minutes. Season to taste with salt and black pepper, stir in the chopped parsley and pour over the pork rolls before serving.
Serves 5–6

ROAST PORK WITH APPLE AND WALNUT STUFFING

Taking the trouble to stuff an inexpensive pork joint such as hand, blade bone or even a large piece of belly can transform it into a dish fit for a gourmet.

1.1–1.5 kg (2 1/2 –3 1/2 lb) boned joint of pork
1 large cooking apple
1 squeeze of lemon juice

1 tablespoon sugar
50 g (2 oz) fresh brown breadcrumbs

50 g (2 oz) walnuts or sweet almonds, chopped
1 small egg, whisked
2 cloves of garlic, crushed

300 ml (1/2 pint) beer
1 teaspoon arrowroot or cornflour
salt and black pepper

If the boned joint has been rolled up undo the string and lay the piece of meat out flat.

Peel and grate the apple and put it in a mixing bowl, stirring in a little lemon juice at the same time. Stir in the sugar, breadcrumbs, walnut, egg and sea-soning in that order. Spread the garlic over the meat and then spoon the stuffing on to it or into any pockets in the meat (this will depend on how it has been boned). Roll the meat up round the stuffing and fasten with string or skewers. Smear the joint all over with oil, score the thick skin well with a sharp knife if not already done, and rub with coarse salt to make good, crisp crackling.

Heat the oven to Gas Mark 8/230°C/450°F. Put the joint in a roasting pan towards the top of the oven for 20 minutes, then move it to the centre of the oven and turn the heat down to Gas Mark 4/180°C/350°F for another 2–2½ hours, basting occasionally.

Half to three-quarters of an hour before you remove the joint, tip out the fat and pour the beer into the roasting pan. This will produce a delicious gravy which you can thicken with the arrowroot or cornflour dissolved in a little water and bubbled up with the juices in the pan when you have removed the joint.

Serves 8–10

ROAST PORK WITH TOMATO AND TARRAGON SAUCE

This rich tomato sauce is no trouble to make but adds greatly to the succulence and flavour of the meat.

1.25 – 1.75 kg (3 – 4 lb) joint of pork on the bone	*juice of 1 lemon*	*For the sauce:*	*1 teaspoon sugar*
3 – 4 cloves of garlic, chopped finely	*sunflower or groundnut oil*	*398 g (14 oz) can of tomatoes*	*2 teaspoons dried tarragon*
	salt and black pepper	*1 large glass of red wine*	*juices from the meat*
		2 teaspoons French mustard	*1 dessertspoon cornflour*
			salt and black pepper

Make deep incisions in the meat and poke the chopped garlic in as far as you can. If not already done by the butcher, score the thick fat closely with a sharp knife. Mix the lemon juice and twice as much oil with salt and black pepper in a cup and smear all over the meat. Put the joint in a roasting pan and if possible cover the meat with foil. Leave for at least two hours at room temperature, spooning the juices over the meat again once or twice.

Heat the oven to Gas Mark 9/240°C/475°F. Remove foil from the meat. Rub the scored fat with salt and a little extra oil (this should produce golden crisp crackling) and roast at the high heat for 20 minutes, then turn down the oven to Gas Mark 3/160°C/325°F and cook for a further 2–2¼ hours.

Before the meat is quite ready, put the tomatoes, wine, mustard, sugar and tarragon into a saucepan. Blend the cornflour until smooth with a little water and add to the mixture. Bring to the boil, stirring, and bubble for 2 –3 minutes. Add salt and black pepper.

When the meat is ready, pour the excess fat from the pan and add the meat juices to the sauce. If the sauce seems too thick add a little more wine or water. Pour the sauce into a serving jug and pour over the meat when carved.

Serves 6–8

ANGLO-CHINESE PIE

At first sight this is a deception. What looks like a traditional, hearty
English pie is put on the table. Then you look closer and see that the crisp
pastry is studded with sesame seeds. Once cut, the crust reveals a golden
sweet and sour mixture of turkey, pork and water chestnuts, smelling
wonderful. I serve the pie with rice and a salad;
it makes a popular family meal.
Pictured on pages 54/5.

For the filling:
3 tablespoons groundnut oil
500 g (1 lb) boneless turkey breast, sliced thinly
500 g (1 lb) boneless pork shoulder steaks, sliced thinly
2 large cloves of garlic, chopped finely
5 cm (2-inch) piece of fresh ginger, chopped finely
¼ teaspoon cayenne pepper
300 ml (½ pint) water
1½ tablespoons of soft dark brown sugar
4 tablespoons tomato ketchup
2 tablespoons tomato purée
1 tablespoon rich soy sauce
1 tablespoon wine vinegar
1 level tablespoon cornflour
227 g (8 oz) can of water chestnuts, drained and sliced thinly
salt

For the pastry:
175 g (6 oz) strong plain flour, plus extra for rolling
½ teaspoon salt
125 g (4 oz) ground rice
3 tablespoons sesame seeds
75 g (3 oz) butter
125 g (4 oz) white vegetable fat
a little groundnut oil

Preheat the oven to Gas Mark 8/230°C/450°F. Heat 2 tablespoons of the oil in a large frying pan over a high heat. Add the turkey and pork slices and stir around just to seal them all over. Then turn down the heat, and, using a slotted spatula, transfer the meat to a casserole and leave it on one side.

Add the remaining tablespoon of oil to the pan and stir the chopped garlic and ginger around over a fairly low heat for about 2 minutes. Then stir in the cayenne pepper, the water, the brown sugar, the tomato ketchup and purée, the soy sauce and the vinegar. Remove the pan from the heat. Mix the cornflour in a cup with 2 tablespoons of water and stir it until smooth. Add this to the pan mixture, put the pan back on the heat and stir it constantly until it is bubbling and thickened. Continue stirring for about 2 minutes. Then pour the sauce into the casserole with the meat, stir it in and cover the casserole. Put the dish in the centre of the oven for 20 minutes and then turn down the heat to Gas Mark 1/150°C/275°F and cook for another hour.

Remove the casserole from the oven and add a little salt to taste. Stir the water chestnut slices into the meat mixture. Then turn the filling into a 1.2–1.5-litre (2–2½-pint) tradtitional pie dish and leave until cold.

Meanwhile, prepare the pastry. Sift the flour, salt and ground rice into a bowl. Stir in the sesame seeds. Add the butter and fat, cut into small pieces, and rub them in lightly (or do it all in a food processor). Stir in 3 – 4 tablespoons of very cold water with a knife until the mixture only just begins to stick together. Then press the dough into a ball and roll it out on a floured surface into a piece big enough to cover the pie dish. Moisten the edges of the pie dish and lay the pastry on it. Cut round the edge neatly and mark it all around with the back of a knife. Roll out the pastry trimmings and cut them into shapes to decorate the top of the pie. Make two small incisions to allow steam to escape.

Refrigerate the pie for 30 minutes or more and preheat the oven to Gas Mark 6/200°C/400°F. Just before cooking, brush the pie crust lightly with cold water and a little groundnut oil. Cook it in the centre of the oven for 25 –30 minutes until browned.
Serves 6

MARINATED AND SPIKED ROAST LEG OF PORK

1 leg of pork
3 large cloves of garlic
5 cm (2-inch) piece of fresh
ginger

grated rind and juice of
2 oranges
3 tablespoons whole-grain
mustard

4 tablespoons thick honey
3 teaspoons ground
coriander
1 teaspoon ground cloves

oil
caster sugar
sea salt and black pepper

Line a roasting pan with a large piece of foil which comes a long way over the edges of the pan. Using a very sharp knife, score the skin of the pork in a criss-cross pattern all over. Then insert the knife into the flesh of the pork in several places to make pockets for flavourings. Put the leg on the foil in the roasting pan. Peel the garlic and ginger and chop them finely together. Mix them in a bowl with the grated orange rind and 1 tablespoon of the mustard. Now press this mixture into the deep incisions you have made in the pork flesh. Then mix the orange juice with the remaining mustard, the honey and the ground spices in another bowl. Season with plenty of black pepper and rub the mixture all over the joint but not on the hard skin. Bring the foil up all round the pork but leave the hard skin exposed. Leave in a cool place overnight.

When you are ready to cook the joint, heat the oven to Gas mark 5/190°C/375°F. Smear the hard skin with oil and sprinkle it with caster sugar and sea salt. Cover the joint loosely with greaseproof paper, tucking it into the foil. Cover the shank (thin) end completely with foil, so it does not dry out. Put the pork into the centre of the oven for 25 minutes per pound plus 25 minutes, opening up the foil and removing the paper completely for the last 30 minutes or so. If the hard skin hasn't crisped you can turn up the oven to its highest setting for about 15 minutes.
Serves 12–15

SWEET SPICED GAMMON

4.95 kg (11 lb) smoked
gammon on the bone
3 tablespoons black treacle
2 tablespoons dark brown
sugar

3 teaspoons black
peppercorns
2 teaspoons allspice berries
1 teaspoon cloves

2–3 teaspoons juniper
berries
750 g (1½ lb) plain flour
water

For the glaze:
3 teaspoons French mustard
1 tablespoon redcurrant jelly

Soak the gammon in a large sink of cold water, if possible overnight, changing the water once or twice. Take it out and pat it dry. In a bowl, put the black treacle and the dark brown sugar. Grind the black peppercorns, the allspice and the cloves in a coffee grinder or with a pestle and mortar. Mix them into the black treacle and sugar. Roughly crush the juniper berries and press them into any cracks in the gammon. Smear the treacle and spice mixture thoroughly over the flesh.

Mix the flour with enough cold water to make an elastic dough. Roll the dough out on a floured board into a piece large enough to wrap up the gammon. Wrap it very loosely – since it shrinks while cooking – and press the edges to seal. Patch up any cracks or holes with foil. Put the parcel into a roasting pan join-sides uppermost. Heat the oven to Gas Mark 4/180°C/350°F, put the pan on a low shelf and bake for 20 –25 minutes per 500 g (1 lb).

When the gammon is cooked, break off the flour crust and cut off the hard skin while it is still hot. Using a sharp knife cut a diamond pattern in the fat. Turn the oven up to Gas Mark 6/200°C/400°F. For the glaze, mix the mustard and redcurrant jelly in a bowl and then brush the mixture over the fat. Put the gammon back in the oven for 15 –20 minutes until well glazed. Leave until cold.
Serves 15–20

SWEET AND TENDER LAMB COOKED IN BEER

Here is a shoulder of lamb with a tasty sweet and savoury stuffing of dates
and anchovies. It is marinated in beer for 1–2 days and then cooked in the
marinade. This produces meat so soft and moist that you should hardly
have to bite it. Shallots are cooked with the lamb and combine with the
beer to make the most delicious gravy.

50 g (2 oz) stoned dates	1 can of anchovy fillets	1 tablespoon wine or cider	oil
2 tablespoons chunky	1 onion	vinegar	2 rounded teaspoons honey
marmalade	2–2.5 kg (4½ –5½ lb)	600 ml (1 pint) can of lager	25 g (1 oz) cornflour
	shoulder of English lamb	250 g (8 oz) shallots	salt, sea salt and black
			pepper

Chop the dates finely and put in a bowl. Add the marmalade. Open the can of anchovies and empty it with the oil into the bowl. Cut up the onions finely and stir them into the mixture. Season with salt and black pepper and mix thoroughly. Using a sharp knife, cut 3 – 4 deep pockets in the underside of the lamb. Spoon the date and anchovy mixture into these pockets. Then rub the meat with the vinegar and season with salt and pepper. Turn the lamb over and put in a roasting pan. Pour the beer into the pan. Cover with cling film and leave in the fridge to marinate for at least 24 hours.

Next day heat the oven to Gas Mark 3/160°C/325°F. Rub the top of the lamb with a little oil and sea salt and cook with the marinade in the centre of the oven for 2–2 ½ hours. After 30 minutes, peel and add the whole shallots to the juices, stirring in the honey at the same time.

When the lamb is cooked transfer it to a carving board. Using a slotted spoon, scoop up the shallots and put them in a serving bowl. Skim the pan juices if there is a lot of oil. Mix the cornflour with a tablespoon of water to a smooth paste and stir it into the pan juices. Continue stirring over a medium heat, letting it bubble for 2–3 minutes until thickened. Pour this gravy into the bowl with the shallots and spoon it over the carved lamb.
Serves 8 –10

SPRING LAMB PIE

Here is an excellent alternative to shepherd's pie: although the flavours are
more sophisticated it seems to please both adults and children just as
much. It has a certain Russian character, with a layer of beetroot and a
soured cream sauce topping the spiced lamb. It has won high marks in our
family.

750 g (1½ lb) lamb fillet or	2 teaspoons caraway seeds	300 ml (½ pint) milk	500 –625 g (1–1¼ lb)
ground lamb	1 teaspoon ground cinnamon	284 ml (½ pint) carton of	baking potatoes, unpeeled
2 tablespoons olive oil, plus	500 g (1 lb) cooked	soured cream	and cut into 2.5 –5 cm
a little extra	beetroot, sliced thinly	juice of 1 lemon	(1–2-inch) slices
2 large cloves of garlic,	5 tablespoons cornflour		salt and black pepper
chopped finely			

Preheat the oven to Gas Mark 5/190°C/375°F. If using lamb fillet, mince or chop in a food processor. Heat the olive oil in a large frying pan to a high heat.

Add the lamb and stir around to brown all over; then add the chopped garlic and the spices. Continue stirring around for another minute or two, until any liquid has evaporated. Season with salt and black pepper. Turn the mixture into a large ovenproof gratinée dish and spread level. Arrange the sliced beetroot all over the top.

Now put the cornflour in a saucepan and mix to a smooth paste with 4 tablespoons of the milk. Gradually stir in the remaining milk and then whisk in the soured cream until smooth. Bring to the boil, stirring all the time with a wooden spoon; then bubble, still stirring, for 3 minutes. Remove from the heat and gradually stir in the lemon juice. Then season to taste with salt and black pepper. Pour this thick sauce all over the beetroot layer in the dish and spread even.

Put the sliced potatoes in a bowl and coat with a little olive oil and salt, using your hands. Arrange the potatoes higgledy-piggledy on top of the soured cream sauce. Bake in the centre of the oven for 1–1¼ hours, until the potatoes are browned and soft when you insert a small knife. Keep the pie warm in a low oven if necessary and serve simply with one green vegetable.

Serves 6 – 8

LAMB AND AUBERGINE DOME WITH FRESH TOMATO SAUCE

This is a sort of meat and vegetable loaf, with a lovely flavour and soft texture, studded with crunchy pieces of almond. It is served with a brilliant tomato sauce and I like it accompanied by a salad and either boiled potatoes or good fresh bread.

500 – 625 g (1–1¼ lb) aubergines	*2 medium-size onions, peeled and chopped finely*	*2 large eggs (size 1–2), beaten*	*1 tablespoon olive oil*
a little over 1 tablespoon olive oil	*375 g (12 oz) lamb mince*	*salt and black pepper*	*25 g (1 oz) butter or margarine*
a good knob of butter or margarine	*50 g (2 oz) cheese, grated*	*a sprinkling of flour*	*2 tablespoons tomato purée*
	50 g (2 oz) blanched almonds, chopped roughly		*3 tablespoons water*
		For the tomato sauce:	*1 rounded teaspoon sugar*
		4 tomatoes	*salt and black pepper*

Peel the aubergines and slice into rounds. Rub all over with salt and leave in a colander in the sink for half an hour or more to let the bitter juices drain away. Preheat the oven to Gas Mark 5/190°C/375°F.

Meanwhile, heat 1 tablespoon of the olive oil and the butter or margarine in a frying pan and fry the onions gently until golden. Leave on one side.

Rinse the salt from the aubergines. Bring a pan of water to the boil. Cover and boil the aubergine slices for only 2 minutes, just until tender. Rinse with cold water, drain and chop up finely. If the aubergines are still hot, let them cool.

Pound the lamb well with a wooden spoon until it is pasty, or whizz it briefly in a food processor. Put it in a mixing bowl and add the fried onions, aubergines, grated cheese and chopped almonds. Season well, add the beaten eggs and mix all together thoroughly.

Spoon the mixture into a shallow, round ovenproof dish and, with wet hands, shape into a smooth dome shape. Smear with the extra oil and sprinkle all over with flour. Cook in the centre of the oven for 1 hour.

While the dome is cooking, make the tomato sauce. Pour boiling water over the tomatoes, drain them, skin and chop the flesh finely. Heat the olive oil and butter or margarine in a heavy saucepan, add the chopped tomatoes and stir over the heat for a minute. Then add the tomato purée, water, sugar and a good seasoning of salt and black pepper. Cover the pan and simmer very gently for about half an hour. Pour into a jug and keep warm until ready to serve.

Serves 6

BULGHUR FLAN WITH PINE KERNELS

I associate pine kernels more than anything with Lebanese food, although they are used all over the Middle East. Bulghur (cracked wheat) is another Lebanese favourite, and this combination of cracked wheat and lamb, enhanced by cumin and mint and topped with golden pine kernels, was one of my favourite tastes when I lived in that part of the world. This is an easy dish to make and I find it very useful for family lunches, accompanied by a salad and some yogurt and chopped cucumber to spoon on as a sauce.

175 g (6 oz) bulghur (cracked wheat)
500 g (1 lb) lean lamb mince

1 medium-size onion, chopped finely
a handful of mint leaves, chopped

2 teaspoons ground cumin
1 egg, whisked
1 clove of garlic

25 g (1 oz) pine kernels
salt and black pepper

Soak the cracked wheat in a bowl of water for 30 – 45 minutes. Preheat the oven to Gas Mark 4/180°C/350°F. Drain and squeeze it dry and put it into a mixing bowl with the minced lamb, the chopped onion, the chopped mint leaves and the cumin. Season generously with salt and black pepper and mix together thoroughly with a wooden spoon. Then mix in the whisked egg. Turn the mixture into a 25 cm (10-inch) earthenware flan dish and press it down evenly. Peel the garlic and slice it across as finely as possible. Scatter the slivers of garlic and the pine kernels on top of the meat mixture, pressing them down a bit with the flat of your hand. Put the flan towards the top of the oven for about 45 minutes until browned on top. Serve cut in slices like a normal flan. **Serves 6**

LAMB MEATBALLS POACHED IN TOMATO AND CHICK-PEA SAUCE

500 g (1 lb) lamb mince
4 cloves of garlic
grated rind and juice of 1 lemon
1 teaspoon ground cumin

2 teaspoons ground cinnamon
a large handful of fresh mint leaves, chopped finely
25 g (1 oz) fresh breadcrumbs

oil for frying
397 g (14 oz) can of chopped tomatoes
1 tablespoon tomato purée
432 g (15 oz) can of chick-peas, drained

1 teaspoon crushed coriander seeds
salt and black pepper

Put the lamb in a bowl. Peel and chop two cloves of garlic finely and add them to the lamb, with the grated lemon rind, the ground cumin and cinnamon, the chopped mint leaves and the breadcrumbs. Season with salt and plenty of black pepper and mix thoroughly together with a wooden spoon. Using damp hands, form the mixture into walnut-sized balls. Heat a little oil in a frying pan, and fry the balls over a fairly high heat just to brown them all over. Remove from the heat and put the balls on some absorbent kitchen paper towelling.

Empty the chopped tomatoes into an iron or other flameproof casserole, stir in the tomato purée and the lemon juice and add the drained chick-peas. Season with black pepper and a little salt. Put in the fried meatballs. Cover the casserole and bring it to the boil over a high heat; then turn the heat down to as low as possible and cook it for 30 minutes. Lastly, peel the remaining two cloves of garlic, cut them in half and slice them thinly. Heat a very little oil in a frying pan over a fairly high heat. Add the garlic and the crushed coriander seeds and toss around until they are dark brown. Scatter on top of the meatballs and sauce. **Serves 4**

Bulghur Flan with Pine Kernels; Lamb Meatballs Poached in Tomato and Chick-pea Sauce

PERA PALAS PIE

When I first arrived in Turkey with a girlfriend at the age of eighteen, we went to the Pera Palas Hotel in Istanbul, the legendary spies' hotel. It was certainly a hotel to capture our imagination, with its much faded grandeur: huge and shabby reception rooms, marble floored bathrooms and the ornate, gilded lift. The hotel was almost empty when we stayed there, and I shall always remember our first evening when the two of us sat completely alone in the dining room with a neat row of waiters staring at us curiously from the far end of the room.

Until that meal, I had always thought of dill weed as a Scandinavian herb and pine kernels as something characteristically Lebanese. In Istanbul, however, you will find fresh dill weed and pine kernels mixed with rice, lamb and fish. In this dish I have used them to make an exceptionally good type of moussaka with a Turkish flavour. The aubergine is surely to Turkey what the leek is to Wales and the smooth curd cheese topping of this dish is dotted with pieces of aubergine and toasted pine kernels. I serve it with rice and a green salad or vegetable and to make it more substantial I sometimes put a layer of sliced cooked potatoes between the meat and the topping.

1 large aubergine weighing about 375 g (12 oz)	*3 tablespoons olive oil*	*2 cloves of garlic, chopped finely*	*50 g (2 oz) plain flour*
lemon juice or white wine vinegar	*25 g (1 oz) pine kernels, plus a few extra*	*2 teaspoons paprika*	*600 ml (1 pint) milk*
	500 g (1 lb) lean lamb mince	*a good handful of fresh chopped dill or 3 teaspoons dried dill*	*250 g (8 oz) curd cheese*
			salt and black pepper

Cut the unpeeled aubergine into 1 cm (½-inch) slices and smear them all over with the lemon juice or vinegar. Then rub the slices with salt and leave them in a colander in the sink for half an hour. Preheat the oven to Gas Mark 5/190°C/375°F.

After half an hour, rinse the slices well, dry them with paper towels and cut them into small cubes. Heat 2 tablespoons of the olive oil in a large frying pan over a high heat, add the aubergines and stir them around for a few minutes until soft and browned. Transfer to a plate on one side. Now empty the 25 g (1 oz) pine kernels into the pan, stir them for a minute or two until browned and empty them on to another plate. Heat the remaining tablespoon of oil in the frying pan over a fairly high heat. Add the minced lamb and fry it, breaking the meat up, for a few minutes until any liquid has evaporated and the meat is browned. Add the chopped garlic and the paprika, cook for another minute or two and then remove the pan from the heat. Stir in the chopped dill weed and empty it into a shallow, ovenproof dish.

To make the topping, put the flour into a saucepan away from the heat and stir in a little of the milk with a wooden spoon until you have a smooth paste. Then stir in the remaining milk and bring it to the boil, stirring all the time, and let it bubble, still stirring, for 2–3 minutes. Then remove the pan from the heat, add the curd cheese and stir or whisk thoroughly until blended into the sauce. Season to taste with salt and pepper. Stir in the reserved fried aubergines and pine kernels and pour the sauce evenly over the lamb in the dish. Scatter a few more unfried pine kernels on top. Cook the pie towards the top of the oven for about 30 minutes until it has browned on top, then serve.

Serves 6

DREAM OF DAMASCUS

Children nearly always love meatballs and as a child in Syria I had the opportunity to try an enormous variety of them. The ones I liked best were the kibbeh: a mixture of pounded lamb and cracked wheat, which were often stuffed and either fried, stewed in a sauce or even eaten raw. I make a spicy kibbeh mixture into larger balls than usual, which I stuff with a luscious centre of marinated chicken breast. The balls are cooked in a thick yogurt sauce and the result is universally popular. I serve my kibbeh with long-grain rice and a mixed salad. If you have any pine kernels, toss a handful of them in a dry, hot frying pan for a minute or two to brown them and then scatter them over the meatballs before serving.

250 g (8 oz) skinless chicken breast fillets
3 tablespoons lemon juice
2 tablespoons olive oil
1 tablespoon fresh chopped mint leaves

125 g (4 oz) bulghur (cracked wheat)
500 g (1 lb) lean lamb mince
2 teaspoons ground coriander

1 teaspoon ground cumin
2 cloves of garlic, peeled and chopped roughly
3 –4 pinches of cayenne pepper
1 tablespoon tomato purée

plain flour
sunflower oil
2 x 240 g (8 oz) cartons of Greek yogurt
2 teaspoons cornflour
1 tablespoon water
salt and black pepper

Chop the chicken fillets into smallish pieces. Into a fairly shallow dish or bowl put the lemon juice, the olive oil, a good sprinkling of black pepper and the chopped mint. Stir in the chopped chicken, cover the container and leave it to marinate at room temperature for at least half an hour. Leave the cracked wheat to soak in a bowl of water. Preheat the oven to Gas Mark 5/190°C/375°F.

When the chicken has marinated, drain the cracked wheat thoroughly. Put the minced lamb into a food processor with the ground spices, the chopped garlic, some cayenne pepper, the tomato purée and a sprinkling of salt. Whizz until the meat is pasty. Add the drained, cracked wheat and whizz until it is evenly mixed. Divide the mixture into eight pieces, form them into balls and then flatten into circles like wide, fairly thin hamburgers. Spoon the marinated chicken into even piles in the middle of each flattened piece of lamb mixture and then carefully draw up the sides in order to enclose the chicken, cupping it gently in your hands to form a ball and pressing together any

cracks which may appear. Put some plain flour into a mixing bowl and put the meatballs into it one at a time to coat them generously with flour. Pour about 5 mm (¼ inch) sunflower oil into a large frying pan and put over a high heat until it smokes. Then gently add the meatballs and fry them, turning them carefully with a spatula just until they are browned all over. Transfer the meatballs with a slotted spatula to an ovenproof dish, not too shallow, in which they will fit in one layer.

Put the yogurt into a saucepan. Mix the cornflour in a cup with the water and stir it into the yogurt with a little salt. Bring to the boil, stirring all the time with a wooden spoon in one direction only. Then turn down the heat and let the mixture only just bubble in the open pan for 10 minutes. Season with a little cayenne pepper. Then pour the yogurt sauce into the dish with the meatballs, trying to pour it in between them rather than on top. Cover with foil or a lid. Bake in the centre of the oven for 50 –55 minutes.

Serves 4

TURKISH MEATBALLS IN EGG AND LEMON SAUCE

I was given this recipe by a private chef in Istanbul. It is a peasant dish
which he was brought up on but still makes today for his rich employers.
The smooth, lemony sauce is delicious and I find it an ideal family dish.

*a handful of parsley,
chopped finely
1 onion, chopped finely*

*500 g (1 lb) lamb (or pork
or beef) mince
125 g (4 oz) rice*

*1 egg
juice of 2 small lemons
2 level dessertspoons plain
flour*

*1 teaspoon paprika
25 g (1 oz) butter
salt and black pepper*

Mix the chopped parsley and onion with the minced
meat. Stir in the rice, salt and plenty of black pepper.
Form into small balls, each the size of a marble (this
is easier to do with wet hands).

Bring 1 litre (1 ¾ pints) salted water to the boil
in a large pan. Drop in the meatballs and when the
water returns to the boil remove any scum. Simmer
gently for half an hour.

In a small saucepan whisk the egg, lemon juice,
125 ml (4 fl oz) water and the flour. Bring to the boil
slowly, stirring all the time. If it seems to thicken too
much, add just a little more water. Then stir the
mixture gradually into the meatballs and water.

Before serving, melt the butter with the paprika,
cook gently for 3 minutes and trickle it over the top.
Serves 3–4

MINCED LAMB WITH CREAMY CHEESE TOPPING

This is most suitable for a large family meal at weekends. It takes very
little time to make, and both adults and children enjoy the mixture of the
tasty lamb with its toasted cheese topping.

*1 teaspoon cooking fat or oil
1 medium-size onion, sliced
and chopped roughly
750 g (1½ lb) fresh lamb
mince*

*1–2 cloves of garlic,
chopped or crushed
2 teaspoons dried thyme (or
a little more fresh thyme)
25 g (1 oz) ground almonds*

*salt and black pepper

For the topping:
600 ml (1 pint) milk*

*25 g (1 oz) cornflour
125 g (4 oz) grated cheese
a little butter or margarine
salt and black pepper*

Heat the fat or oil in a large frying pan. Fry the onion
for a minute or two and then add the lamb, garlic and
thyme. Cook quickly over a strong heat, stirring the
mixture constantly; then pour off any excess fat and
add plenty of salt and black pepper to taste. Lastly, stir
in the ground almonds. Transfer the mixture to an
overproof dish, pat down and keep warm.

Put the milk in a saucepan, blend the cornflour
with a little cold water and stir into the milk. Bring

to the boil, stirring all the time and simmer for about
2 minutes. Stir in all but a tablespoon of the cheese,
salt and black pepper and continue stirring until the
cheese has melted.

Pour the sauce over the lamb and sprinkle the
remaining cheese on top. Dot with butter or margarine. Put under a medium grill until golden brown
and serve with a green salad or green vegetable.
Serves 6–8

Turkish Meatballs in Egg and Lemon Sauce

MARINATED LEG OF LAMB WITH PORCINI AND TOMATO SAUCE

In the early summer in Italy I first tasted fresh porcini; the flesh is soft and rich and literally melts in your mouth. When fresh, the large mushrooms can be simply roasted in the oven, but dried porcini, although never quite so melting in consistency, retain their wonderful smell and taste, making all the difference in sauces and stews. Available from delicatessens, they are expensive, but worth it, and a wonderful treat for dinner parties.

For the marinade:
finely grated rind and juice of 1 orange
1 rounded teaspoon ground mace
1 rounded tablespoon tomato purée
2 tablespoons extra-virgin olive oil
a small bunch of fresh thyme
1 leg of lamb weighing 2–2.5 kg (4½–5 lb)
salt and black pepper

For the sauce:
125 g (4 oz) packet of dried porcini, ceps, or any dried mushrooms
1 tablespoon extra-virgin olive oil
1 large clove of garlic, chopped finely
397 g (14 oz) can of chopped tomatoes
juice of 1 large orange
150 ml (¼ pint) double cream
salt and black pepper

To mix the marinade, put the orange rind and juice into a bowl. Add the ground mace, the tomato purée, the olive oil, a little salt and plenty of black pepper. Pull the leaves off the thyme (you can use dried thyme in winter), add half to the orange and tomato mixture, and press the remaining leaves into 3 – 4 deep incisions in the leg of lamb.

Lay the lamb on a large piece of foil and smear the orange and tomato marinade all over it. Bring the foil up to enclose the lamb and put in the fridge (or, in winter, a cold place) for several hours or overnight, bringing it to room temperature an hour or so before you want to cook it.

Meanwhile soak the dried porcini, broken up a bit if they are in large pieces, in tepid water, changing the water two or three times, for an hour or more.

Heat the oven to Gas Mark 5/190°C/375°F. Unwrap the lamb and put into a roasting pan in the centre of the oven for 15 minutes per pound for pale pink lamb.

Start the sauce while the lamb is cooking. Put the olive oil in a heavy-based medium-sized saucepan over a medium heat. Add the chopped garlic and stir around. Then add the canned tomatoes and the orange juice. Season with plenty of black pepper and with salt. Add the drained porcini, bring to the boil, then cover the saucepan and simmer for ¾–1 hour.

When the lamb is ready, add the double cream to the sauce and simmer for a minute or two. Pour the excess fat from the roasting pan and then pour the juices and any scraped-out residue into the sauce. Check for seasoning, and pour into a sauce boat.
Serves 8

LAMB'S LIVER WITH PARSLEY AND BUTTERED LEEKS

An extremely simple dish of thinly cut parsleyed liver on a bed of buttery leeks, both nutritious and delicious. The important thing is to cut the liver as finely as possible, using your sharpest knife.

2 large leeks
75 g (3 oz) butter
500 g (1 lb) lamb's liver, sliced thinly
flour for coating
1 tablespoon olive or sunflower oil
a handful of fresh parsley, finely chopped, or 1 tablespoon dried parsley
1 small orange, cut into wedges
salt and black pepper

Remove the outer leaves from the leeks and slice very thinly in rounds. Wash well and drain. Melt 50 g (2 oz) butter in a large frying pan and fry the leeks very gently, tossing now and then, until soft. Transfer to a fairly shallow serving dish, sprinkle with salt and black pepper, cover with foil and keep warm.

Season the sliced liver with salt and pepper and dust with flour. Melt the remaining 25 g (1 oz) of the butter with the oil in the pan and toss the liver over a fairly high heat for 3–4 minutes. Then, still over the heat, add the parsley. Stir thoroughly together and then transfer to the serving dish on top of the leeks.

Decorate the border of the dish with the small wedges of orange for people to squeeze on the liver before eating. Mashed potatoes go well with this dish. **Serves 4**

MARINATED SHOULDER OF LAMB STUFFED WITH SWISS CHARD, WITH A TOMATO, BRANDY AND CREAM SAUCE

If you can't find Swiss chard, substitute spinach instead. The cooking time in this recipe produces lamb which is tender and very pale pink – if you like your lamb a darker pink reduce the cooking time by 15–20 minutes.
Pictured on pages 54/5.

2.25–2.5 kg (5–5½ lb) shoulder of lamb, boned but not rolled
juice of 2 lemons

4 tablespoons olive oil
5 cm (2-inch) piece of fresh ginger, peeled and chopped very finely

500 g (1 lb) Swiss chard leaves with stems
500 g (1 lb) tomatoes
4–5 tablespoons brandy

300 ml (½ pint) double cream
salt and black pepper

Several hours before, or even the night ahead, put the lamb into a roasting pan. Put the lemon juice and the olive oil into a bowl and stir in a sprinkling of black pepper and a little salt. Rub all the flesh (but not the skin) part of the lamb with the chopped ginger and then smear on the lemon juice and oil, using it all up. Leave the joint skin side downwards in the pan, cover with cling film and leave in a cool place or the fridge for several hours or overnight.

Then cut up the Swiss chard, chopping the leaves into smallish pieces and the stems into very small pieces. Plunge into a saucepan of boiling salted water and simmer for only 1–2 minutes, just until the leaves are limp. Drain and rinse with cold water to cool. Pat the chard dry with a cloth, and then press it into the pockets of the boned lamb. Sometimes the lamb is boned and cut right open, in which case you have to put the chard on the flesh and then bring up the lamb and enclose it as well as you can, tying it together with string. If the lamb has been boned neatly leaving a large pocket, just stuff all the chard into the pocket, and then enclose by securing with 2 or 3 skewers. Rub the skin with olive oil and salt.

Heat the oven to Gas Mark 3/160°C/325°F. Put the lamb on the centre shelf and cook for about 1¾ hours, basting occasionally. Put the tomatoes in a bowl, pour boiling water over them, leave for a minute, then drain, skin and chop up finely. Put the chopped tomatoes into the roasting pan around the lamb and return to the oven for another 20 minutes.

Remove from the oven, manoeuvre the lamb on to a carving board and leave it to sit while you make the sauce. Pour away some excess fat from the roasting pan but make sure you leave the juices behind. Add the brandy to the tomatoes and juices and simmer in the pan on top of the stove for a minute, then pour in the cream and boil up again, stirring for a minute or two. Season to taste with salt and black pepper, and pour into a sauce boat. **Serves 10**

LAMB COOKED IN MILK

This casserole can be made using the cheapest stewing lamb. It has a mild,
delicate flavour and smooth consistency.

a little cooking fat or oil
1 teaspoon sugar
625–750 g (1¼ –
1 ½ lb) stewing lamb

1 level tablespoon plain flour
600 ml (1 pint) milk
25 g (1 oz) pearl barley

5–6 sticks celery, sliced
1 onion, sliced thinly in
rings
a little butter or margarine

a little top of the milk
juice of half a lemon
¼ –½ whole nutmeg,
grated
salt and black pepper

Preheat the oven to Gas Mark 9/240°C/475°F. Melt a little fat in a large frying pan, add the sugar and fry the lamb until browned all over. Drain off the fat and transfer the meat to a casserole dish. Blend the flour in a jug or bowl with a little of the milk until smooth. Add the rest of the milk, season with salt and black pepper and pour over the lamb. Add the pearl barley and celery. Cover and cook in the oven until simmering (15–20 minutes) and, turning the oven down to Gas Mark 2/150°C/300°F, cook for another 1¼– 1½ hours.

Fry the onion in a little butter over a strong heat until golden brown. Stir some top of the milk, the lemon juice and the nutmeg into the casserole, sprinkle the fried onions on the top and serve accompanied by minty green peas and new potatoes or buttered noodles.
Serves 4

LEVANTINE LAMB PIE

This pie, which looks rather like a cake made out of curling autumn
leaves, reminds me of visits to Morocco. It is made with the irresistible
thin, crip filo pastry, which you buy ready made. The sweet, spiced lamb
and spinach filling is a rich feast of flavour. I would serve the pie with rice
and a tomato or mixed salad.
Pictured on the front cover.

500 g (1 lb) spinach
750 –875 g (1½ –
1 ¾ lb) lamb neck fillets
1 tablespoon sunflower or
groundnut oil

100 g (3½ oz) butter
2–3 large cloves of garlic,
chopped finely
2 teaspoons ground cumin
2 teaspoons ground
cinnamon

375 g (12 oz) onions,
peeled and chopped fairly
small
125 g (4 oz) sultanas
1 heaped tablespoon
thick cut marmalade

500 g (1 lb) filo pastry
salt and black pepper
300 ml (½ pint) carton of
natural yogurt (the Greek
kind if possible), to serve

Wash the spinach well and take the stalks off. Bring a large pan of salted water to the boil and plunge in the spinach leaves for just a minute or so until limp. Drain well, pressing out all the liquid you can, and then chop up small.

Cut up the lamb into very small cubes. Heat the oil and 15 g (½ oz) of the butter in a large frying pan. Stir in the chopped garlic and the spices. Add the meat and stir around over a high heat until sealed. Then stir in the onions and the sultanas. Cover the pan tightly with foil and leave just bubbling over a low heat for ¾–1 hour or until the meat is tender to bite, stirring round now and then, especially towards the end when the juices evaporate. (If all the liquid hasn't evaporated by the time the meat is tender, increase the heat, remove the foil and bubble until it has.)

Remove the pan from the heat and season with salt and black pepper. Stir in the marmalade. Lastly, stir in the chopped spinach and leave until cold. Preheat the oven to Gas Mark 4/180°C/350°F.

Gently melt the remaining 75 g (3 oz) butter in a saucepan. Brush a loose-based 7–7½ inch (18 –19 cm) diameter, deep cake tin thinly with butter. Lay in a whole sheet of filo pastry, press it down in the tin and let the ends hang right over the sides. Brush the pastry within the tin thinly with butter. Lay another sheet across the other way so that the tin is completely lined. Continue like this in layers, buttering each sheet and letting the pastry hang out all round the edge of the tin. Spoon in the cold lamb cubes. Then bring in the overlapping pastry sheet by sheet loosely over the top, buttering each piece. The top 2–3 layers should be specially crumpled, sticking up towards the centre.

Cook in the centre of the oven for about 30 minutes, until the top is well browned. Then put the tin on a narrower round object and push the pie carefully up and out. Using a wide spatula, lever it carefully off the base on to an ovenproof serving plate and put it back in the oven for another 20–30 minutes. If more convenient you can make the pie in advance and keep it warm in a low oven for at least an hour. Serve the yogurt in a bowl with the pie.
Serves 6 – 8

GRILLED AROMATIC LAMB FILLET WITH FRESH CORIANDER YOGURT

If you cook them in the right way, lamb neck fillets are like the most exquisite little noisettes. If you grill them quickly and then slice them thickly across they are juicy and pink in the centre and smoky on the outside. This aromatic paste, smeared on well ahead, will permeate and tenderise the meat. Basmati rice and a crisp salad are the perfect accompaniments. During the summer this is also a good barbecue recipe.

1 teaspoon whole-grain mustard
⅓ teaspoon whole cumin seeds
¾ teaspoon ground coriander seeds

2 teaspoons lemon juice
1 teaspoon light tahina (sesame seed paste)
1 tablespoon groundnut oil
1 small clove of garlic, chopped finely

375 g (12 oz) lamb neck fillets
150 g (5 oz) carton of Greek yogurt

a small handful of fresh coriander leaves, chopped finely
cayenne pepper and sea salt

In a small bowl put the mustard, the cumin seed, the ground coriander seed, the lemon juice and the tahina paste. Stir in the oil and the chopped garlic and season with a good pinch of cayenne pepper and a sprinkling of sea salt. Mix thoroughly with a wooden spoon until the paste thickens a little. Put the lamb fillets into a shallow dish or pan and smear the paste all over them. Cover the dish with cling film and leave at room temperature for two hours or in a fridge for longer, even overnight.

Make the yogurt sauce by putting the yogurt into a mixing bowl and seasoning with a good pinch of cayenne pepper and a sprinkling of sea salt. Then stir the chopped coriander into the yogurt, turn into a serving bowl and put in the fridge until needed.

About 20 minutes before you start your meal put the prepared lamb fillets under the hottest possible grill for about 5 – 8 minutes on each side until blackened in patches. Then turn off the grill and rest the lamb for 5 minutes or so. Have a large, flat, warmed serving plate ready. Put the lamb fillets on to a board, and, using a very sharp knife, cut across in 1 cm (½-inch) slices and arrange a single layer on the plate.
Serves 2

SUMMER CHICKEN

A simple but succulent dish of golden chicken with an exciting aroma,
reminiscent of a Middle Eastern feast.

juice of 1 lemon
2–3 tablespoons olive or
sunflower oil
2 large cloves of garlic,
crushed
1 teaspoon ground turmeric

2–3 teaspoons powdered
cumin
1 large handful fresh mint
leaves, chopped finely, or
1 tablespoon dried mint

6 joints of chicken or a
2 kg (4 ½ lb) chicken
jointed into 6
150 g (5 oz) carton of
natural yogurt

salt and black pepper

In a small bowl mix together the lemon juice, oil, crushed garlic, turmeric, cumin, mint and salt and black pepper. Rub or brush this mixture all over the chicken pieces. Lay them in a wide, preferably shallow, ovenproof dish. Pour over any extra oil and lemon mixture. If possible, leave to marinate for an hour or more at room temperature. Preheat the oven to Gas Mark 4/180°C/350°F.

Cover the dish with foil or a lid and cook in the centre of the oven for 1¼–1½ hours.

Before serving, spoon the yogurt on top of the chicken. Serve with new potatoes or long-grain rice and a mixed salad.

Serves 6

THE MEMSAHIB'S CURRIED CHICKEN

2.5 cm (1-inch) piece of
fresh ginger or 1 teaspoon
ground ginger
1 small green chilli
1 large clove of garlic

2 cardamom pods or 1
teaspoon coriander seeds
juice of ½ lemon
1 tablespoon natural yogurt
4 chicken joints, thawed if
frozen

2 tablespoons cooking oil
2 hard-boiled eggs, shelled
and sliced
salt

For the sauce:
1 tablespoon dried milk
powder
5 tablespoons single cream
5 tablespoons natural yogurt
chopped parsley, to garnish

Roughly peel the fresh ginger, if used, and cut open the chilli and discard all the seeds. Then peel the garlic and chop all these ingredients together as finely as possible. Remove the seeds from the cardamom pods if used and grind these or the coriander seeds in a pestle and mortar, or crush with a rolling pin between two sheets of greaseproof paper. Mix the lemon juice and the tablespoon of yogurt together and stir in the prepared spices, including the ground ginger, if used. Score the chicken joints all over with a knife and coat all over with the yogurt and spice mixture. Leave in a covered dish to marinate overnight, or for several hours, in the fridge. Then sprinkle the joints with salt to season.

Preheat the oven to Gas Mark 4/180°C/350°F.

Heat the oil in a pan and fry the joints over a medium heat until pale golden on both sides. Transfer to a casserole dish with the oil and spices from the pan. Cover the casserole and cook in the oven for ¾–1 hour, or until cooked. Then transfer the chicken joints to a warm serving dish and arrange the slices of hard-boiled egg amongst them.

Pour off any excess fat from the casserole juices and boil the juices in a saucepan for 2–3 minutes until reduced and thickened. Stir in the milk powder, cream and the 5 tablespoons of yogurt and heat gently but don't boil. Pour the sauce over the chicken and sprinkle with chopped parsley. Serve with long-grain rice or new potatoes, and a salad.

Serves 4

CHICKEN AND MUSHROOM PAPRIKA

I often make this mild, creamy dish for our supper because it is so quick
and easy, but it is equally suitable for a special occasion. Serve with it
either long-grain rice and a green salad or a bright green, lightly cooked
vegetable such as broccoli which will look beautiful in contrast to the
smooth, pinky sauce.

*500 g (1 lb) boned chicken
or turkey breasts
juice of 1 lemon*

*2 teaspoons paprika
40 g (1½ oz) butter or
margarine*

*175 g (6 oz) mushrooms,
sliced finely or halved if
small*

*300 ml (½ pint) single
cream
a little chopped parsley
salt and black pepper*

Remove the skin from the breasts and cut them into small, thin slices. Put into a bowl with the lemon juice, paprika and salt and black pepper and stir up thoroughly. Melt the butter in a large frying pan, add the chicken pieces and cook over a gentle heat, stirring now and then, for 10–15 minutes.

Add the prepared mushrooms to the pan. Then pour in the cream and stir. Heat and simmer gently for a minute or two.

Taste the sauce, add extra seasoning if needed and pour into a serving dish. Sprinkle with the parsley.
Serves 4

CHICKEN ROASTED IN YOGURT

This way of roasting a chicken produces a very succulent flavour. You can
vary the taste by adding your own choice of herbs, garlic or spices to the
yogurt – it is particularly good with curry paste stirred into it. Here is one
version which everyone seems to like.

*1.5 –2 kg (3 ½ –4 ½ lb)
chicken, well thawed if
frozen*

*juice of 1 lemon
2 teaspoons ground
cinnamon*

*2 teaspoons fresh, or
1 teaspoon dried, thyme*

*150 g (5 oz) carton of
natural yogurt
salt and black pepper*

Make deep cuts in the breast and legs of the chicken and sprinkle with the lemon juice. Leave for at least half an hour at room temperature.

Preheat the oven to Gas Mark 6/200°C/400°F. Then mix the cinnamon, thyme and salt and black pepper into the yogurt and spread thickly all over the chicken. Roast in the centre of the oven for 1¼–1½ hours, until cooked. Cover the breast with foil if it browns too quickly.

Serve with new potatoes or buttered noodles and fresh courgettes or broccoli.
Serves 4–6

CHICKEN BAKED IN A SALT CRUST WITH ROSE-TINTED SAUCE

The simple method of baking in salt is thought to originate, as do so many clever ways of cooking, in China. These days, however, the place you would be most likely to find a perfect chicken or fish prepared in this way would be in France, or possibly Spain. Don't imagine that the chicken turns out at all salty to taste; the salt simply acts as an insulating crust and cooks the bird to a perfection hard to achieve in any other way. You need quite a lot of coarse salt to bury the bird with, but you can keep the salt to use again; once you have used this method I feel sure you will want to repeat it. In fact I use the very coarse salt which I buy in huge bags for my dishwasher.

1.1–1.25 kg (2½ –3 lb) fresh chicken (corn fed if possible)
6 cloves of garlic, peeled and chopped roughly

coarse salt

For the sauce:
750 g (1½ lb) tomatoes
50 g (2 oz) butter

2.5 cm (1-inch) piece of fresh ginger, peeled and chopped finely

150 ml (5 fl oz) carton of double cream
salt and cayenne pepper

Preheat the oven to Gas Mark 8/230°C/450°F. Choose a deep, ovenproof casserole in which the chicken will fit with 2.5–5 cm (1–2 inches) to spare all around it. Line the base of the dish with two layers of foil, bringing it up well over the edges. Put the chopped garlic into the body cavity of the chicken. Put a thickish layer of coarse salt into the dish, put the chicken in breast-side downwards and then pour in enough salt to bury the bird completely. Cover the dish tightly and then put it in the centre of the oven for about 2 hours or until cooked.

Shortly before the chicken is cooked, make the sauce. Put the tomatoes into a bowl, pour boiling water over them, leave for a minute, and then drain and peel the tomatoes and chop them up very small. Melt the butter in a heavy saucepan over a medium heat. Add the chopped ginger and the tomatoes and bubble them gently in the open saucepan, stirring frequently, for 10–15 minutes until they are cooked and mushy. Put the pan on one side.

When the chicken is ready take the dish out of the oven and spoon the top layer of salt into a large bowl; then lift out the chicken with the help of the foil, tipping all the rest of the salt into the bowl as you do so. Wipe any grains of salt off the chicken and put it on a serving dish in a low oven to keep warm while you finish the sauce. Using a wooden spoon rub the tomato and ginger thoroughly through the sieve into another saucepan. Stir in the cream and boil, stirring, for 3 – 4 minutes until the sauce is slightly thickened. Remove it from the heat and season to taste with salt and cayenne pepper. Just before serving pour the sauce evenly all over the chicken.

Serves 4 –5

Chicken Baked in a Salt Crust with Rose-tinted Sauce; Rabbit and Pumpkin with Mustard and White Kidney Beans (page 102)

CRISPY CHICKEN JOINTS WITH PIQUANT SAUCE

This method of boiling the chicken pieces before frying seems to make
the skin particularly crispy. The sauce is a vague echo of a famous
Mexican dish in which a small amount of chocolate enriches a piquant
sauce and gives it a unique flavour.

4 chicken breast joints
6–8 cloves of garlic, peeled and cut in half

3 sticks of celery, cut up roughly
300 ml (½ pint) water groundnut oil

1–2 medium-size green chillies
397 g (14 oz) can of chopped tomatoes

15 g (½ oz) plain chocolate, broken up
a good handful of parsley
salt

Put the chicken joints into a saucepan with the garlic
and celery and pour in the water. Bring to the boil,
cover the saucepan and then simmer gently for 30
minutes. Take out the chicken and pat dry thoroughly with absorbent paper. Save the liquid.

Heat about 5 mm (¼ inch) depth of oil in a frying
pan and fry the joints over a medium heat on both
sides until golden brown – be careful, as they may spit
a bit. Then transfer the chicken to a serving dish and
put in a low oven to keep warm.

Cut the chillies in half under running water,
discard the seeds and put the halved chillies in the
saucepan with the chicken juices, the garlic and the
celery. Add the tomatoes, bring to the boil in the open
pan and boil briskly for 10 minutes, until reduced a
bit. Then remove from the heat and add the chocolate, stirring it round in the sauce until melted.

Pour the sauce into a food processor or liquidiser
and whizz until smooth. Pour back into the saucepan,
add salt to taste and reheat. Take out a few whole
sprigs of parsley to garnish the chicken, chop the rest
finely and stir into the sauce. Serve the sauce in a
separate bowl or jug to spoon over the chicken.
Serves 4

HARVESTER'S CHICKEN

Even though children love it, it's easy to get tired of chicken as it can so
often be rather characterless. Marinating these chicken joints in wine
vinegar improves and slightly changes the flavour. But the point of this
dish is the fruity sauce, a combination of tomatoes and apples which
works remarkably well. Serve with rice and peas or beans.

4 large chicken thighs
3 cloves of garlic
red wine vinegar

500 g (1 lb) tomatoes
1 tablespoon olive oil
125 g (4 oz) butter

3 x 2.5 cm (3 x 1-inch) sticks of cinnamon
4 dessert apples

1 tablespoon caster sugar
oil
sea salt and black pepper

Make two small incisions in the flesh on the underside
of each of the chicken thighs and insert 2 slices of
garlic (from 1 clove) in each. Sprinkle the flesh with
black pepper. Pour some wine vinegar into a small
roasting pan, enough to cover the bottom about 5
mm (¼ inch) deep, and lay the chicken thighs in it
flesh side down. Rub the skin with oil and sea salt.
Leave at room temperature for 1–2 hours.

Preheat the oven to Gas mark 6//200°C/400°F.
Put the chicken towards the top of the oven for 30–35
minutes until browned, basting carefully now and
then. Meanwhile, pour boiling water over the tomatoes in a bowl. After a minute, drain, peel the tomatoes and chop up roughly. Heat the olive oil and 50 g
(2 oz) of the butter in a saucepan over a gentle heat.
Chop the remaining 2 garlic cloves finely and add
them to the saucepan with the cinnamon sticks. Stir
round and then add the chopped tomatoes.

Leave the tomatoes in the open pan over a low
heat while you peel the apples and cut them up

roughly. Add the apples to the saucepan, turn up the heat a little and simmer steadily in the open pan, stirring now and then until the apples are very soft and the tomato liquid has reduced a little. Then remove from the heat and add the remaining 50 g (2 oz) butter and the caster sugar.

The chicken should be ready about the same time as the sauce. Pour the chicken pan juices into the sauce and then season to taste with salt and black pepper. Pour the sauce into a shallow, oblong serving dish and place the chicken pieces on top.
Serves 4

PRIZE PUMPKIN

Sometimes I feel that an idea has proved a real triumph. This is one
example. It is a spectacular party piece; a large golden pumpkin is used as a
cooking pot, an edible one, for a creamy mixture of chicken and spices.
The sweet flesh of the pumpkin almost melts into the chicken and spices
as it cooks, and the combination is mouthwatering in the extreme.
Wonderfully festive in appearance, this will be a talking point at any party.
Serve it with a crisp green vegetable or green salad
and new potatoes, if possible.
Pictured on page 2.

7 cm (3-inch) piece of fresh ginger, peeled
8 cardamom pods
1–2 fresh green chillies

8 skinless chicken breast fillets weighing about 875 g (1¾ lb)
125 g (4 oz) butter

625 –750 g (1¼ –1½ lb) onions, sliced thinly
6–8 cloves of garlic, sliced thinly
125 g (4 oz) button mushrooms

50 g (2 oz) plain flour
450 ml (¾ pint) milk
1 large pumpkin 3.25 –3.50 kg (7½ –8 lb)
sunflower oil
sea salt

Cut the ginger into small, thin slices. Extract the seeds from the cardamom pods and grind them in a pestle and mortar. Cut open the chillies under running water, discard the seeds and chop the flesh up finely. Slice the chicken breasts across in 1 cm (½-inch) slices.

Now melt three-quarters of the butter in a large heavy pan on top of the stove, add the onions, and cook over a low heat, stirring now and then until the onions are soft. Then add the prepared ginger, garlic, cardamom and chilli. Add the remaining butter until melted, then add the sliced chicken and the button mushrooms and stir around to coat with butter. Stir in the flour, then gradually add the milk and season with sea salt. Bring to the boil, stirring all the time until very thick. Then remove from the heat.

Now, using a large and very sharp knife, cut the top off the pumpkin. Using a big spoon with sharp edges, scoop out the pumpkin seeds and all the stringy interior leaving only the firm orange flesh. Heat the oven to Gas Mark 9/240°C/475°F. Spoon the chicken mixture into the pumpkin, put it into a roasting pan and put the top back on the pumpkin. Smear the pumpkin skin with sunflower oil and put it back in the oven.

After 25 –30 minutes turn the heat down to Gas Mark 4/180°C/350°F for about 1¼ hours. Using a wide spatula, and holding the pumpkin with a cloth, carefully lift and move it from the roasting pan to a large, round serving plate. To serve, scoop out the flesh of the pumpkin with the chicken mixture.
Serves 8

CHICKEN AND SMOKED OYSTERS WITH GRILLED PEPPERS IN SAFFRON AND FRESH LIME SAUCE

This is a very quick dish to make. The chicken breast, cooked briefly but gently, is white and tender. The oysters add a smoky flavour to the saffron cream sauce and the peppers a full sweetness. You need to serve either a bowl of rice or noodles with this to absorb the juices, and I would add a simple green salad.
Pictured on page 107.

1 large yellow or green pepper
1 large red pepper
6 chicken breast fillets, skinned

4 tablespoons olive oil
juice of 1 large or 2 small limes

300 ml (½ pint) double cream
1 packet of powdered saffron

2 very large, flat mushrooms, sliced across
1 can of smoked oysters
salt and black pepper

Cut the peppers in half lengthways. Put them under a hot grill, skin side up, for 10–20 minutes until blackened – the peppers should be fairly soft. Rinse them under cold water until cool enough to handle and peel. Then cut into thin strips. Cut the chicken breasts across into 1 cm (½-inch) pieces. Lay the pieces face down between 2 large sheets of oiled greaseproof paper (you may have to do this in two lots). Bash the chicken pieces through the paper until fairly thin, with a flat heavy knife or a rolling pin.

Heat the olive oil in a large saucepan over a very low heat. Add the lime juice. Then add the chicken pieces, stir around to coat them in the oil and juice,

cover the saucepan and cook for 5–8 minutes, just until the chicken is white.

Remove from the heat and add the sliced peppers, the cream and the saffron. Then add the sliced mushrooms and season with salt and pepper. Put back on the heat and bring to bubbling in the open saucepan over a medium heat. Bubble, stirring around gently, for 2–3 minutes. Drain the oil from the oysters, add them to the saucepan and remove from the heat.

If not ready to eat leave the mixture in the saucepan and briefly reheat later before pouring into a warmed serving dish.
Serves 6

CHICKEN AND FISH CASSEROLE WITH LEMON

The flavours of chicken and smoked fish are delicious together, making this simple dish into something special.

4 smallish joints of chicken, with the skin removed
250 g (8 oz) cooking tomatoes, chopped
1 green or red pepper, chopped

1 large lemon, sliced in rounds
1–2 cloves of garlic, chopped (optional)
about 250 ml (8 fl oz) chicken stock

4 pieces of smoked cod, haddock or whiting, weighing about 300 g (10 oz)

2 teaspoons chopped fresh or dried tarragon
salt and black pepper

Preheat the oven to Gas Mark 6/200°C/400°F.

Put the chicken joints into a casserole dish. Add the tomatoes, pepper, lemon and garlic, with salt and pepper, to the chicken. Pour over the chicken stock.

Put the lid on the dish and cook for 20 minutes. Add the fish and tarragon and continue cooking for another 25–30 minutes. Serve with rice.
Serves 4

CHICKEN STUFFED WITH COUSCOUS

Couscous is eaten all over North Africa. Subtly spiced and studded with
almonds and dried fruit it tastes delicious.

75 g (3 oz) couscous
50 g (2 oz) butter
*1 clove of garlic, peeled
and chopped finely*

*40 g (1½ oz) blanched
whole almonds*
*2 teaspoons ground
cinnamon*
*1 teaspoon whole cumin
seeds*

25 g (1 oz) seedless raisins
*1.25 kg (3 lb) maize-fed
chicken*
2 teaspoons paprika
2 tablespoons olive oil

*2 teaspoons clear or set
honey*
1 tablespoon lemon juice
1 tablespoon tomato purée
150 ml (¼ pint) water
salt and black pepper

Put the couscous in a bowl. Pour in plenty of hot
water, soak for about 10 minutes until it is puffed up
and then drain it in a sieve. Melt the butter in a
medim-sized saucepan over a low heat, add the
chopped garlic and the almonds and stir over a low
heat for about 2 minutes. Add the cinnamon and
cumin seeds and stir for another minute. Add the
drained couscous and the raisins and season with salt
and black pepper. Cover the pan and continue cooking over a low heat for about another 8 minutes.

Meanwhile, preheat the oven to Gas Mark
6/200°C/400°F. Leave the couscous to cool slightly

and then spoon it into the body cavity of the chicken,
pressing it in. Mix the paprika with the olive oil and
smear it all over the chicken. Put the chicken in a
roasting pan and cook in the centre of the oven for
1–1¼ hours.

When cooked, remove the chicken to a carving
board. Pour any excess fat from the pan and stir the
honey, lemon juice, tomato purée and water into the
pan juice. Bubble everything together on top of the
stove, stirring for a minute or two. Season to taste
with salt and pepper and then pour into a gravy jug.
Serves 4–5

CREAMY CHICKEN PASTA

300 g (10 oz) pasta shapes
40 g (1½ oz) butter
1 tablespoon cooking oil

*300 –375 g (10 –12 oz)
boned chicken breast,
skinned and cut into
2.5 cm (1-inch) pieces*

*1 medium-size onion,
chopped*
*125 g (4 oz) mushrooms,
sliced finely*
*300 ml (½ pint) single
cream*

*2–3 teaspoons fresh, or
2 teaspoons dried, chopped
tarragon*
salt and black pepper

Boil the pasta in plenty of salted water according to
the pack instructions or for 10 –15 minutes, until
tender. Drain and rinse through with hot water. Put
into a serving bowl and stir in 15 g (½ oz) of the
butter. Cover and keep warm in a very low oven
while you make the sauce.

Melt the remaining 25 g (1 oz) butter with the oil
in a large frying pan and toss the chicken pieces in it

over a fairly high heat for 3–4 minutes. Add the
chopped onion and cook over a lower heat until the
onion is just soft. Then add the sliced mushrooms,
tossing for another minute. Finally add the cream,
tarragon and plenty of salt and pepper. Allow the
cream to get just hot and then mix the sauce with the
pasta. Serve with a salad.
Serves 4–6

CHICKEN NOODLES WITH CASHEW NUTS IN THE BURMESE WAY

Snack food in Burma, as in many Eastern countries, is excellent and in the
markets we always found little establishments where you could eat a bowl
of noodles with chicken and vegetables.

*2 large skinless chicken
breasts
2 tablespoons oyster sauce
1 level tablespoon soft dark
brown sugar*

*3–4 pinches of cayenne
pepper
25 g (8 oz) Chinese egg
noodles
375 g (12 oz) carrots*

*2 tablespoons groundnut oil
2.5 cm (1-inch) piece of
fresh ginger, peeled and
chopped finely
2 cloves of garlic, chopped
finely*

*1 teaspoon ground turmeric
75 g (3 oz) unsalted cashew
nuts
leaves of a small –
medium-size bunch of fresh
coriander, chopped finely*

Cut the chicken breasts across in thin slices and put
them in a bowl with 1 tablespoon of the oyster sauce,
the brown sugar and the cayenne pepper. Stir the
slices to coat them evenly, cover the bowl and leave
to marinate while you prepare the other ingredients.
Cook the noodles according to the directions on the
packet, drain them and leave them on one side. Peel
and slice the carrots very finely, using a food processor
if possible. Put the oil in a wok or a large iron or other
flameproof casserole over a medium heat. Add the

chopped ginger and garlic, the turmeric and the
cashew nuts and stir around for a minute. Then add
the marinated chicken and stir around for 3 – 4
minutes, until the chicken is just cooked. Add the
sliced carrots, stir for another minute, and, lastly, add
the reserved noodles and the remaining tablespoon of
oyster sauce; stir until everything is just warmed
through. Very roughly mix in the coriander leaves
and serve immediately.
Serves 4 –5

MOGHUL CHICKEN

This is my simple-to-make version of an elaborate dish eaten on feast days
in India. Serve with basmati rice and a vegetable curry, and perhaps a
bowl of yogurt with added cucumber and mint to refresh the palate.

*50 g (2 oz) desiccated
coconut
50 g (2 oz) blanched
almonds
2.5 cm (1-inch) piece of
fresh ginger, peeled*

*½ teaspoon chilli powder
300 ml (½ pint) hot water
2 large onions
75 g (3 oz) butter or
margarine*

*6 chicken joints
6 –8 whole cardamom
pods, crushed lightly
5 –7 cm (2–3-inch) sticks
of cinnamon
6 whole cloves*

*6 tablespoons plain yogurt
salt
25 g (1 oz) flaked almonds
a few chopped coriander
leaves or a little chopped
parsley, to garnish*

Put the coconut, blanched almonds, peeled ginger
and chilli powder into a liquidiser, add the hot water
and whizz until smooth.

Peel and slice the onions into rings. Heat the
butter in a flame-proof casserole, add the onions and
fry over moderate heat until soft and golden.

Heat the oven to Gas Mark 4/180°C/350°F. Add
the mixture from the liquidiser to the casserole and
stir. Add the chicken joints, the whole spices and the

yogurt and season with salt. Mix thoroughly over the
heat, then cover the dish and cook in the oven,
stirring occasionally for 1½ –2 hours until the
chicken is very tender.

Just before serving fry the flaked almonds in a little
butter for a minute until golden, and sprinkle over the
top, together with the chopped coriander leaves or
parsley.
Serves 6

STEAMED CHICKEN PUDDING WITH CHICORY, LEMON AND GINGER

Here is an exciting twist to a traditional dish. What could look more old-fashioned and English than a steamed pudding presented in its basin, wrapped in a white linen napkin? The light crust of this pudding is made with butter instead of suet; it is spiced and full of taste. Once broken into, the crust reveals not steak and kidney but a filling of lemony chicken with chicory which is mouthwatering and delicate. I serve the pudding simply with a green salad or green beans.

1 kg (2 lb) boned and skinned chicken (breast, thigh or both)
25 g (1 oz) plain flour, plus extra for rolling
2 tablespoons olive oil
175 g (6 oz) self-raising flour

3 teaspoons paprika
1 teaspoon ground mace
2 teaspoons dried dill
3–4 good pinches of cayenne pepper

125 g (4 oz) fresh white breadcrumbs
175 g (6 oz) frozen butter, plus extra for greasing
1 egg
water

5 cm (2-inch) piece of fresh ginger
2 large cloves of garlic
3 heads of chicory
coarsely grated rind and juice of 1 lemon
salt and black pepper

Cut the chicken into largish chunks. Put the plain flour into a bowl and season it with salt and black pepper. Add the chicken and turn it around to coat it with flour. Heat the olive oil in a large frying-pan over a high heat. Add the chicken pieces and fry just to brown them on all sides; then remove from the heat and leave in a bowl on one side to cool.

Put the self-raising flour in a bowl and mix in the spices, the dill, the cayenne pepper and salt. Stir in the breadcrumbs. Holding the frozen butter in a cloth at one end, coarsely grate it into the flour and breadcrumb mixture, mixing it in lightly with your fingertips. Whisk the egg lightly in a measuring jug and bring it up to 175 ml (6 fl oz) with water. Gradually stir the liquid into the flour mixture. Bring together and form a ball. Cut off a little over a quarter of the dough for the lid. Roll out the larger piece of dough fairly thinly on a floured board into a large circle 33–36 cm (13–14 inches) across. Butter a 1.75-litre (3-pint) pudding basin. Carefully lift the large piece of pastry and line the basin, pressing it together if it tears and leaving the excess hanging over the edge.

Put a large saucepan half full of water on to boil. Peel the ginger and garlic and chop finely. Cut the chicory across into thickish slices. Mix the chopped ginger and garlic, the lemon rind and the sliced chicory with the browned chicken. Add the lemon juice and season with salt and black pepper. Spoon the mixture into the lined basin, piling it up in a mound at the top. Fold the overlapping pastry over the filling and dampen the folded-over edges. Roll out the reserved dough in a circle big enough for the top. Press the edges lightly to seal them. Butter a piece of greaseproof paper, make a pleat in the middle and put it over the top of the pudding. Put a piece of foil fairly loosely over the paper and tie both securely round the basin with string. Make a string handle and then lower the basin into the saucepan of boiling water. Cover and boil gently for 3–3½ hours (or 1 hour in a pressure cooker) topping up the water now and then so that it doesn't boil away.

Serves 6

RABBIT AND PUMPKIN WITH MUSTARD AND WHITE KIDNEY BEANS

Rabbit seems to be eaten much more in France than in England, where people often look rather apprehensive if you suggest having rabbit for supper. But since it is possible to buy excellent fresh rabbit nowadays, I think one should disregard any hesitation and show people how good it can be. In France, more often than not, it is cooked with mustard, which certainly goes well with rabbit and for this casserole I have added a base of pumpkin purée flavoured with caraway seeds.
Pictured on page 95.

1 tablespoon olive oil
2 teaspoons caraway seeds
750–875 g (1½ –1¾ lb) fresh rabbit joints

4 cloves of garlic, chopped roughly
125 g (4 oz) butter
1 kg (2 lb) piece of pumpkin, peeled, de-seeded and chopped

2 teaspoons green peppercorns, crushed
4 teaspoons Dijon mustard
a little more than 150 ml (¼ pint) white wine or water

400 g (13 oz) can of white kidney beans (cannellini beans)
150 ml (5 fl oz) carton of soured cream
continental parsley
salt

Preheat the oven to Gas Mark 4/180°C/350°F. Heat the olive oil in a largish iron or other flameproof casserole over a medium heat, add the caraway seeds and stir them around for a moment. Then add the rabbit joints and seal them on both sides. Stir in the chopped garlic, stir around for half a minute and then turn off the heat. Add the butter, cut into pieces. When the butter has melted in the hot casserole, add the chopped pumpkin, the crushed green peppercorns, the mustard, the white wine or water and a sprinkling of salt. Stir with a wooden spoon to mix thoroughly. Cover the casserole with a tight-fitting lid and cook it in the centre of the oven for 1¼ hours.

Stir the casserole with a wooden spoon to break up the pumpkin until it becomes a purée. Drain the canned kidney beans and add them to the dish. Cover the dish again and continue cooking in the oven for another 20–30 minutes. Just before serving, pour the soured cream roughly over the top and sprinkle with a few whole leaves of continental parsley, if available, or ordinary parsley.
Serves 4

CHINOISERIE OF RABBIT WITH JERUSALEM SLICES

These joints of rabbit are cooked with the famous, and blissful, Chinese combination of fresh ginger and garlic and have a glossy sauce dotted with brilliant green spring onions. The non-Chinese element is the thin crunchy slices of lightly sautéed jerusalem artichokes which, used in this way, taste as if they were invented for Chinese dishes. I would serve this dish with rice and some thinly sliced cabbage, steamed or boiled but still crunchy.
Pictured on page 107.

oil	*2 large cloves of garlic,*	*soy sauce*	*salt and black pepper*
butter	*peeled and chopped finely*	*1 tablespoon cornflour*	
1 kg (2 lb) fresh rabbit joints	*150 ml (¼ pint) boiling*	*a bunch of spring onions,*	
4 –5 cm (1½–2-inch) piece	*water*	*chopped small, using plenty*	
of fresh ginger, peeled and	*500 g (1 lb) jerusalem*	*of green stalk*	
chopped finely	*artichokes*		

Preheat the oven to Gas Mark 4/180°C/350°F. Heat a little oil and butter in a large frying pan. Fry the rabbit joints over a high heat on both sides just until golden grown. Transfer with a slotted spatula to a casserole dish. Leave the frying pan with the fat on one side. Sprinkle the chopped ginger and garlic over the rabbit and season with salt and a little black pepper. Pour in the boiling water, cover the dish and put in the oven for 30 – 40 minutes.

Meanwhile, wash and scrub the jerusalem artichokes but don't bother to peel. Cut across into very thin slices. Add a little more oil and butter to the frying pan and heat. Add the sliced artichokes and stir around with a wooden spoon over a high heat for 4–5 minutes. The artichokes should still be rather crunchy, though some of the smaller slices will start to break up a bit. Spoon into a large shallow dish and sprinkle with a little salt.

Using a slotted spatula, transfer the rabbit joints and arrange them on top of the artichokes. Strain the casserole juices into the saucepan. Add a sprinkling of soy sauce and the cornflour mixed to a smooth paste in a cup with a little water. Put over the heat and bring to the boil, stirring. Then bubble for 2–3 minutes, stirring a bit. Lastly, stir in the chopped spring onions and remove from the heat. Spoon the sauce over each rabbit joint like a thick glaze, and serve.
Serves 6

DUCK WITH GOOSEBERRY AND BRAZIL NUT STUFFING

If you are a small family and decide to have duck at Christmas, this
gooseberry and nut stuffing and sauce makes a nice change from the
traditional orange sauce. Made in a slightly larger quantity
it is also good for goose.

*2–2.5 kg (4½ –5½ lb)
duck*

*For the stuffing:
50 g (2 oz) pearl barley*

*coarsely grated rind and
juice of 1 small orange
1 small can of gooseberries
heart and liver of the duck,
chopped finely*

*50 g (2 oz) brazil nuts,
chopped finely
50 g (2 oz) melted butter
1 (size 4) lightly whisked
egg
salt and black pepper*

*For the sauce:
juice from the gooseberries
1 small glass of sweet
vermouth or sherry
about 2 level teaspoons
arrowroot or cornflour
salt and black pepper*

Boil the pearl barley in unsalted water, until tender
but still slightly nutty. Rinse through with cold water
and then mix thoroughly with the rest of the stuffing
ingredients. Season well. Stuff the whole of the duck
with this mixture and truss up or stick skewers in to
keep down the loose skin of the neck and hold the
legs together. Heat oven to Gas Mark
6/200°C/400°F. Rub a little salt all over the skin of
the duck and roast in the centre of the oven, first on
one side for 30 minutes then the other side for 30
minutes and finally on its back for 40–50 minutes.

Transfer the duck to a serving plate and keep
warm. Then pour off the fat from the juices (keep the
fat, as it is wonderful for fried and roast potatoes) and
pour the juices into a saucepan. Add the gooseberry
juice and vermouth. Blend the arrowroot (this will
make a transparent, shiny sauce) or cornflour with a
little water and stir into the juices. Bring to the boil
and bubble, stirring, for 2–3 minutes. Season with salt
and pepper. Serve in a sauce jug with the duck. Don't
forget to spoon all the delicious stuffing out.
Serves 4–6

SPICED DUCK WITH PRUNE AND HAZELNUT STUFFING

Duck always seems a rich, luxurious food and yet frozen duck is often
surprisingly inexpensive. If it is carefully flavoured and stuffed it can be a
real delicacy. You need not stick to the old stand-by of cooking the duck
with oranges. For a change, spice it with cinnamon and stuff it with this
moist and unusual mixture – you will then have an impressive dinner
party dish without having slaved away all day preparing it.

*175 g (6 oz) prunes,
soaked in water overnight
50 g (2 oz) hazelnuts,
chopped finely
75 g (3 oz) carrots, grated*

*50 g (2 oz) fresh brown
breadcrumbs
2 teaspoons ground
cinnamon
25 g (1 oz) butter*

*2–2.5 kg (4½ –5½ lb)
duck, thawed if frozen and
with the heart and liver
removed and sliced finely
1–2 large cloves of garlic,
crushed or chopped finely*

*1 egg, beaten
150 ml (¼ pint) sweet
dessert wine, e.g. Muscatel
150 ml (¼ pint) water
2 teaspoons cornflour
salt and black pepper*

Stone the prunes, chop up and put into a bowl with
the prepared hazelnuts, carrot, breadcrumbs and
1 teaspoon of the cinnamon.
    Melt the butter in a small pan and toss the heart

and liver with the garlic over a medium heat for 1–2
minutes. Stir into the bowl of chopped ingredients,
season well with salt and black pepper and bind
together with the egg. Press the stuffing right into the

body cavity of the duck and skewer to enclose.

Heat the oven to Gas Mark 5/190°C/375°F. Rub the duck all over with the other teaspoon of cinnamon and with salt. Put it on one side on a rack over a roasting pan and roast just above the centre of the oven for 40 minutes, then turn on to the other side for another 40 minutes. Finally, lay the duck on its back, breast-side upwards, for another 40–50 minutes, or until it is cooked. You can test this by inserting a skewer between the leg and body – if clear juices run out it is cooked.

To make a good gravy, pour the fat out of the pan and pour the dessert wine and water into the pan. Stir the cornflour in a little water until smooth and add to the wine, water and pan juices. Bring to the boil and simmer for 2–3 minutes, stirring all the time, until thickened and smooth. Season to taste.

I think plain boiled potatoes and a fresh green vegetable go best with this rich dish.
Serves 4–6

ROASTED MALLARDS WITH SWEET ONION AND OYSTER MUSHROOMS

Mallards are so different from commercially reared duck that it is hard to think of them as from the same family. They are dark-fleshed, with a wonderful gamey flavour, and are less fatty than ordinary duck – a real treat for a formal dinner party. They are easy to prepare with this creamy mixture of onions and oyster mushrooms as an accompaniment.

1 lemon
2 mallards
25 g (1 oz) butter
1 tablespoon olive oil, plus extra for greasing

500 g (1 lb) onions (red ones if available), sliced roughly
4 large cloves of garlic, sliced roughly

1 tablespoon demerara sugar
150 ml (¼ pint) double cream
1 teaspoon dried oregano

125 g (4 oz) oyster mushrooms, halved if large
sea salt and black pepper

Cut the lemon in quarters and put two quarters inside each of the two mallards. Rub them with olive oil and sea salt and put into a roasting pan. Heat the oven to Gas Mark 6/200°C/400°F. Put the mallards on the centre shelf and cook for 45 minutes (this should give you moist pink flesh which is as it should be), basting now and then. Meanwhile put the butter and 1 tablespoon olive oil in a large frying pan.

Melt over a gentle heat, add the onions and garlic and cook slowly, stirring now and then, until the onions are completely soft. Then stir in the sugar and continue to stir over the heat for a minute or two until dissolved. Add the cream and oregano, season with sea salt and black pepper and bring to the boil. Then add the mushrooms and stir around over the heat for a few minutes until the mushrooms are cooked.

When the mallards are ready, pour the juices from the pan and from the inside the birds into the onion and mushroom mixture, and stir together. Check for seasoning and spoon the mixture into a warmed serving bowl to accompany the mallards.
Serves 4–6

DUCK POACHED IN TEA AND HONEY

Earl Grey tea is wonderfully aromatic and gives this duck a really subtle
flavour. Because of the method of cooking it is also very moist without
being fatty and the flesh should still be slightly pink. The reduced juices
make a delicious, dark, shiny sauce which has pieces of apple in it. This is
a simple recipe but as it is done in two stages start well in advance.
I usually serve the duck with brown rice or egg noodles and
any slightly crunchy vegetables.

*2–2.5 kg (4½ –5 lb)
whole duck
1 medium-size onion,
peeled and chopped roughly*

*1 lemon
3 tablespoons Earl Grey
tea-leaves
2 tablespoons honey*

*sunflower or groundnut oil
2 cloves of garlic, chopped
finely
1 large dessert apple*

*2 teaspoons wine vinegar
salt and black pepper*

Preheat the oven to Gas Mark 6/200°C/400°F. Wash
the duck. Sprinkle the body cavity with about 1
teaspoon of salt and put in the chopped onion. Pierce
holes all over the lemon with a skewer and use it as a
stopper to keep the onion in. Place the duck, breast
side down, in an oval casserole dish.

Put the tea-leaves in a measuring jug and pour in
600 ml (1 pint) boiling water. Stir and leave for 3
minutes. Strain the tea into the casserole dish. Pour
another 600 ml (1 pint) boiling water on to the used
tea-leaves, leave again for a few minutes and then
strain over the duck. Finally pour in the honey,
dissolved in a glass of hot water. The duck should
now be almost covered with liquid. Cover the dish
and cook in the oven for 1–1¼ hours.

Carefully lever the duck from the juices and put
on a rack over a roasting pan. Leave on one side.
Strain the juices through a fine sieve into a bowl and
leave to cool before putting in the fridge. Leave there
until the fat can be skimmed off the top. Then pour
the liquid into a large saucepan.

Reheat the oven to Gas Mark 9/240°C/475°F.
Rub the duck with a little sunflower or groundnut
oil, the crushed garlic and about 1 teaspoon of salt.
Put towards the top of the oven and cook for 25–30
minutes, basting once or twice.

Meanwhile, make the sauce from the juices. Boil
the juices in the pan fiercely until very much reduced
and looking dark and syrupy – this may take 15–25
minutes. Remove from the heat and season to taste
with salt and black pepper. Peel and core the apple,
chop up fairly small and stir into the syrupy juices. Put
back on the heat and boil for another 2–3 minutes.
Finally, remove from the heat, stir in the vinegar and
pour into a sauce boat to serve with the duck.
Serves 4–5

Chicken and Smoked Oysters with Grilled Peppers in Saffron and Fresh Lime Sauce (page 98); Chinoiserie of Rabbit with Jerusalem Slices (page 103); Duck Poached in Tea and Honey

ROAST DUCK WITH RED ONIONS AND ARTICHOKE HEARTS

Gently cooked red onions combined with artichoke hearts and toasted
hazelnuts, mixed with the juices of the duck, acts both as a delicious sauce
and as an extra vegetable. When you can, buy the fresh French Barbary
ducks. They are excellent: very tender and a little more 'gamey' in flavour.

1.75–2 kg (4 –4½ lb) duck	2 tablespoons olive oil, plus a little extra	1 tablespoon caster sugar, plus a little extra	juice of ½ lemon a handful of parsley,
375 g (12 oz) red onions	400 g (13 oz) can of	250 ml (8 fl oz) water	chopped
50 g (2 oz) hazelnuts	artichoke hearts	1 tablespoon cornflour	salt and black pepper

Preheat the oven to Gas Mark 7/220°C/425°F.
Smear the duck with a little oil and rub all over with
salt and a little caster sugar. Put on a rack over a
roasting pan and cook just above the centre of the
oven for 1–1¼ hours.

Meanwhile, peel the onions and chop up into
fairly small pieces. Roughly chop the hazelnuts. Heat
the olive oil in a large frying pan over a fairly high
heat, add the hazelnuts and stir around briefly until
toasted brown, then turn the heat down low and add
the onions. Cook gently, stirring around now and
then until the onions are very soft.

Drain the artichoke hearts, rinse thoroughly with
water and cut in quarters. When the onions are soft
add the artichokes and stir in the caster sugar. Season
with salt and black pepper. Turn off the heat and leave
on one side until the duck is cooked.

Empty the juice from the inside of the duck into
the onion mixture together with the water. In a cup
mix the cornflour with a little water and stir until
smooth. Stir this into the onion mixture and put back
on the heat. Bring to bubbling, stirring. Add the
lemon juice and just before serving, the parsley.
Serves 4

GRILLED DUCK BREAST SLICES WITH PARSNIP AND WINE SAUCE

Now that you can buy duck breast fillets in this country it is possible, as
the French have done for years, to cook these tender marinated slices so
that they are slightly rare, something which is impossible to achieve with a
whole bird without seriously undercooking the leg joints.

6 duck breast fillets	juice of 1 orange	1 tablespoon fresh or	125 g (4 oz) small
175 ml (6 fl oz) plus 2	1 teaspoon ground mace	2 teaspoons dried chopped	parsnips, peeled
tablespoons white wine	2 teaspoons ground cinnamon	dill 3–5 cloves of garlic	sea salt and black pepper

Using a sharp knife, score the skin of the duck fillets
at 1 cm (½ inch) intervals across the fillet. Pour 175
ml (6 fl oz) of wine into a measuring jug, add the
orange juice, the spices and the dill, and season with
a little sea salt and plenty of black pepper.

Pour the mixture into a roasting pan or dish just
big enough to hold the duck fillets in one layer closely
together. Put the duck fillets into the marinade flesh
side down. Slice the garlic cloves across as finely as

possible. Insert a thin slice of garlic into each scoring
cut in the skin. Spoon some of the marinade over the
skin so that it sinks in between the cracks. Cover the
dish and leave in the fridge or a cool place for several
hours or overnight.

Boil the parsnips in salted water until soft, and
then put into a food processor with 2 tablespoons of
white wine, and whizz to a purée. Turn into a bowl
and leave on one side. When you are ready to cook

the duck, heat the grill to its highest point. Lift the duck breasts from the marinade and put under the grill, flesh side up, for 5 – 8 minutes until browned.

Meanwhile pour the ducks' marinade into the bowl of parsnip purée, stirring it in to mix smoothly. Turn the duck breasts over so they are skin side up and grill for another 5–8 minutes until brown. The duck flesh should still be pale pink inside. Pour the parsnip and marinade into a frying pan and stir in the juices from the grilled duck. Bubble the mixture fiercely, stirring around in the frying pan for 3 – 4 minutes. Then check for seasoning and add salt and pepper if necessary.

Using a very sharp knife cut the breasts lengthways in thin slices and arrange neatly on a heated serving dish or on individual plates. Spoon the parsnip sauce on to the plates at the side of the duck. **Serves 6**

ROAST BARBARY DUCK STUFFED WITH RED CABBAGE AND MUSHROOMS

If you can't get Barbary duck you can use an ordinary duck for this recipe, but a Barbary duck is less fatty and has a better texture and taste. The stuffing of sweet and sharp red cabbage makes a perfect accompaniment to the rich meat. If you are having a larger dinner party, simply double the recipe, using two ducks instead of one.

2.5–5 cm (1–2 inch) piece of fresh ginger, peeled
2 large cloves of garlic
2 rounded tablespoons crab-apple, apple or redcurrant jelly

2 tablespoons red wine vinegar
1 level teaspoon caraway seeds
175 g (6 oz) red cabbage, chopped finely

125 g (4 oz) mushrooms, sliced finely
25 g (1 oz) fresh brown breadcrumbs
1.5 kg (3½ lb) Barbary duck

olive oil
2 teaspoons arrowroot, soaked with 1 tablespoon water
250 ml (8 fl oz) unsweetened apple juice
sea salt and black pepper

Chop the ginger and garlic finely together. Put the crab-apple jelly and the wine vinegar into a saucepan over a medium heat and stir until the jelly has melted. Then bring to the boil and boil for a minute. Add the caraway seeds and then the cabbage and mushrooms. Stir around, cover the pan and leave to simmer gently for 5 minutes. Then season with salt and black pepper and boil fiercely, uncovered, for a few minutes until the juices have almost evaporated. Remove from the heat and stir in the breadcrumbs. Leave until cool and then spoon into the body cavity of the duck. Then rub the duck all over with a little oil and salt.

Heat the oven to Gas Mark 6/200°C/400°F. Put the duck breast downwards on a rack on a roasting pan. Roast on the centre shelf for half an hour, then turn the duck the right way up and continue to cook for a further half hour. Then remove the duck and put on a carving board. Pour off as much fat as you can, leaving any brown juices and sediment in the pan. Add the arrowroot and apple juice and boil vigorously on top of the stove for 3 – 4 minutes, stirring all the time. Now try the sauce and add salt and black pepper to taste. Pour into a sauce boat. **Serves 4**

TURKEY BALLS KIEV

These balls of minced turkey resemble a tiny version of Chicken Kiev but they are poached and served with a cream and egg yolk sauce instead of being coated in breadcrumbs and fried. However, in the same irresistible way they burst forth with liquid butter as you cut them open. Serve with a green vegetable, such as broccoli, broad beans or petits pois, and new potatoes or egg noodles.

375 g (12 oz) turkey breast fillets, skinned
75 g (3 oz) fresh white breadcrumbs

2–3 cloves of garlic, crushed
2 eggs, separated
40–50 g (1½ – 2 oz) butter, cold from the fridge

150 ml (5 fl oz) carton of soured cream
1 tablespoon single cream or top of the milk

1 tablespoon chopped fresh, tarragon or dill
salt and black pepper

Mince the turkey fillets or chop them in a food processor. Put in a bowl with the breadcrumbs and garlic and season with plenty of salt and black pepper. Add the unbeaten egg whites and work in thoroughly with a wooden spoon. With damp hands, form the mixture into balls each the size of a large marble. Then cut off little squares of butter, form a hole in each ball, insert the butter and press the mixture round again to enclose it.

Bring a large pan of water to the boil. Drop in the turkey balls and continue boiling vigorously for a few minutes until all the balls rise to the top. Lift them out with a slotted spoon and put closely together in a shallow ovenproof dish. Cover with foil and keep hot in a low oven while making the sauce.

Before serving, put the egg yolks, the soured cream, the cream or top of the milk and the tarragon or dill in a small saucepan with salt and black pepper. Heat very gently, stirring and not allowing to bubble, for a few minutes until the sauce thickens a little. Pour over the turkey balls and serve.
Serves 4–5

GUINEA FOWL COOKED IN ARTICHOKE PURÉE WITH SHALLOTS AND LYCHEES

Guinea fowl has a taste similar to pheasant and, like pheasant, it can be dry. The best way to cook it is to braise it in a casserole. Here it is cooked in a purée of jerusalem artichokes with shallots and bacon. The lychees added at the end add a slight sweetness which goes well with the delicately flavoured bird. Serve with sautéed or baked potatoes and a green vegetable.

500 g (1 lb) jerusalem artichokes
6 large, unpeeled cloves of garlic

175 g (6 oz) thinly sliced, rindless, streaky bacon
250 g (8 oz) shallots
425 g (14 oz) can of lychees

2 teaspoons dried, or
2 tablespoons chopped, fresh tarragon
about 1.1 kg (2½ lb) guinea fowl

plain flour
soft butter or margarine
5–6 tablespoons double cream
salt and black pepper

Scrub the artichokes but don't bother to peel them. Put in a saucepan of salted water with the garlic and boil until the artichokes are soft. Roll the bacon up into tight little rolls. Peel the shallots.

When the artichokes are cooked put in a food processor with the garlic cloves, popped out of their skins, and the strained juice of the lychees. Add the tarragon and season well with salt and black pepper.

Preheat the oven to Gas Mark 4/180°C/350°F.

Pour the artichoke mixture into a casserole dish. Rub the guinea fowl with flour and then smear with soft butter. Put the bird in the casserole and sprinkle with salt and black pepper. Place the peeled shallots all round the bird, interspersed with the bacon rolls. Cover the casserole and cook in the centre of the oven for 1½ – 1¾ hours, until tender.

Remove the bird and put it in the centre of a large warmed serving dish. Strain off excess fat from the artichoke mixture, stir in the drained lychees and then only very roughly stir in the double cream. Spoon the mixture around the bird and serve.

Serves 4

TURKEY IN PUFF PASTRY

Meat wrapped in a glazed pastry case is always an impressive dish to serve at a dinner party, although using packet puff pastry it is simple to prepare. In this recipe the breast of turkey stuck with thyme and a little garlic is covered with a layer of liver sausage or pâté, then encased in the crisp golden pastry and served with a soured cream sauce. Remember to start it in good time, as the meat has to be precooked and cooled before the pastry stage.

1 clove of garlic
4 teaspoons fresh or
2 teaspoons dried thyme

1 kg (2 lb) breast fillet of turkey, rolled and tied up cooking oil
150 ml (¼ pint) vermouth or white wine

250 g (8 oz) continental liver sausage or soft liver pâté
400 g (13 oz) frozen puff pastry, thawed

1 egg yolk
1 teaspoon cornflour
150 ml (5 fl oz) carton of soured cream
salt and black pepper

Heat the oven to Gas Mark 3/160°C/325°F. Chop the garlic finely and mix with the thyme. Press the mixture deep into the gaps in the meat with your fingers. Cover the meat generously with oil and sprinkle all over with salt and black pepper. Roast the joint in the centre of the oven for about 2 hours, basting occasionally and adding the wine to the pan about half an hour before the end.

Take out the meat and leave to cool completely, reserving the juices in a small saucepan. When the meat is cold cut off the string.

Heat the oven to Gas Mark 6/200°C/400°F. Take the skin off the liver sausage and press it (or the pâté, if used) all over the meat, making the surface as even as possible. Roll out the pastry to a piece big enough to wrap the meat in, about 38 cm (15 inches) square. Lay the meat in the centre, cut off a 5 cm (2-inch) square at each corner, dampen the edges and wrap up the joint like a parcel, making sure that there are no more than two thicknesses of pastry in any one place. Cut decorations from the pastry trimmings.

Put the pastry parcel in a greased roasting pan and brush all over with the egg yolk. Cook in the centre of the oven for 25–35 minutes, until a rich golden brown and puffed up.

Before serving, blend the cornflour with a little cold water and stir with the soured cream into the pan juices. Bring gently to the boil, stirring until thickened. Test for seasoning and add salt, pepper and a little more thyme if you wish. Pour into a sauce boat and serve with the meat. I normally serve new potatoes with this dish and broccoli, broad beans or a good mixed salad.

Serves 4–6

STUFFED TURKEY BREASTS IN CHINESE PASTIES

From the outside this looks like a steamed Cornish pasty, but the enticing
smell tells you immediately it has Far Eastern connections. The turkey
breast is stuffed with beansprouts and flavoured with oyster sauce.

75 g (3 oz) plain flour, plus extra for kneading
75 g (3 oz) strong white flour
½ teaspoon salt
175 ml (6 fl oz) boiling water
4 boneless turkey breast steaks weighing about 750 g (1½ lb)
2 cloves of garlic
2.5 cm (1-inch) piece of fresh ginger
125 g (4 oz) fresh beansprouts
1 teaspoon ground coriander
1 teaspoon mustard seeds
3 tablespoons oyster sauce
oil for greasing
lettuce leaves and soy sauce, to serve

Sift the flours and salt into a bowl. Stir in the boiling water with a wooden spoon until the dough sticks together. Knead it with the palm of your hand on a floured surface until the dough is smooth and elastic. Wrap the ball of dough in cling film and leave to rest for 1½–2 hours.

Meanwhile, prepare the filling. Using a very sharp knife, carefully cut a deep pocket in the turkey steaks. Peel the garlic and ginger and chop them together very finely. Put the beansprouts in a bowl and add the chopped garlic and ginger, the ground coriander, the mustard seeds and 1 tablespoon of oyster sauce. Spoon the beansprout mixture into the cavities in the turkey breasts, pressing it in.

When the dough has rested, divide it into four pieces and roll these into four balls. Roll out one ball fairly thinly on a floured surface to a circular shape.

Place a stuffed turkey breast on one side of the circle, moisten the edge on one side of the circle and bring the pastry over to enclose the piece of turkey and make a semicircular shape like a pasty. Press the edges to seal. Repeat the process with the other three balls of pastry.

Brush the remaining 2 tablespoons of oyster sauce on both sides of the pasties and place them on an oiled steaming tray or trays. (If your steamer is small you may have to cook the pasties in two batches, and keep the first lot warm in a covered dish in a low oven.) Steam the pasties for 20–25 minutes. Lift the pasties carefully out of the steamer with a spatula and put them in a warmed serving dish on a bed of lettuce leaves. Just before putting them on the table, sprinkle on a little soy sauce.
Serves 4

TURKEY-STUFFED MUSHROOM PUFFS

500 g (1 lb) turkey breast fillets
50 g (2 oz) butter
1–2 green chillies, de-seeded and chopped finely
25 g (1 oz) plain flour
scant 275 ml (9 fl oz) milk
75 g (3 oz) whole hazelnuts
2 teaspoons chopped tarragon
125 g (4 oz) frozen petits pois
250 g (8 oz) packet of puff pastry, thawed if frozen
4 extra large flat mushrooms
a little butter for greasing
1 egg yolk
salt

Mince the turkey breasts or chop in a food processor. Melt the butter in a saucepan, stir in the chopped chillies and remove from the heat. Stir in the minced turkey; then stir in the flour and add the milk gradually. Bring to bubbling, stirring all the time with a wooden spoon; then simmer gently, stirring often, for another 10 minutes. Add salt to taste. Then add the hazelnuts and remove from the heat. Stir in the chopped tarragon and the frozen petits pois, turn into a bowl and leave until cold.

Roll out the pastry very thinly into a large piece, as square as possible. Cut the piece of pastry into four rough squares. Cut the stalks off the mushrooms. Lay each mushroom out black side up on a square of pastry and spoon a quarter of the cold turkey mixture on to each one, piling it on. Bring the corners of the pastry up one by one to the centre top, covering the filling. Moisten the top to seal but don't fold over the sticking-out sides of pastry. There should be small gaps at each corner of the base so that the mushroom juices can run out. Lay the parcels on a buttered baking sheet. If you have time, keep in the fridge until ready to cook. Preheat the oven to Gas Mark 7/ 220°C/425°F.

Brush the parcels all over with egg yolk and cook in the centre of the oven for 20 minutes until a rich golden brown. Transfer the parcels carefully on to a serving plate with a wide spatula, letting any water from the mushrooms run away.

Serves 4

STEAMED TURKEY BALLS WITH SCARLET SAUCE

These are made with turkey breast. Lightly spiced with nutmeg and flavoured with parmesan cheese they make an original change from fried meatballs. The red pepper and tomato sauce is delicious and looks beautiful.

For the turkey balls:
750 g (1½ lb) turkey breast fillets, skinned
25 g (1 oz) unsalted butter, softened
25 g (1 oz) fresh white breadcrumbs
a large handful of parsley, chopped finely

¼ whole nutmeg, grated
3 tablespoons freshly grated parmesan cheese
1 egg, whisked
salt and black pepper

For the sauce:
1 medium-size red pepper

25 g (1 oz) butter
1 tablespoon olive oil
2 cloves of garlic, chopped finely
250 g (8 oz) tomatoes, cut small
397 g (14 oz) can of chopped tomatoes

2 tablespoons tomato purée
salt and chilli powder
whole basil leaves (when in season) and chopped fresh basil or parsley, to garnish

Mince or chop finely the turkey breast. Put in a mixing bowl and add all the remaining turkey ball ingredients. Mix well with a wooden spoon and season generously with salt and black pepper. Using oiled hands form the mixture into small balls the size of ping-pong balls and lay in the top of a steamer. Cover and steam for 20 –25 minutes.

Meanwhile, make the sauce. Cut the pepper in half, discard the seeds and chop as finely as possible, in a food processor if you have one. Heat the butter and olive oil in a saucepan, add the chopped pepper and garlic and stir over a medium heat for a minute or two. Then add the fresh tomatoes to the pan and cook for another few minutes until mushy. Add the can of tomatoes and the tomato purée. Cover the pan and simmer gently for another 15–20 minutes. Season to taste with salt and chilli powder. When the turkey balls are ready, pile them on a heated serving plate, spoon the sauce over the top and sprinkle with chopped basil or parsley. Decorate the plate with whole basil leaves.

Serves 6

PHEASANTS WITH FENNEL SAUCE

2 tablespoons groundnut oil
25 g (1 oz) butter
2 pheasants
2 large bulbs of fennel
2 teaspoons ground cumin

2 teaspoons ground coriander
2 large cloves of garlic, finely chopped
2 tablespoons plain flour

300 ml (½ pint) tomato juice
300 ml (½ pint) single cream
coarsely grated rind and juice of 1 orange and 1 lemon

10 −12 juniper berries, crushed
a good handful of fresh parsley, chopped finely
salt and black pepper

Heat the oil and butter in a large, deep frying pan. Fry the pheasants in the pan over a high heat, turning them just until browned all over. Remove them and put into a fairly large casserole. Cut the fennel into about 8 pieces lengthways, discarding the stalks and base, and arrange the pieces in the casserole dish around the pheasants. Put the frying pan back over a gentle heat and stir the ground cumin, the coriander and the chopped garlic into the oil and butter.

Stir in the flour and continue stirring over the heat for a minute. Then remove the pan from the heat and gradually stir in the tomato juice, the cream and the orange and lemon rind and juice. Put the pan back on the heat and bring up to boiling point, stirring all the time until the sauce thickens. Season to taste with salt and black pepper and stir in the crushed juniper berries.

Heat the oven to Gas Mark 3/160°C/325°F. Now pour the sauce over the fennel pieces round the pheasants in the casserole dish. Cook in the centre of the oven for 1½ hours or until the pheasants are tender. To serve, remove the pheasants from the casserole with a slotted spoon and a fork and put on to a carving board. Stir the chopped parsley into the casserole dish and pour the sauce, with the fennel in it, into a serving bowl. Carve the pheasant on to the plates and spoon some of the sauce over it.
Serves 6 −7

PHEASANTS IN SAFFRON SAUCE

Pictured on pages 54/5.

2 good pinches of saffron strands
125 ml (4 fl oz) very hot water
6 large cloves of garlic

50 g (2 oz) butter
500 −625 g (1−1 ¼ lb) onions, chopped roughly
juice of 1 lemon

150 ml (¼ pint) apple juice
3 hen pheasants
1 tablespoon olive oil
2 medium − large red peppers

1 rounded teaspoon caraway seeds
150 ml (¼ pint) double cream
salt and black pepper

Put the saffron strands into a measuring jug and pour the hot water over them. Leave on one side. Chop 4 cloves of the garlic roughly. Melt the butter in a large frying pan, add the chopped onions and garlic and cook, stirring often, over a fairly gentle heat until the onions are translucent and very soft without being burnt at the edges. Then put them into a food processor with the lemon and apple juice and whizz very thoroughly until as smooth as possible.

Using your sharpest large knife, cut the pheasants down the centre along the breast bone and then cut each in two. If you have difficulty, bang the knife with a wooden rolling pin. Add the olive oil to the pan you cooked the onions in, and put over a fairly high heat. Fry the joints 4 or 5 at a time just to brown them on each side. When they are browned, use a slotted spatula to transfer them to a large casserole dish.

Heat the oven to Gas Mark 3/160°C/325°F. Cut the peppers in half lengthways, discard the seeds and stem and cut across finely. Scatter the pepper slices amongst the pheasant joints. Now pour the puréed onions into a bowl and stir in the saffron strands and their water. Then add the caraway seeds. Peel the remaining 2 cloves of garlic, chop finely and stir into the mixture. Season with salt and black pepper.

Then pour the sauce over the pheasants and peppers, cover the dish and cook in the centre of the oven for 1½ –2 hours until the pheasant is tender, turning the joints around in the juices once or twice during the cooking. Then transfer the pheasant joints with a slotted spatula to a large serving dish with the pieces of red pepper mostly on top. Pour the cream into the sauce, and boil for 2–3 minutes. Check for seasoning and pour the sauce over the pheasant just before serving.

Serves 6–8

PHEASANT BREAST WITH BRANDY SAUCE

In season you can now buy jointed pheasant breast which makes a perfect treat for two people. To serve, don't carve the breast in the usual way; I simply slice it in half with a very sharp knife. In this recipe pheasant is impregnated with tarragon and garlic butter beneath the skin and accompanied by a luxurious creamy brandy sauce flavoured with sieved fresh tomatoes. If you can, serve the pheasant with wild rice and lightly cooked broccoli or mangetout peas. If you want to serve the dish to a small party of people, simply multiply the quantities.

25 g (1 oz) unsalted butter
a good handful of fresh tarragon
1 clove of garlic, crushed
1 hen pheasant breast joint
olive oil
3 medium-size tomatoes
4 tablespoons double cream
3 tablespoons brandy
sea salt and black pepper

Soften the butter by mashing it with a fork in a small bowl. Pull the leaves off the tarragon stalks and chop all but a few of them very finely. Mix the finely chopped tarragon and the crushed garlic into the softened butter, and season with black pepper and a little sea salt. Push your fingers under the skin of the pheasant breast, pull it gently back and make two deep cuts along the breast on each side with a small, sharp knife. Press the tarragon butter into these cuts and also smear some all over the breast. Pull the skin back over the breast and secure down with a small skewer if necessary. Smear the joint with olive oil and sprinkle the skin with a little crushed sea salt. Put into a roasting pan and heat the oven to Gas Mark 6/200°C/400°F. Cook the pheasant breast in the centre of the oven for 45 –55 minutes until rich golden brown. Meanwhile prepare the sauce.

Put the tomatoes into a bowl, pour boiling water over them, leave for a minute or two, then drain and skin them. Whizz them to a purée in a food processor and then press them through a sieve into the bowl again. Stir in the cream and the brandy. Chop the reserved whole tarragon leaves roughly and add them to the mixture together with plenty of black pepper and a sprinkling of sea salt.

When the pheasant is ready, remove it from the pan and put it on to a warmed serving plate, or simply cut it in half and put on to two warmed plates. Pour most of the excess fat from the roasting pan (keep it for future cooking), leaving any juices or sediment in the pan. Pour the sauce mixture into the roasting pan and bring to bubbling on top of the stove, stirring all the time. Simmer fairly gently, stirring, for 4 –5 minutes, then pour into a sauce boat or straight on to the breasts of pheasant.

Serves 2

STUFFED BONED SHOULDER OF VENISON WITH CREAMY ONION SAUCE

I often serve a mixture of celeriac, potato and parsnip with venison, mashed with plenty of butter, spread in a gratinée dish, sprinkled with cheese and browned above the venison in the oven for ½ – ¾ hour. As well as this a plain, crisply steamed green vegetable is a good accompaniment.

125 g (4 oz) dried apricots, chopped finely
4 large cloves of garlic, chopped finely
5 – 7 cm (2–3 inch) piece of fresh ginger, peeled and chopped finely
175 g (6 oz) rindless streaky bacon, chopped
2 teaspoons ground cinnamon
2 teaspoons ground cumin
2 teaspoons ground paprika
1 orange
6 tablespoons olive oil
1.25–1.5 kg (3 –3½ lb) boned shoulder of venison
3 tablespoons red wine vinegar
50 g (2 oz) butter
500 g (1 lb) onions, sliced thinly in rings
300 ml (½ pint) double or single cream
salt and black pepper

Put the apricots, garlic, ginger and bacon into a bowl with the cinnamon, cumin and paprika. Coarsely grate the orange zest and add it to the mixture with 3 tablespoons of the olive oil. Season with black pepper and salt and mix thoroughly with a wooden spoon. If the venison is already rolled, undo the string and lay out flat. Press the stuffing all over it. Roll the joint up loosely and then secure together with string.

Squeeze the orange juice into a bowl, add the wine vinegar and the remaining 3 tablespoons olive oil and season well with black pepper. Put the stuffed joint into a casserole and pour over the orange juice mixture, rubbing it all over the joint. Cover the casserole and leave in a cool place until next day, basting the joint with the liquid whenever you re-member.

To cook, heat the oven to Gas Mark 3/ 160°C/325°F. In a large frying pan melt the butter over a medium heat, add the onions and cook, stirring until soft. Open the casserole, add a sprinkling of salt to the liquid, coat the venison once more and then lift it up and spread the fried onions on the bottom of the casserole. Then put the venison back on top, cover and put just below the centre of the oven for 2½ hours, basting often. Remove the joint from the casserole and put on to a carving board.

If the casserole is flameproof, boil up the juices fiercely on top of the stove for about 3 minutes to reduce slightly (or pour into a saucepan to do this). Then stir in the cream and simmer for another minute or two. Season to taste with salt and black pepper, and pour the sauce into a serving bowl to spoon over the venison on your plates. Use a sharp knife for the venison – and make sure that everyone has both meat and stuffing.

Serves 8

PIGEONS WITH A COMPOTE OF RED CABBAGE

2 rounded tablespoons plain
flour
4 wood pigeons
2 tablespoons sunflower oil,
plus extra if necessary

4 tablespoons olive oil
salt and black pepper

For the compote:
2 largish onions

50 g (2 oz) butter
500 g (1 lb) red cabbage
5 cm (2-inch) piece of fresh
ginger
2 large cloves of garlic

2 teaspoons caraway seeds
125 g (4 oz) pitted prunes,
cut in half
150 ml (1/4 pint) red wine
salt

First make the compote. Peel the onions and chop them roughly. Melt the butter in a large flameproof casserole over a medium heat, add the onion and cook until soft and just beginning to brown. Meanwhile chop up the red cabbage finely. Peel the ginger and the garlic and chop them together finely. When the onion is soft add the chopped ginger and garlic followed by the cabbage. Add the caraway seeds, the halved prunes and the wine. Season with salt. Cover the casserole dish with a lid and remove it from the heat.

Put the flour into a bowl and season with salt and black pepper. Dip the pigeons in the flour to coat them thoroughly. Heat the sunflower oil in a large frying-pan over a high heat and fry the pigeons just to brown them on all sides, adding more oil if necessary. Arrange them on top of the red cabbage and spoon a tablespoon of olive oil over each one. Heat the oven to gas Mark 3/160°C/325°F. Cook, covered, in the centre of the oven for about 1½ hours.
Serves 4

GINGER PIGEON WITH HONEY, APRICOTS AND WALNUTS

125 g (4 oz) dried apricots
2 wood pigeons
2 pig's kidneys

5 −7.5 cm (2–3-inch) piece
of fresh ginger
4 −5 cloves of garlic
25 g (1 oz) fat for frying

50 g (2 oz) shelled walnuts
1 rounded tablespoon
thick, or 2 tablespoons
clear, honey

1 red or green pepper
a little chopped mint or
parsley
salt

Put the dried apricots in a bowl, cover with 300 ml (½ pint) hot water and leave for 2 hours or more. Using a very sharp knife, cut the pigeons in half down the breast bone. Skin the kidneys, cut away the cores and then slice in half lengthwise. Peel the ginger and garlic, slice roughly, put in a liquidiser with a little water and whizz to as smooth a paste as possible. (If you have no liquidiser just chop as finely as you can.)

Heat the fat in a large, heavy saucepan. Put in the pieces of pigeon and cook until just brown on both sides. Then add the ginger and garlic paste and the kidneys and stir for a minute. Add the apricots with their soaking water, the walnuts and another 600 ml (1 pint) of water. Stir in the honey and season with

salt. Bring to the boil, cover the pan and simmer gently for about 1½ hours or until the pigeon is tender. Then lift out the pigeon and kidney with a slotted spoon and arrange on a warm, shallow dish.

Strain the remaining juices into another saucepan and spoon the apricots and walnuts around the pigeon joints. Slice the pepper across in very fine rings, cut into semi-circles and arrange in an overlapping pattern round the edge of the dish. Cover with foil and keep warm. Boil up the juices in the pan fiercely for 8 −10 minutes until well reduced and thickened. Just before serving, spoon this sauce over the pigeons, etc. and sprinkle with a little chopped mint or parsley.
Serves 4

FISH SAUSAGES IN A GOLDEN SAUCE WITH SPRING ONIONS

These are delicate little white fish sausages in a rich cheesy sauce. You can
either serve them as a hot first course, in which case the dish would
probably stretch to 8 servings, or as a main course with a crisp green
vegetable such as broccoli and with new or sautéed potatoes.

For the sausages:		For the sauce:	
500 g (1 lb) cod fillets, fresh	1 teaspoon baking powder	a bunch of spring onions	450 ml (¾ pint) milk
or thawed from frozen	3 pinches of chilli powder	50 g (2 oz) butter	125 g (4 oz) Red Leicester
2 large egg whites (size 1–2)	finely grated rind of	1 teaspoon paprika	cheese, grated coarsely
½ oz (15 g) cornflour	1 orange	scant 25 g (1 oz) plain flour	2 large egg yolks (size 1–2)
	salt		salt and black pepper

Skin the cod fillets and put in a food processor with
the egg whites, cornflour and baking powder. Season
with salt and the chilli powder and whizz until
smoothly blended. Then stir in the grated orange
rind. Using wet hands, take up bits of the mixture and
form into small fat sausages. Bring a large saucepan of
water to the boil. Drop in the fish sausages and simmer
for 7 minutes. Drain in a colander and then put in a
rather shallow ovenproof dish. Preheat the oven to
Gas Mark 2/150°C/300°F.

To make the sauce, chop up the spring onions
fairly small, using as much as of the green part as
possible. Melt the butter with the paprika in a saucepan. Remove from the heat and stir in the flour with
a wooden spoon until smooth. Stir in the milk, put
back on the heat and bring to the boil, stirring.
Bubble, still stirring, for about 3 minutes. Add the
grated cheese amd stir until melted; then stir in the
egg yolks. Season to taste with salt and pepper and add
the chopped spring onions.

Pour the sauce over the fish sausages. Heat the
grill to high and put the dish under it for 2–4 minutes
until speckled dark brown. Finally, put the dish on
the centre shelf of the oven and cook for 30 minutes
before serving.
Serves 4–5

SQUID LEQUEITIO

Sliced squid should have only a few minutes cooking, and it will then be
tender and delicious.

2 tablespoons olive oil	juice of 1 large orange	1 kg (2 lb) squid, prepared	2 teaspoons dried oregano
500 g (1 lb) spanish	2 tablespoons tomato purée	and cleaned	salt and cayenne pepper
onions, chopped very finely	150 ml (¼) pint water		

Heat the olive oil in an iron or other flameproof
casserole dish on top of the stove over a medium heat.
Add the chopped onions and stir them around for 2 or
3 minutes; then stir in the orange juice, the tomato
purée and the water. Cover the pan and cook the sauce
over a very low heat for 30–45 minutes until it is soft
and mushy. Meanwhile, make sure the fishmonger has
extracted the transparent bone from the squid and
taken out all the soft innards. Then slice the bodies of
the squid across in thin rings and cut the tentacles up
roughly. When the onion sauce is ready, add the squid
and the oregano, increase the heat again, cover and
cook for another 5 minutes or so until the squid is just
opaque. Remove from the heat, season to taste with
salt and a pinch or two of cayenne pepper.
Serves 4

FISH BAKED IN CABBAGE LEAVES

This unusual way of cooking fish in tasty, tender cabbage leaves makes it
especially succulent and the slices of sharp apple add a titillating tang.

*500 g (1 lb) cod, whiting
or haddock fillets*

*1 fairly large but loosely
packed green cabbage,
weighing about 500–625 g
(1–1¼ lb)*

*25–50 g (1–2 oz) butter
or margarine, plus extra for
greasing*
1 teaspoon paprika

*1 large cooking apple, about
250 g (8 oz) weight, peeled
and sliced thinly*
salt and black pepper

If the fish is frozen, thaw it slightly and remove the
skin. Take the whole leaves off the cabbage and
submerge them – you may do this in two or three
batches – in a large pan of boiling salted water for
2 minutes. Drain and rinse with cold water.

Butter a large, but not too deep, ovenproof dish.
Preheat the oven to Gas Mark 5/190°C/375°F. Lay
about half of the cabbage leaves on the bottom, letting
them come up and overlap the sides of the dish. Lay
the fish fillets on top of the cabbage leaves. Sprinkle
with the paprika and with salt and pepper. Arrange
the apple slices on top of the fish and dot with butter.
Fold the cabbage leaves over the fish and apples and
cover with the remaining leaves, pushing the cabbage
in round the edges so that the fish is completely
encased. Dot with some more butter, cover with foil
or a lid and cook in the centre of the oven for 1 hour.
Serves 6

STUFFED FILLETS OF PLAICE

Fish and rice go well together and this way of stuffing tender fillets of
plaice with a nutty pilaf rice mixture under a light, creamy sauce makes a
substantial dish.

*15 g (½ oz) butter or
margarine, plus a little extra*
*1 small onion, chopped
finely*

*1 teaspoon chopped fresh or
dried thyme*
125 g (4 oz) easy-cook rice
4 tablespoons water

½ lightly beaten egg
*4 plaice fillets (if frozen,
allow to thaw first)*
*150 ml (5 fl oz) carton of
single cream*

1 teaspoon lemon juice
salt and black pepper
*a little chopped parsley, to
garnish*

Melt the butter in a heavy-based saucepan and gently
cook the onion in it until just softened. Add the thyme
and a good sprinkling of salt and black pepper. Stir in
the rice and the water. Bring to the boil, cover and
simmer gently for 10–15 minutes, until the rice is
cooked but still has a slight bite to it. Allow to cool
and then bind the rice together with the egg.

Preheat the oven to Gas Mark 6/200°C/400°F.
Butter an ovenproof dish and lay out the plaice fillets
in it one by one, spooning a mound of rice on to each
one and then rolling the fish loosely up round the rice
– it doesn't matter if it bursts out each side. Arrange
the stuffed fillets closely together in a dish, dot with a
little extra butter and sprinkle with salt and pepper.
Cover with foil or a lid and cook in the oven for
25–30 minutes.

Warm the cream gently and gradually stir in the
lemon juice, which will thicken it. Do not overheat
the cream or it will curdle. Season to taste with salt
and pepper, pour the sauce over the stuffed fillets and
serve, garnished with a little chopped parsley.
Serves 4

MONKFISH KEBABS WITH AUBERGINE AND YOGURT SAUCE

Chicken kebabs, well seasoned, are often delicious, but fish kebabs are my real favourite. Driving up the banks of the Bosporus beyond Istanbul there are a string of waterside restaurants and on a hot summer night they are a wonderful escape from the turmoil and dirt of the city. In one of these restaurants I had the ultimate fish kebabs. They used swordfish – which I had seen earlier in the day in Istanbul market – staggeringly arranged, fanning outwards like silver catherine wheels. So these kebabs were literally swordfish served on a sword. Another firm-fleshed fish, monkfish, is an excellent alternative to swordfish. I serve the kebabs with brown rice and a salad.

1 medium-size aubergine
750 g (1½ lb) filleted monkfish
2 large bulbs of fennel

7 tablespoons olive oil
juice of 1 large lemon
2 rounded teaspoons ground coriander

1 clove of garlic, peeled and chopped finely
240 g (8 oz) carton of Greek yogurt

2 tablespoons chopped fresh dill
salt and black pepper

First cut the unpeeled aubergine into 1 cm (½ inch) slices, rub the slices all over with salt and leave them in a colander in the sink for half an hour. Then cut the monkfish into 4–5 cm (1½–2-inch) chunks and cut the fennel into 5–7.5 cm (2–3 inch) pieces. Put 5 tablespoons of olive oil and the lemon juice into a mixing bowl, stir in the coriander and season with salt and black pepper. Add the pieces of fish and fennel and stir them around to coat them in the oil mixture. Leave in a cool place on one side.

After half an hour wash all the salt off the aubergine slices, pat them thoroughly dry with paper towels and cut them into 1 cm (½ inch) cubes. Now heat the remaining 2 tablespoons of olive oil in a frying pan over a medium heat, add the aubergine pieces and toss them around for a few minutes until they are browned on all sides and soft. Then add the chopped garlic, stir for another half a minute and put the pan on one side, off the heat. When the aubergine has cooled slightly, gently stir the yogurt in a mixing bowl until smooth, season it with salt and black pepper and then lightly stir in the aubergine, garlic and oil, lastly adding the chopped dill weed. Turn into a dish.

Now thread the monkfish and fennel alternately on four to six long skewers, starting and finishing each skewer with a largish piece of fennel. Put the skewers under a very hot grill or on a barbecue grill, basting with any oil and lemon remaining in the bowl, for 5–7 minutes on each side, until the fish is blackened on the edges. Serve on or pushed off the skewers. Pour any cooking juices left in the grill over the top of the kebabs.
Serves 4

SALMON FILLETS WITH A SPECIAL CREAM SAUCE

As they have to be served soon after cooking, fillets of fish with a sauce are difficult for a large dinner party, However, they are an ideal treat when there are only two of you. The most important thing with salmon is that it should not be overcooked, as it can create an unpleasant tackiness when you chew it.

For this recipe you should ask for the salmon to be filleted and skinned for you at the fish counter – ask to keep the skin and bones too. With them you make stock in which the salmon is poached and which then also makes the basis of a wonderful sauce. Serve with new potatoes if possible and a crisp green vegetable.

1 kg (2 lb) piece of salmon, filleted and skinned
2.5 –5cm (1–2 inch) piece of fresh ginger

1 small onion
2 pinches of chilli powder
450 ml ($^3/_4$ pint) water
6–7 strands of saffron

2 tablespoons white wine vinegar
125 ml (4 fl oz) double cream

1 rounded tablespoon fresh tarragon, chopped
salt

Put the salmon skin and bones into a saucepan. Chop up the washed but unpeeled ginger roughly. Cut the unpeeled onion into quarters. Put the ginger and onion into the saucepan with the fish bits and add a sprinkling of salt, the chilli powder and water. Bring to the boil, then cover the pan and simmer gently for 20–25 minutes. Now strain the liquid into a bowl in which you have put the saffron strands, and leave to infuse for ½ hour or more, then stir in the vinegar.

When the saffron has infused into the liquid, lay the salmon fillets in the bottom of a saucepan and pour the liquid over them. Cover the saucepan and bring to the boil; after half a minute remove from the heat and let the fish sit in the liquid for 5 minutes. Then transfer the fillets carefully with a slotted spatula to a fairly shallow, heated serving dish. Cover and keep in the oven at the lowest possible setting while you make the sauce – if you aren't quite ready to start the sauce you can leave the fish in a low oven for 20–30 minutes.

To make the sauce, bring the fish juices to the boil in the saucepan and boil fiercely for about 4 – 6 minutes until the liquid is reduced, thick and syrupy – you should be left with 2–3 tablespoons of liquid. Stir the cream into this concentrated liquid, bring to the boil, throw in the chopped tarragon and allow to boil for about half a minute. Check for seasoning, though the sauce probably won't need adjusting. Finally, spoon the sauce over the salmon fillets and serve at once.

Serves 2

ANCHOVY-STUFFED MULLET WITH VEGETABLE STEW

Red mullet is an excellent and pretty fish, much eaten in Spain. In this recipe, the fish are stuffed with little strips of anchovy and served with a Spanish-style mixture of vegetables: an easy and satisfying dish. I serve it either with baked potatoes, or with good, crusty bread, warmed in the oven.

2 fairly large aubergines
lemon juice
6 small to medium-size red mullet
50 g (1¾ oz) can of anchovies in oil

3 tablespoons olive oil
2 large cloves of garlic, chopped roughly
375 g (12 oz) tomatoes, chopped fairly small

1 teaspoon caraway seeds
1 teaspoon paprika
500 g (1 lb) french beans, topped and tailed
432 g (15 oz) can of chick-peas, drained

300 g (10 oz) large flat mushrooms, sliced thinly
salt and black pepper

Cut the unpeeled aubergines across into fairly thin slices. Sprinkle them with lemon juice, rub them all over with salt and leave them in a colander in the sink for half an hour.

If the fish have not been prepared by the fishmonger, gut them, but leave the heads on. Wash them well and rub off any scales. Pat them dry with kitchen paper towelling. Using a small sharp knife, cut slanting slits across the fish on both sides about 2 cm (¾ inch) apart. Slice the anchovy fillets into thin strips and slip a slice down each slit in the red mullet. Then smear the fish generously with olive oil and any oil left from the anchovy can.

Rinse the aubergine slices with cold running water to remove all the salt. Put the remaining oil into a large saucepan and heat it over a medium heat; add the garlic and stir it round, then add the tomatoes, the aubergines, the caraway seeds, the paprika and the prepared french beans. Stir around for a minute, cover the saucepan and let it bubble very gently for about 20 minutes until the aubergines are soft and the beans are cooked. Add the drained chick-peas and the mushrooms to the saucepan and season with salt and black pepper. Cover the saucepan and cook for another five minutes only; remove from the heat.

Heat the grill to high and grill the stuffed fish for 4 – 5 minutes on each side: they should be speckled brown. To serve, spoon the vegetable stew into a warmed serving dish and arrange the fish on top.
Serves 6

Anchovy-stuffed Mullet with Vegetable Stew

BOSPORUS MUSSEL STEW

For me, two ingredients epitomise meals I have eaten in Turkey over the years since my first visit; first and above all aubergines, and second the plump, orange-fleshed mussels of the Bosporus.

500–625 g (1–1¼ lb) aubergines	300 ml (½ pint) water	397 g (14 oz) can of chopped tomatoes	15 g (½ oz) pine kernels or
white wine vinegar	250 g (8 oz) small onions (red ones if available), sliced	2 tablespoons tomato purée	25 g (1 oz) blanched almonds, split
salt	finely in rings	3 tablespoons olive oil	2 heaped tablespoons
1 kg (2 lb) fresh mussels	2 large cloves of garlic, sliced finely	black pepper	chopped fresh dill or 3 teaspoons dried dill

Cut the aubergines across in slices and then cut the slices in half, sprinkling them with the vinegar as you do so. Rub the slices all over with salt and put them in a colander to drain.

Wash and scrub the mussels, discarding any that are open. Pour the water into a large saucepan and bring it to the boil. Add the mussels, cover them, and boil for 2 minutes until all the shells have opened. Discard any that do not open. Pour the liquid from the mussels into a largish iron or other flameproof casserole. Extract the mussels from their shells and put them in a bowl on one side.

Rinse all the salt from the aubergines with running water. Bring the mussel liquid in the casserole up to the boil. Add the rinsed aubergines, the onions, the garlic, the canned tomatoes, the tomato purée, the olive oil and a generous sprinkling of black pepper. Stir together thoroughly, cover the dish and simmer it gently on top of the stove for about 45 minutes.

Check the dish for seasoning, though no added salt should be necessary. Add the mussels to the dish just to warm while you heat a small dry frying pan and toss the pine kernels or almonds in it for a minute or two to brown them. Just before serving, add them to the dish with the chopped dill weed and remove it from the heat. Serve with rice and either spinach or a green salad.
Serves 6

BURMESE FISH CURRY

Burmese food is like a mixture of Chinese and Indian, which to me is a good combination. The Burmese would add more chillies or cayenne pepper to the following curry, so if you have fiery tastes you can do so too. Serve with plenty of rice, boiled potatoes or Chinese noodles to soak up the delicious juices. I find steamed whole-leaf spinach is a particularly good vegetable for this dish.

5 tablespoons groundnut oil, plus a little extra	5 cm (2-inch) piece of ginger, chopped finely	250 g (8 oz) tomatoes, skinned and chopped small	450 ml (¾ pint) water juice of 1 lemon
1 teaspoon turmeric	2 large cloves of garlic,	½ teaspoon cayenne pepper	a bunch of spring onions,
2 teaspoons salt	chopped finely	1 good tablespoon oyster	cut in 5 cm (2-inch) pieces
1–1.1 kg (2¼ –2½ lb) cod fillet		sauce	

In a large mixing bowl, put 3 tablespoons groundnut oil, the turmeric and the salt and stir them together.

Skin the cod and cut it into large chunks. Put the fish into the mixing bowl and rub it all over with the oil and turmeric mixture. Heat a thin film of oil in a large frying pan to a high heat. Then add the pieces of fish and fry for a minute on each side to seal them, turning gently. Remove from the heat and set aside, while you prepare the other ingredients.

Pour any remaining oil and turmeric from the mixing bowl into an iron or other flameproof casserole and add the remaining 2 tablespoons groundnut oil. Heat to a medium heat. Add the chopped ginger and garlic and stir them around for a minute or two until just beginning to brown. Add the chopped tomatoes and the cayenne pepper and stir over the heat for another 2 minutes. Stir in the oyster sauce and then remove the pan from the heat. Add the water and lemon juice and stir before carefully adding the fish and any pan juices. Cover the casserole and allow it just to bubble over a very low heat for 15 minutes. Add the spring onions, cover, and cook for another 2–3 minutes.

Serves 6

QUENELLE-STUFFED PINK TROUT

In this recipe I fill the fish with a light smoked cod quenelle mixture and serve it with a creamy leek sauce. New potatoes go best with it, and either a lightly cooked green vegetable or a simple salad of frisé or crisp lettuce which avoids other last-minute cooking when you are making the sauce.

1 large pink-fleshed trout, weighing 1.1–1.25 kg (2³/4–3 lb), gutted but with the head left on
250 g (8 oz) smoked cod fillet

2.5 cm (1-inch) piece of fresh ginger, peeled and chopped finely
300 ml (1/2 pint) double cream

1 large egg (size 1–2), separated
25 g (1 oz) butter, plus extra for greasing
125 g (4 oz) leeks, trimmed and chopped finely

3 teaspoons raspberry or red wine vinegar
chilli powder
salt and black pepper
fennel or watercress, to garnish

Wash the trout in plenty of cold running water, and then pat dry inside and out with absorbent paper and lay the fish on a large piece of generously buttered foil. Skin the cod fillet and put the fish into a food processor. Add the ginger to the cod with 2 tablespoons of cream and the white of an egg, reserving the yolk. Finally add a good pinch of chilli powder.

Whizz until the mixture is very smooth. Then, using damp hands, take up the fish purée and stuff it into the entire body cavity of the fish, patting it into a long shape. Wrap up the fish completely, but not too tightly, in the buttered foil; lay it in a roasting pan.

Heat the oven to Gas Mark 5/190°C/375°F, then cook the fish on the centre shelf for 40 – 45 minutes. Put the butter into a smallish saucepan and melt over a medium heat. Add the chopped leeks and stir around for 8–10 minutes until thoroughly softened. Remove from the heat, stir in the vinegar and leave on one side until the fish is cooked. Then carefully open the foil and pour the juices into the saucepan with the leeks.

Gently slip the fish onto a warmed serving plate, garnish with fennel, watercress or other leaves if you like. Stir the reserved egg yolk into the leek and fish juices with a wooden spoon and put over a medium heat. Add the cream, stirring all the time and continue just below boiling point for a minute or two. Finally, season the sauce with salt and black pepper to taste and pour into a sauceboat to serve with the fish.

Serves 6

SCALLOP AND MONKFISH WITH FENNEL IN SAFFRON YOGURT CREAM

2 large bulbs of fennel
2 large spanish onions
225 g (7 oz) carton of
natural yogurt

2 rounded teaspoons
cornflour
2 tablespoons milk
10 –14 strands of saffron

4 –5 pinches of chilli
powder
300 ml (½ pint) double
cream
1 kg (2 lb) monkfish,
filleted

8 large scallops
fresh fennel or chives,
chopped
salt

Cut the stalks and ends from the fennel bulbs, chop them, and reserve. Take off any marked outer pieces. Cut the bulbs lengthways into 6 – 8 pieces each. Peel the onions and slice across in rings. Pour the yogurt into a fairly large iron or other flameproof casserole. Mix the cornflour wth the milk in a cup until smooth, and then mix into the yogurt.

Put the dish over a medium heat and bring to the boil, stirring all the time in one direction only. Simmer, still stirring, for about 2 minutes. Then add the saffron, salt and the chilli powder and stir in the cream. Add the sliced fennel and onion. Bring to the boil again, cover the casserole and simmer gently over a very low heat, stirring now and then, for 30 – 40 minutes until the fennel and onion are very soft.

Slice the monkfish in fairly large pieces, removing any skin. Slice the scallops across in 5 mm (¼ inch) pieces and slice the orange coral in half lengthways. Now you can either complete the cooking or remove the casserole from the heat and leave on one side until shortly before you are ready to eat it.

If you do this bring the contents of the casserole to the boil again, drop in the monkfish pieces, cover the pan and simmer very gently for 10 –15 minutes until the fish is just cooked, then add the sliced scallops and simmer for another 4 –5 minutes only. Finally, stir in the chopped fennel leaves and serve at once. **Serves 6**

ROASTED MONKFISH WITH AUBERGINE AND CREAM SAUCE

Monkfish is a beautifully firm-textured fish which can be cooked in many different ways. Here is an easy and impressive recipe for a dinner party. The 'joints' of fish are roasted whole, smeared with a delicious coating of tomato, olive oil, garlic and spices. They smell wonderful as they cook, and the creamy sauce with slices of soft aubergine is a perfect accompaniment.

2 rounded tablespoons
tomato purée
3 tablespoons olive oil, plus
a little extra
1 rounded teaspoon ground
cinnamon

1 teaspoon caraway seeds
2–3 large cloves of garlic
5 –7 cm (2–3 inch) piece of
fresh ginger, peeled
2 monkfish tails weighing
about 1.1 kg (2½ lb)

2 tablespoons lemon juice
2 large aubergines weighing
1.1 kg (2½ lb)
300 ml (½ pint) single or
double cream

salt and black pepper
feathery fennel leaves or
lovage, to garnish

Put the tomato purée into a bowl with the olive oil, the ground cinnamon and the caraway seeds. Chop the garlic and ginger finely together, add to the bowl and stir. Smear this mixture all over the monkfish tails, and leave on a plate on one side.

Put the lemon juice into a fairly large saucepan of salted water and put over a high heat. Meanwhile slice the aubergines across in thin rounds. When the water in the saucepan is boiling, add the aubergine slices, cover the pan and simmer for 5–8 minutes until the slices are soft. Drain the slices in a colander and rinse with cold water. Then lay the slices on the bottom of a large roasting pan and lay the monkfish tails on top. Dribble a little olive oil over the aubergine slices not covered by the monkfish.

Heat the oven to Gas Mark 6/200°F/400°F. Put the monkfish in the centre of the oven and cook for 35 – 40 minutes, basting once or twice. Then using a wide spatula, transfer the cooked fish carefully on to a warm serving plate and garnish. Pour the cream into the roasting pan with the aubergine slices and heat to bubbling, stirring all the time. Bubble for about 12 minutes, season to taste with salt and black pepper and then pour into a warmed serving bowl to serve with the fish.

Serves 6

THE VEGETARIAN INDIAN

If you are travelling in India on a limited budget – which in that country I feel is much the most interesting thing to do – you nearly always eat best if you stick to the vegetarian dishes. Chicken is delicious in India but it is expensive, and meat is often very tough indeed. The variety of vegetable dishes can make a very satisfying meal. This recipe for spinach and chick-peas cooked in spices and tamarind with eggs is substantial enough to be a complete supper.

1 teaspoon cumin seeds
2 teaspoons coriander seeds
1 heaped teaspoon tamarind
concentrate, or 4 teaspoons
lemon juice
2 tablespoons groundnut oil

25 g (1 oz) butter
2–3 cloves of garlic, chopped
500 g (1 lb) tomatoes,
chopped roughly

500 g (1 lb) fresh spinach,
washed thoroughly
2 teaspoons mustard seeds
(optional)
¼ teaspoon cayenne pepper

432 g (15 oz) can of
chick-peas, drained
4 medium–large eggs
(size 2–3)
1 rounded tablespoon
desiccated coconut
salt

Put the cumin and coriander seeds in a coffee grinder and grind them finely. Mix the tamarind concentrate with 2 tablespoons of very hot water in a cup stirring with a teaspoon until smooth. Put the oil and butter in an iron or other flameproof casserole dish and heat them over a medium heat. Add the garlic and ground spices and stir for a minute; add the chopped tomatoes and bubble, stirring all the time, for about 5 minutes until the tomatoes have softened to a mush.

Stir in the tamarind juice or lemon juice and then put in the whole leaves of spinach (you needn't bother to take off the stalks.) Cover the casserole and cook over a medium heat for a few minutes until the spinach has gone limp. Then uncover, stir around, add the mustard seeds, the cayenne pepper, the drained chick-peas and a sprinkling of salt. Cook in the open dish over a medium to high heat for about 8 minutes, stirring around all the time.

Lower the heat, break the eggs on top of the spinach mixture, cover the dish again and cook for 6 – 8 minutes until the eggs are just set. Meanwhile, heat a small dry frying pan and toast the dessicated coconut for a minute or two until golden. When the eggs are ready, scatter the toasted coconut on top and serve.

Serves 4

PUMPKIN AND GOAT'S CHEESE LASAGNE WITH YOGURT AND CARDAMOM

When people ask me what they should serve at a buffet party, I frequently recommend a lasagne. It is such a satisfying dish and it can be made well ahead and re-heated if convenient; it is easy to eat with only a fork, even if you cannot avoid standing up and holding your plate in one hand! I think this is the best lasagne I have ever made. It has a wonderful flavour and is lighter in texture, less rich and more sophisticated than usual. Also, as it is a vegetable dish, it will cater for any vegetarian guests. If you want to have it at a smaller meal, simply divide the quantities given.
Pictured on pages 54/5.

300 g (10 oz) oven-ready lasagne sheets
cooking oil
1.75 kg (4 lb) piece of pumpkin
3 medium–large onions

4 tablespoons olive oil
8 –10 cardamom pods
4 teaspoons dried green peppercorns, crushed
2 teaspoons caster sugar

500 g (1 lb) small white goat's cheese logs
4 rounded tablespoons cornflour
4 tablespoons milk

2 x 450 g (15 oz) cartons of Greek yogurt
4 heaped tablespoons coarsely grated parmesan cheese
salt and black pepper

Put the lasagne sheets into a large bowl of hot water, to which you have added a good sprinkling of cooking oil, to prevent the pasta sticking together. Leave to soak while you prepare the other ingredients. Remove any seeds or string from the pumpkin. Cut off the skin and slice the flesh into 5 –7 cm (2–3 inch) pieces. Steam or boil the pieces until soft. Meanwhile slice the onions fairly thinly and then chop up roughly. Heat 2 tablespoons of the olive oil in a large frying-pan and fry them over a gentle heat, stirring frequently, until soft and translucent.

Extract the seeds from the cardamom pods and grind in a coffee grinder or pestle and mortar. Crush the green peppercorns. When the pumpkin is soft, drain and mash roughly in a bowl with a fork. Stir in the ground cardamom, crushed green peppercorns and the caster sugar. Season to taste with salt. Then stir in the fried onions. Spread the remaining 2 tablespoons olive oil on the bottom of a very large, fairly shallow ovenproof dish which has a 2.75–3.5 litre (5 – 6 pint) capacity, or you can use two dishes.

Slice the goat's cheese across in thin slices without cutting off the rind. Drain the lasagne sheets and put a layer of them on the bottom of the oiled ovenproof dish. Then spoon one third of the pumpkin and onion mixture evenly over the lasagne. Now arrange one-third of the goat's cheese slices on top of the pumpkin. Put on another layer of lasagne sheets and continue as before, ending with a layer of lasagne.

If cooking immediately, heat the oven to Gas Mark 6/200°C/400°F. Put the cornflour in a saucepan, add the milk and stir until smooth. Stir in the yogurt. Put on the heat and bring to the boil, stirring in one direction only. Allow to simmer, still stirring, for 2–3 minutes. Then season very sparingly with salt and black pepper and spoon the yogurt sauce evenly over the lasagne. Lastly, sprinkle with the grated parmesan. Cook the dish in the centre of the oven for about 35 minutes until speckled brown on top.
Serves about 14

STAR LEEK PIE

Here is one delicious answer if you have vegetarian guests, and it should
certainly please non-vegetarians too. The golden pastry is made with
cheese and paprika, and the soft leek filling has an added sweetness of
onion. Caraway seeds, which seem to have an affinity both with cheese
and with many vegetables, certainly create a wonderful effect here. I
usually serve the pie at an informal occasion, accompanied simply with
a tomato salad.

For the pastry:	125 g (4 oz) mature	For the filling:	1 rounded teaspoon caraway
375 g (12 oz) plain flour	Cheddar cheese, grated	750 g (1½ lb) leeks	seeds
3 rounded teaspoons paprika	175 g (6 oz) cold butter	1 large onion	milk or egg yolk to glaze
3–4 pinches of chilli powder	1 large egg (size 1–2)	50 g (2 oz) butter, plus	pastry
½ teaspoon salt	3 tablespoons cold water	extra for greasing	sea salt and black pepper

To make the pastry, sift the flour, paprika, chilli
powder and salt into a bowl. Using a fork or knife,
stir in the grated cheese. Cut the butter into small
pieces, stir into the flour and then rub with your
fingertops until the mixture is like breadcrumbs.
Using a fork, lightly whisk the egg with the water and
pour it gradually into the flour mixture, mixing in
with the fork until it sticks together.

Press the dough into a ball, wrap it in clingfilm
and refrigerate while you make the pie filling. Slice
the leeks into approximately 2.5 cm (1-inch) pieces,
using as much of the green part as possible. Peel the
onion and cut into 2.5 cm (1-inch) pieces. Melt the
butter in a large frying pan, add all the sliced leeks and
onion and the caraway seeds and cook over a low to
medium heat, stirring fairly often until the leeks and
onion are completely soft. Season with sea salt and
plenty of black pepper and leave until cold.

Butter a large, flat, ovenproof circular plate or
pizza tray. Cut the pastry in half, form into two balls
and roll out one ball on a floured surface into a rough
circle approximately 23 –34 cms (9–9½ inches) in
diameter. Turn over the edges a little to make a more
even circle and place on the buttered plate. Spoon on
the cooled leeks within about 1.5 cm (¾ inch) of the
edge of the pastry. Roll out the second half of the
pastry into a similar circle but this time, using a sharp
knife, cut all round the outside in a pointed zig-zag
pattern, rather like a simple childen's drawing of a fat,
many-pointed star.

Lay this piece of pastry on top of the leeks and
press gently to seal on to the bottom circle of pastry
– there should be a few gaps between the points
where steam will be able to escape. Press the pastry
trimmings together, roll out and cut out decorations
for the pie – perhaps another star or two. Moisten the
decorations and arrange them on top. If you are not
ready to cook, refrigerate the pie. Then heat the oven
to Gas Mark 7/220°C/425°F. Brush the pie with
milk, or egg yolk if you want a really high gloss, and
bake in the centre of the oven for about 30 minutes.
Serves 6

Part 4

SIDE DISHES AND ACCOMPANIMENTS

Red Cabbage, Parsnip and Hazelnut Salad (page 132);
Baked Aubergines with Fresh Mint Chutney (page 143);
Chinese Leaf and Broad Bean Salad (page 140);
Chinese Salad Dressing (page 144);
Orient Onions (page 137);
Potatoes Roasted in their Skins with Olive Oil (page 135)

STRAW LEEKS WITH SPICED MUSHROOMS

Mushrooms take very well to spices, and cultivated mushrooms in particular are greatly enhanced by them. The contrast of the rich mixture of chopped and spiced mushrooms topped with a pile of briefly cooked strips of leek is excellent. The dish goes perfectly with any roast or grilled meat, poultry or game. You can prepare and cook the mushrooms in advance; it will only take a few minutes to boil or steam the leeks and assemble the mixture at the last moment.

75 g (3 oz) unsalted butter
4 rounded teaspoons ground coriander
2 teaspoons ground mace

½ teaspoon cayenne pepper
500 g (1 lb) mushrooms, chopped small

2.5 cm (1-inch) piece of fresh ginger, peeled and chopped finely
2 tablespoons tomato purée

750 g (1½ lb) leeks, trimmed
6 tablespoons creamed smetana
salt

Put the butter into a large saucepan and melt it over a medium heat. Then add the ground coriander, mace and cayenne pepper and stir for half a minute.

Next add the chopped mushrooms, the chopped ginger and the tomato purée. Stir around to mix together, then cover the pan and leave over a fairly low heat for abut 15 minutes. Then remove from the heat, add salt to taste and leave on one side. Wash the leeks and cut across into 7 cm (3-inch) pieces, then cut these pieces lengthways into fairly thin strips.

Shortly before serving, steam or boil the leek strips for 5 – 8 minutes until soft. Drain. Then quickly reheat the mushrooms, stirring them around. Remove them from the heat and only roughly stir in the smetana. Spread the mixture on the bottom of a shallow, heated dish and pile the leeks up in the centre, sprinkled with a little salt if they have been steamed.
Serves 6

RED CABBAGE, PARSNIP AND HAZELNUT SALAD

The subtle, sweet flavour of the parsnip is an important part of this excellent winter salad.
Pictured on pages 130/1.

For the salad:
1 medium-size red cabbage
250 g (8 oz) small parsnips, boiled and cut in quarters

50 –75 g (2–3 oz) hazelnuts
1 dessertspoon dried fennel or tarragon

For the French dressing:
3 tablespoons red wine vinegar
6 tablespoons olive oil

1 teaspoon soft brown sugar
1 clove of garlic, crushed (optional)
salt and black pepper

Simply slice the red cabbage very finely and mix in a bowl with the boiled parsnips and hazelnuts. Sprinkle over the dried fennel; I find the easiest way to mix the French dressing is to shake the ingredients in a jam jar with a tight-fitting lid kept for the purpose.
Serves 8

GOLDEN PURÉE WITH A GRATINÉE OF GOAT'S CHEESE

This is one of my favourite vegetable purées. It is a rich mixture of carrot and parsnip topped with bubbling goat's cheese. As an accompanying dish it goes especially well with all game or pork. I often serve it instead of potatoes, and it is useful as it can be made ahead and kept warm. It is also excellent as the one hot element in a lunch of cold meats and salads.

750 g (1½ lb) carrots, chopped roughly
500 g (1 lb) parsnips, chopped roughly

75 g (3 oz) butter, cut up roughly
¼ –½ a whole nutmeg, grated

125 g (4 oz) white round goat's cheese

sea salt and black pepper

Steam or boil the carrots and parsnips until soft. Put into a food processor and add the butter, the grated nutmeg, sea salt and plenty of black pepper. Whizz to a purée. Then spoon into a wide gratinée dish. Slice the goat's cheese across in thin rounds and arrange all over the top of the purée. Sprinkle with black pepper. Put the dish under a hot grill until the cheese is bubbling and speckled with brown. Keep warm in a low oven until ready to serve.

Serves 6

SAFFRON AND GARLIC MASHED POTATOES WITH GRATED COURGETTES

Saffron adds its unique flavour and clear yellow colour to these garlicky mashed potatoes which look beautiful in a wide dish edged with the brilliant green flakes of tender courgettes. The mixture goes specially well with any fish dishes and with lamb, too. I would serve buttered baby carrots as the other accompanying vegetable.
Pictured on the front cover.

a good pinch of saffron strands
150 ml (¼ pint) milk

2 tablespoons extra-virgin olive oil
4 cloves of garlic

1 kg (2 lb) potatoes, boiled until soft
75 g (3 oz) butter

500 g (1 lb) courgettes, grated coarsely
salt and black pepper

At least half an hour in advance put the saffron strands in a small saucepan with the milk. Bring to the boil, stirring, then remove from the heat, cover the saucepan and leave on one side.

Heat the olive oil in a small frying pan over a medium heat, add the chopped garlic and stir around for a minute or so until browned. Leave on one side. Add the saffron milk and the garlic with its oil to the potatoes on their saucepan, and stir around. Then cover the pan and put back over a medium heat for about 5 minutes, stirring around once or twice. Then add 50 g (2 oz) of the butter and mash well with a fork or old-fasioned masher (never try to mash potatoes in a food processor as they turn to glue).

Season to taste with salt and black pepper, and spoon into a wide serving dish. Cover the dish wth foil and put to keep warm in a low oven until almost ready to eat. Then briefly cook the courgettes. To do this, bring salted water to the boil, add the grated courgettes and cook for only one minute, just until the courgettes turn brilliant green. Then drain and mix in the remaining 25 g (1 oz) butter. Spoon the grated courgettes round the edge and serve.

Serves 6–8

SMOKY AUBERGINE PURÉE WITH PINE KERNELS

For a more sophisticated Sunday lunch, this hot purée of aubergines with
soft white cheese is an excellent accompaniment to roast lamb. The subtle
smoky flavour of the purée is achieved by grilling whole aubergines until
their skins are burnt black and cracked. Alternatively, this can be served as
a first course, with toast or pitta bread.

about 1 kg (1–2¼ lb) large aubergines	*125 g (4 oz) full fat soft cheese with garlic*	*4 –5 pinches of cayenne pepper*	*25 –50 g (1–2 oz) pine kernels*
50 g (2 oz) butter			*salt*

Put the whole, unpeeled aubergines under the hottest
possible grill for about 15 –20 minutes, turning them
until they are black all over and the skin has blistered
or cracked. Then hold the hot aubergines in a cloth,
break them open, and spoon and scrape all the flesh
out with a metal spoon into a food processor. Add the
butter and the soft cheese and whizz to a smooth
purée. Season to taste with the cayenne pepper and
salt. Spoon the mixture into a warm serving bowl.

Heat a small, dry frying pan over a fairly high heat,
add the pine kernels, and toss around for a minute or
two until toasted dark brown. Scatter on top of the
aubergine purée. Sprinkle a little cayenne pepper on
top, if you wish, cover the dish with foil and keep
warm in a low oven until ready to eat.
Serves 6

SPROUT SNOW

This is really just a way of using up leftover brussel sprouts; in this recipe
they are made into a light mousse which can be served as a first course or
as part of a meal. You should only use sprouts which have not been
over-cooked and which are still bright green.

3 tablespoons water	*300 ml (½ pint) milk*	*¼ of a whole nutmeg, grated*	*375 g (12 oz) lightly cooked sprouts*
11 g (⅓ oz) sachet of gelatine	*3 large eggs (size 1–2)*		*chopped parsley*
	salt and black pepper		

Put the water in a small bowl and sprinkle in the
gelatine. Set the bowl in a pan of water over a low
heat and stir until the gelatine dissolves. Allow to cool.
Put the milk into a saucepan and bring to the boil.
Remove from the heat. Separate the eggs, putting the
whites in a large bowl and the yolks in the top of a
double saucepan (or into a mixing bowl which you
can set over a pan of water). Pour the hot milk on to
the egg yolks, whisking thoroughly. Put the eggs
yolks and milk over a saucepan of gently simmering
water and stir constantly with a wooden spoon until
thickened to a custard. Turn the custard into a large
bowl and season it heavily with black pepper and salt.
Stir in the grated nutmeg and allow to cool. Stir in
the gelatine.

Now chop up the sprouts finely and stir them into
the custard. Whisk the egg whites to soft peaks and then
fold them into the sprout mixture and turn into a
900 ml –1.2-litre (1½–2-pint) ring mould or loaf tin.
Refrigerate until set. Twenty minutes before serving,
dip the mould or tin briefly in a sink of hot water and
then turn it out, giving it a good shake, on to a serving
plate. Sprinkle the top with chopped parsley.
Serves 6

POTATOES ROASTED IN THEIR SKINS WITH OLIVE OIL

If you like you can mix some very finely sliced onion amongst the
potatoes before cooking them. Try to use waxy, not floury, potatoes such
as the red-skinned Desirée for this recipe, as they will hold their shape
far better.
Pictured on pages 130/1.

The day before your meal, cook your potatoes, whole and unpeeled, either by steaming or boiling them. While the potatoes are hot cut them up into fairly small cubes and put these in a large mixing bowl. Now, depending on how many potatoes you are cooking, pour in enough olive oil to be absorbed evenly by the hot potatoes, as you turn them around with a wooden spoon. Season them with salt and black pepper, then spoon onto a large, shallow, oven-proof dish and leave in a cool place until needed.

If possible cook the potatoes in a hot oven at Gas Mark 9/240°C/475°F on the top shelf for 20 –30 minutes at the beginning, turning them around gently before continuing to cook them at a lower temperature. In any case let them cook above the roast until you think they look brown and crisp enough, and then put them under the roast at the bottom of the oven where they should gently crisp up some more.

PERUVIAN POTATOES

The best potatoes I have ever tasted came from the mountains of Peru;
they had a close waxy texture and were quite a deep yellow colour. The
nearest thing to those Peruvian potatoes that I have been able to find are
Italian waxy potatoes which have a pale yellow colour and appear in the
shops here during the winter; in the summer Jersey potatoes would do
well. You could serve this as an accompaniment to meat or chicken
or as a light lunch dish together with a salad.

*1 smallish onion, a red one
if possible
4 tablespoons lemon juice*

*2 pinches of cayenne pepper
2 fresh green chillies
750 g (1½ lb) small to
medium-size potatoes*

*2 tablespoons olive oil
175 g (6 oz) cottage cheese
150 ml (5 fl oz) carton of
double cream*

*1 level teaspoon turmeric
4 hard-boiled eggs
salt*

Peel the onion and slice it very thinly in rings. Put it in a shallow bowl and stir in the lemon juice, the cayenne pepper and a little salt. Cover the bowl and leave it on one side. Cut the chillies open under running water, discard the seeds and stem and then chop them up very finely. Wash but don't peel the potatoes and steam or boil them until they are cooked but not falling apart.

Meanwhile, gently heat the olive oil in a small pan, and fry the chillies for 2–3 minutes. Put the cottage cheese, cream and turmeric and a little salt into a food processor, add the chillies and pan juices and whizz until smooth. Cut the cooked potatoes in half and arrange on a serving dish. Peel the hard-boiled eggs, cut them in half lengthways and arrange them amongst the potatoes. Pour the sauce over the top, drain the onion rings and add them.
Serves 4–5

TERRINE OF BROCCOLI

This terrine tastes good enough for gourmets, and looks good, too. The
textured green slices look very pretty surrounded by the
smooth carrot sauce.

750 g (1½ lb) sprouting
broccoli, with the tough
stalks removed
¼ whole nutmeg, grated
¼ teaspoon caraway seeds

3 tablespoons grated
parmesan cheese
2 teaspoons green
peppercorns
50 g (2 oz) fresh
breadcrumbs

4 tablespoons natural
yogurt
2 eggs, whisked lightly
2 egg yolks, whisked
lightly
salt and black pepper

For the sauce:
375 g (12 oz) carrots,
peeled and chopped roughly
300 ml (½ pint) creamed
smetana or Greek yogurt
salt and cayenne pepper

Put a roasting pan half full of water on the centre shelf
of the oven and preheat to Gas Mark 4/
180°C/350°F. Steam or boil the broccoli for 5 –7
minutes until just tender. Drain well and chop finely,
either in a food processor or as small as you can by
hand. Turn into a mixing bowl and add the nutmeg,
caraway seeds, parmesan, green peppercorns and
breadcrumbs. Season with salt and a little black pepper. Add the yogurt and the whisked eggs and egg
yolks, mixing in thoroughly with a wooden spoon.
Lightly oil a 1 kg (2 lb) loaf tin and line the base with
a piece of oiled greaseproof paper. Fill the tin with the

mixture and put in the pan of water in the oven. Cook
for 30–35 minutes. Leave in the tin for about 10
minutes; then loosen the edges carefully with a wide
knife and turn out on to a board. Peel off the paper
and leave to cool.

Steam or boil the carrots until soft (5 –7 minutes)
and then purée in a food processor or liquidiser, or
through a sieve. Cool and then mix in a bowl with
the creamed smetana or yogurt and season to taste
with salt and cayenne pepper. Serve slices of the cold
terrine individually, in pools of the sauce.
Serves 6

PARSNIP TIMBALES

At first people find it hard to identify these little moulds – they taste
almost like a light cream cheese mixture, but the unique and excellent
flavour of parsnip emerges after the first mouthful. These timbales are
served cold on blanched chinese leaves, dressed with vinaigrette.

500 g (1 lb) parsnips,
topped, tailed, peeled and
cut up roughly
oil for greasing

6 large flat continental
parsley or mint leaves
1 large egg (size 1–2)
250 ml (8 fl oz) double
cream

¼ nutmeg, grated
1 head of chinese leaves
(keeping the stems)
salt and black pepper

For the vinaigrette dressing:
2 tablespoons white wine
vinegar
5 tablespoons good olive oil,
virgin if possible
salt and black pepper

Preheat the oven to Gas Mark 2/150°C/300°F. Boil
the prepared parsnips in salted water until soft. Generously oil 6 deep ramekin or cocotte dishes (about 125
ml /4 fl oz in capacity) and place a leaf of parsley or
mint on the bottom of each. Drain the parsnips, put
in a food processor with the egg and cream and whizz
until very smooth. (If you don't have a food proces-

sor, press the cooked parsnip through a sieve and then
beat or whisk thoroughly with the egg and cream.)
Season to taste with salt, black pepper and the freshly
grated nutmeg. Spoon the parsnip mixture into the
dishes and cook in the centre of the oven for 20–25
minutes. Remove from the oven and leave until cold.

While the timbales are cooling, take the chinese

leaves and neaten them, cutting off just the base of the stems. Bring a large pan of water to the boil, put in the leaves, cover the pan and boil for 2–3 minutes only. Drain the leaves and leave to cool.

When the timbales are cold, very carefully loosen the sides of the tins with a knife and then, with a gentle shake, turn out on to a flat surface. Arrange the cooled chinese leaves either on individual plates or on one large flat serving dish and place one cold timbale towards the bottom of each leaf. Mix together a dressing of the wine vinegar and olive oil seasoned well with salt and black pepper. Serve the timbales cold but not chilled and just before serving spoon the dressing over the top of the timbales, spreading down on to the chinese leaves.

Serves 6

ORIENT ONIONS

These stuffed onions are eaten cold. They are bursting with a mildly curried filling of onion, almonds and peas and are served in a lake of yogurt, which mingles deliciously with the onions as you eat them. They will make a good vegetarian main course, if you increase the quantity.
Pictured on pages 130/1.

3 large spanish onions, unpeeled
about 4 tablespoons olive oil
2–3 cloves of garlic, chopped finely

3 teaspoons curry powder
125 g (4 oz) blanched whole or split almonds

125 g (4 oz) peas, cooked
1 small handful of parsley, chopped finely

1 tablespoon lemon juice
salt
450 g (15 oz) carton of natural yogurt

Preheat the oven to Gas Mark 6/200°C/400°F. Put the whole, unpeeled onions in a roasting pan and cook in the centre of the oven for 40 – 45 minutes. Leave until cool. Cut off the bottoms and tops of the onions and peel off the hard skin. Cut the onions in half crossways and take out all but the outer shells. Brush the outside of the shells with a little of the olive oil.

Chop the onion insides up into small pieces. Heat 3 tablespoons of the olive oil in a frying pan over a medium heat. Add the chopped onion, chopped garlic, curry powder and almonds. Stir around over the heat for 2–3 minutes and then stir in the cooked peas and cook for another minute. Lastly, stir in the chopped parsley and lemon juice and remove from the heat. Turn into a bowl, cover and leave until cold. Season to taste with salt.

Shortly before serving, stir the yogurt to make sure it is smooth and then spread it in a flat lake on 6 individual serving plates. Put a half onion shell on each plate and spoon in the filling, piling it up. Serve cold but not chilled and, just before serving, spoon a spot more olive oil over each onion.

Serves 6

PEPPERS PAR EXCELLENCE

3 red peppers (choose ones which stand steadily upright)
635 –750 g (1¹/₃ –1¹/₂ lb) aubergines

juice of ¹/₂ lemon
175 g (6 oz) unsalted butter, softened

1 small clove of garlic, crushed
1 teaspoon caster sugar

2–3 pinches of cayenne pepper
¹/₂ cucumber
salt

Preheat the oven to Gas Mark 4/180°C/350°F. Cut the peppers in half cross ways and carefully cut out the seeds, etc. Put in a saucepan of boiling salted water and simmer for 10 minutes. Drain and stuff each pepper half with a roughly crumpled ball of silver foil. Put the peppers in a roasting pan with a little water. Cook in the centre of the oven for 30 – 40 minutes.

Meanwhile, put the aubergines under a very hot grill for about 20 minutes, turning regularly until charred black all over. Peel off the burnt and cracked skin, under cold water as they will be very hot; then put the flesh in a sieve and press down with a wooden spoon to squeeze out as much liquid as possible. Put the hot flesh (it will not at this stage look at all appetising) in a liquidiser or food processor, adding the lemon juice, butter, crushed garlic, caster sugar, cayenne pepper and salt. Whizz until smooth and leave to cool and thicken.

When the peppers are cooked, take them out of the oven and leave to cool. Put each one in the centre of individual serving plates. Spoon the aubergine purée into them. Slice the cucumber into rounds as thinly as you possibly can (you can use the food processor for this) and arrange in an overlapping circle around each pepper. Lastly, arrange three overlapping cucumber circles on the top of each stuffed pepper. Keep in a cool place until ready to serve.
Serves 6

MUSHROOMS STUFFED WITH LEEK AND WATERCRESS PURÉE

You must find the largest flat mushrooms for this, or find your own field
mushrooms if you are lucky. Of the cultivated mushrooms, the giants
have much more of a real mushroom flavour.

8 very large flat mushrooms, with the stalks cut off
250 g (8 oz) unsalted butter

500 g (1 lb) trimmed leeks, sliced in rings
¹/₂ whole nutmeg, grated

1 bunch of watercress
1 small lettuce, with the leaves separated

salt and black pepper
a few sprigs of watercress, to garnish

Put a large pan of salted water on to boil. When the water is boiling briskly, put in the mushrooms, cover the pan, bring to the boil again and immediately remove from the heat. Drain the mushrooms and place them, black side downwards, on a triple layer of kitchen paper towelling to cool and dry off.

Gently melt 125 g (4 oz) of the butter in a large frying pan. Add the sliced leeks and cook over a low heat, stirring around every so often until completely soft. Add the nutmeg and watercress, including its stalks. Stir the watercress around with the leek until the leaves are just limp.

Put in a food processor or liquidiser with the remaining butter and whizz until a smooth purée. Season to taste with salt and plenty of black pepper. Turn into a bowl and leave to cool.

When cold, make a bed of the lettuce leaves on a serving plate. Put the mushrooms on top. Spoon a mound of leek purée on to each mushroom, chill well in the fridge before serving and, lastly, place a sprig of watercress on the top of each.
Serves 8

Peppers Par Excellence; Mushrooms Stuffed with Leek and Watercress Purée

LEEKS IN TWO DRESSINGS

Leeks are a great favourite of mine and this is a particularly good way of
serving them cold. It will do either as a first course or as
part of a salad meal.

500 g (1 lb) thin leeks
1 tablespoon wine vinegar
5 tablespoons olive oil

a bunch of spring onions,
chopped finely
150 ml (¼ pint) double
cream

2 tablespoons mayonnaise
(a good commercial kind
will do)

salt and black pepper

Cutting off and discarding the darker green ends, cut
the leeks into 7 cm (3-inch) pieces and wash well.
Plunge them into boiling salted water for 8–12
minutes, until tender when you insert a small sharp
knife. Drain and arrange in one layer in a fairly
shallow serving dish.

Mix together the vinegar and olive oil, season
with salt and plenty of black pepper and pour this
dressing over the leeks while they are still hot.
Sprinkle over the chopped spring onions, keeping
back a spoonful for garnish, and leave to cool.

Before serving, whisk up the double cream until
thick and then thoroughly stir in the mayonnaise.
Spoon this dressing all over the leeks and sprinkle with
the reserved spring onions.
Serves 4–5

CHINESE LEAF AND BROAD BEAN SALAD

The simplest of salads, with a delicate flavour and a contrast of texture
which will refresh the palate between courses.
Pictured on pages 130/1.

about ½ head of Chinese
leaves

250 g (8 oz) frozen broad
beans

chopped parsley

Chinese Salad Dressing
(page 144)

Slice the Chinese leaves across in thick rounds and put
in a salad bowl. Empty the frozen beans into a bowl,
pour boiling water over them and leave for 1 minute.
Drain the beans and pop them out of their skins into
the salad bowl. Add the Chinese Salad Dressing.
Serves 5–6

RUM BUTTER

When I was a child and didn't like Christmas pudding very much the only
reason I would eat a spoonful was to have a huge dollop of rum or brandy
butter on the top. If you prefer brandy butter make it with icing sugar and
brandy. You can make the butter when you make the pudding, pack it
into a plastic box with a lid and store it in your refrigerator. Take out well
beforehand on Christmas Day.
Pictured on page 203.

250 g (8 oz) unsalted
butter
125–175 g (4–6 oz) soft,
pale brown sugar (to taste)

4–5 tablespoons light rum

Cream the butter until pale and soft. Beat in the sugar.
Add the rum drop by drop, beating all the time so that
it doesn't curdle.
Serves 6 – 8

CHILLED BRANDY SAUCE

This quickly made, light and creamy sauce is an alternative to rum or
brandy butter with the Christmas pudding – in fact it's delicious
with almost any hot pudding.

150 ml (¼ pint) double
cream

1 level tablespoon icing
sugar, sifted
1–2 tablespoons brandy

Simply whisk the cream until thick, then whisk in the
icing sugar and gradually stir in the brandy to taste.
Chill in the refrigerator.
Serves 6–8

ONION. BRANDY AND ORANGE SAUCE

A lovely sauce, perfect to serve with roast goose, duck, pheasant and pork.
As it is a creamy sauce, keep the pan juices from the meat separate to be
served as a thin gravy.

2 large onions
75 g (3 oz) butter
1 teaspoon ground
cinnamon

coarsely grated rind of 1 and
juice of 2 large oranges
1 tablespoon plain flour

2 teaspoons caster sugar
2–3 tablespoons brandy,
to taste

150 ml (5 fl oz) double
cream
salt and black pepper

Peel the onions, cut them in half and then slice them
as thinly as possible. Melt the butter in a large frying
pan over a low heat. Stir in the onion slices and then
stir in the ground cinnamon and the orange rind.
Cook gently until the onions have completely softened. Remove from the heat and stir in the flour,
followed by the orange juice and the caster sugar.

Return to the heat and simmer gently, stirring all the
time, for about 2 minutes. Then add the brandy and
the cream and continue to simmer gently, stirring, for
another 3 minutes or so. Season to taste with salt and
black pepper, adding more brandy if you want. Pour
into a bowl to serve with your roast.
Serves 4–6

APRICOT AND CLEMENTINE SAUCE FOR HAM AND OTHER COLD MEATS

A good sauce can make all the difference to cold meats. Over Christmas, when one begins to tire of bland cold ham or turkey, an interesting sauce is vital to give life to the meat. The following sauce can either be served warm, which I prefer, or cold, but not chilled. Since you will probably want to make it ahead, just gently re-heat it to serve it warm.

250 g (8 oz) dried apricots
4 small clementines or small oranges

1 medium-size onion
4 – 6 cloves
50 g (2 oz) soft brown sugar

water
1 – 2 tablespoons red wine vinegar

2 – 4 pinches of cayenne pepper

Soak the apricots in water for at least 2 hours. Then cut the unpeeled clementines or oranges across in very thin rounds, discarding any pips. Peel the onion and chop it roughly. Put the sliced clementines, onion, cloves, sugar and the drained apricots into a saucepan and pour in water to cover. Bring the liquid to the boil, cover the pan and let it simmer very gently for about 30 minutes until soft and fairly thick. Stir vigorously. Add vinegar and cayenne pepper to taste.
Serves 4 – 6

BROWN BREAD SAUCE

A solid fuel cooker is ideal for this recipe if you have one. Some breads absorb more or less liquid than others, so check from time to time to see if you need add either more milk or a little more crumpled bread. You can make the sauce up to three days in advance, cover the top with greaseproof paper and keep it in the fridge to re-heat when needed. You can always remove the crusts from the bread if you don't like dark flecks in the sauce, but I think it's much nicer if you keep the crusts on.

1 large onion
150 g (5 oz) wholemeal or brown bread
75 g (3 oz) butter

6 cloves
1/4 of a whole nutmeg, grated

900 ml (1 1/2 pints) creamy milk

300 ml (1/2 pint) double cream
sea salt and black pepper

Peel the onion and chop it up small. Tear the bread, including the crusts, into smallish pieces and put these with the onion into a heavy saucepan, or into an ovenproof dish if you want to cook the sauce in the oven. Dot with the butter and cloves, sprinkle with the nutmeg and season with a little salt and black pepper. Mix the milk with the cream and pour it over the other ingredients.

To cook on top of the stove, put the covered saucepan over the lowest possible heat, stirring now and then to break up the bread, for 1 1/2 – 2 hours. To cook in the oven heat the oven to Gas Mark 1/2/130°C/250°F and put the covered dish in for 1 1/2 – 2 hours, stirring round two or three times, until you have a fairly thick sauce. Lastly, check the seasoning, adjust it to taste and remove the cloves, if you can find them.
Serves 6 – 8

BAKED AUBERGINES WITH FRESH MINT CHUTNEY

Pictured on pages 130/1.

4 small aubergines
salt

Fresh Mint Chutney with
Coconut (below)
oil

Cut the aubergines in half lengthways and rub the flesh with salt. Leave in a colander for half an hour to drain away the bitter juices. Then rinse off the salt and smear the cut side of the aubergines with the chutney.

Put them together again, smear the outsides well with oil and put closely together in an oven-proof dish, so that they don't fall apart.

Cover the dish with oiled foil. Heat the oven to Gas Mark 4/180°C/350°F and cook the aubergines for ¾–1 hour – depending on their size – until they are soft and a small sharp knife slides in easily. **Serves 4**

FRESH MINT CHUTNEY WTH COCONUT

This refreshing chutney will keep in a cupboard or in a container in the fridge for a week or so. It is good with lamb or fish and also in the recipe for baked aubergines (above). If you can get fresh coriander leaves instead of mint for the chutney it will be even better.

a large handful of fresh
mint leaves
the flesh of 1 fresh coconut,
grated

1 heaped teaspoon cumin
seeds
6 cloves of garlic

1–2 green chillies,
de-seeded
1 teaspoon sugar

2 teaspoons salt
2 tablespoons lemon juice

Simply put all the ingredients in a food processor or liquidiser and whizz up until smooth.

YOGURT WITH AUBERGINE, MINT AND CUMIN

1 smallish aubergine
1–3 tablespoons sunflower
oil

1 clove of garlic, chopped
finely
1 teaspoon ground cumin

500 g (1 lb) carton of plain
yogurt
salt

a pinch of cayenne pepper
a small handful of fresh
mint leaves, chopped finely

Slice the aubergine across in rings and then into semi-circles. Rub the pieces all over with salt and leave in a colander in the sink for half an hour (to drain away the bitter juices). Then wash the salt off the aubergine and pat dry.

Heat the oil in a frying pan. Add the aubergine and fry over medium heat until soft. Then add the chopped garlic and the cumin. Stir and cook for

another 2–3 minutes. Turn off the heat and leave to cool.

Empty the yogurt into a bowl. Add salt and the cayenne pepper. Stir in the aubergine, scraping every bit of oil and spice from the pan. Then stir in the chopped mint leaves, leaving a few for garnish on top. Keep in the fridge until needed.
Serves 4 – 6

CHINESE SALAD DRESSING

This is a good dressing for finely sliced Chinese leaves or Savoy cabbage,
for watercress and peeled cucumber and for salads with ham, game or
chicken liver in them.
Pictured on pages 130/1.

2 tablespoons lemon juice
1½ tablespoons soy sauce
1 tablespoon caster sugar
1 tablespoon sunflower oil

1 cm (½-inch) piece of
fresh ginger, chopped finely,
or 2 pinches of cayenne
pepper

Mix the lemon juice, soy sauce and sugar together thoroughly. Then stir in the oil and the chopped ginger or cayenne.

FRENCH DRESSING WITH MUSTARD AND GARLIC

This is my husband's favourite dressing, smooth, yellow and tasty.
It is suitable for a wide range of salads.

2 teaspoons white
wine vinegar
2 rounded teaspoons Dijon
mustard

1 small clove of garlic,
crushed

3–4 tablespoons olive oil
or a mixture of olive and
sunflower oil

sea salt and black pepper,
to taste

Mix the ingredients thoroughly by shaking together in a closed screw-top jam jar.

ITALIAN GREEN SAUCE

If you have a liquidiser or food processor this is an instant sauce which
transforms any rather dry or bland cold meat or chicken. Just arrange
thinly carved slices of the meat on a flat plate and pour the sauce over
them before serving. It also makes an extremely good dressing for cold
pasta shapes eaten as a salad. If you don't use all the sauce at once
it keeps well in a closed jar in the fridge.

juice of 1 lemon
6 tablespoons sunflower oil

5 tablespoons olive oil
2 large cloves of garlic,
peeled

75 g (3 oz) mixture of fresh
mint and parsley

40 g (1½ oz) grated
parmesan cheese
salt and black pepper

Simply put all the ingredients into a liquidiser or food processor and whizz up until the sauce is thick and fairly smooth. Season with salt and plenty of black pepper. If you have no machine, chop the garlic, mint and parsley as finely as you can and mix thoroughly together with the other ingredients.

CHAPATIS

Chapatis are the simplest form of wholemeal Indian bread and are eaten
with almost all curries. You tear bits off them and use them as a scoop for
mopping up the juices. They are fun to make and my children used to
love them spread with butter and jam for tea!

*250 g (8 oz) wholewheat
flour, plus a little extra*

1 teaspoon salt

*about 150 ml (¼ pint)
water*

oil for frying

Put the flour and salt into a bowl. Add enough water
to form a rather soft and sticky dough. Knead well for
8 –10 minutes, folding and kneading with the palm
of the hand. Cover the dough with a damp cloth and
leave to rest for at least half an hour.

Knead the dough again, form into balls the size of
ping-pong balls, flatten slightly and dip in a little more
of the wholewheat flour. Roll out each piece of
dough on a well floured board as thinly as you can.

(This is easier if you dip the chapati into flour from
time to time, as otherwise the dough tends to stick.)

Lightly oil a heavy frying pan or griddle and set
over a medium heat. Cook the chapatis one at a time,
turning with a palette knife when you see bubbles
appearing and then cooking the other side until they
puff up more. Pile them on a plate, cover with foil
and keep warm in a very low oven.
Makes about 14

BHATURA BREAD

A puffed-up, deep-fried bread specially good with tandoori dishes and
grilled meats but also delicious to mop up the juices of curry. Once the
dough is made, you can keep it in the fridge and use it as you want it.

*250 g (8 oz) strong white
or wholemeal flour, plus
a little extra*

*2 tablespoons plain yogurt
1 teaspoon baking powder*

*1 rounded teaspoon salt
½ –1 teaspoon chilli
powder*

*water
oil for deep-frying*

Mix the ingredients with sufficient warm water to
make a stiff dough, either with a wooden spoon or
the dough hook of an electric mixer, until it leaves
the sides of the bowl. (If it is still sticky, add a little
more flour.) Knead well, form into a ball and leave
covered at room temperature for 4 – 6 hours.

Roll the dough into a fat sausage and cut off

¼ – ½-inch rounds. Roll out each round on a
floured surface to the size of a saucer. Deep-fry the
bhaturas quickly in smoking oil, patting down gently
(so that they puff up) and turning once. Eat as soon as
possible, though, if you have to, you can keep them
warm in a low oven.
Makes about 14

Part 5

DESSERTS

Chocolate and Fresh Orange Bombe (page 157);
Shiver Me Timbers (page 156);
Strawberry and Pineapple Salad with Orange Cream (page 201);
Black Cherry Mousse Cake (page 160)

APRICOT ICE CREAM WITH TOASTED ALMONDS

Try this divine offering, which combines creamy richness with the strong
flavour of dried apricots, enhanced by the toasted crunch of almonds.

250 g (8 oz) dried apricots
250 g (8 oz) light brown
sugar

150 ml (5 fl oz) water
juice of 1 lemon, strained
3 large eggs (size 1–2),
separated

300 ml (½ pint)
whipping cream
50 g (2 oz) flaked
almonds

a good pinch of salt
75 g (3 oz) icing sugar,
sifted

Soak the apricots in water for 2 hours or more until soft. Drain and chop into small pieces. Dissolve the brown sugar in the water over a low heat. Add the chopped apricots. Bring to bubbling and stir around. Cover the pan, lower the heat and let them simmer very gently for 10–15 minutes, stirring now and then. Remove from the heat and stir in the lemon juice.

Whisk the egg yolks and stir them into the apricot mixture. Put the pan back over a very low heat, stirring constantly, without allowing it to bubble, for 5 minutes. Transfer the mixture to a bowl and leave to cool. Then whisk the cream until thick, but not stiff, and fold it into the apricot mixture. Toast the flaked almonds for a few minutes in a hot oven until brown. Stir in all but a handful of them. Whisk the egg whites with a good pinch of salt until thick. Then add the sifted icing sugar, and whisk until the mixture stands in peaks. Fold in the apricot and cream mixture with a metal spoon. Pour into a pretty 2.1 litre (3½ pint) freezerproof bowl and sprinkle the remaining almonds on top. Freeze for at least 5 hours.
Serves 6 – 8

CHOCOLATE SWIRL ICE CREAM

This is a frothy, soft, white ice with a lemony tang, which is streaked with
dark chocolate. It is quite quickly made and is irresistible for any occasion.

For the chocolate:
150 ml (5 fl oz) hot water
1 teaspoon instant coffee
50 g (2 oz) caster sugar

125 g (4 oz) plain
chocolate, broken up roughly
the yolks of 3 large eggs
(size 1–2)

For the ice cream:
the whites of 3 large eggs
(size 1–2)
½ teaspoon salt
175 g (6 oz) caster sugar

6 tablespoons water
juice of 1 lemon
300 ml (½ pint) double or
whipping cream

To make the chocolate, put the hot water into a bowl set over a saucepan of very hot, but not boiling, water. Add the instant coffee and caster sugar, sift, and then add the chocolate. Stir the mixture in the bowl until completely smooth. Add the egg yolks one at a time. Continue stirring over the hot water for about 5 minutes. Then put the bowl on one side to cool.

When the chocolate is cool, whisk the egg whites with the salt until stiff. In a pouring saucepan, dissolve the caster sugar in the water over a low heat. Then bring to the boil and boil fiercely for 3 minutes. Pour the syrup in a thin stream on to the egg whites and continue whisking until very thick. Then whisk in the lemon juice a little at a time. In another bowl, whisk the cream until thick and then gently but thoroughly fold it into the egg whites with a metal spoon. Spoon the chocolate mixture only very roughly into the egg white mixture in streaks and then pour the mixture into a freezerproof bowl (approximately 1.75-litre/3-pint), glass if possible, and freeze for at least 5 hours.
Serves 8

ICED CHOCOLATE CHARLOTTE

All the joys of chocolate lie in this wonderful ice cream – it makes compulsive eating, yet is neither too rich nor too sweet. It is edged with sponge fingers, and soaked with a fresh orange and lemon syrup which gives an exciting contrast to the smooth chocolate.

juice of 2 oranges
juice of 1 lemon
125 g (4 oz) demerara or soft pale brown sugar
about 1½ packets of sponge fingers

125 g (4 oz) caster sugar
150 ml (5 fl oz) water
150 g (5 oz) plain chocolate, broken up

1 teaspoon instant coffee
1 tablespoon hot water
2 large eggs (size 1–2)
a good pinch of salt

450 ml (¾ pint) whipping cream
a little flaked or grated chocolate, to decorate

Have ready a 19 cm (7½-inch) loose-based cake tin.

Squeeze the orange and lemon juice into a measuring jug and bring up to 150 ml (5 fl oz) with water, if necessary. Strain into a saucepan and add the demarara or soft pale brown sugar. Dissolve the sugar in the orange and lemon juice, stirring over a low heat. Bring to the boil and bubble for 30 seconds.

Leave the syrup until it is not too hot to touch (it cools more quickly if you sit the saucepan in cold water for a minute or two). Then dip the sponge fingers in one by one, just for a moment, as they should not become too soft, and place them around the sides of the cake tin. Pour any extra syrup slowly around the sides, over the top of the sponge fingers. Leave in a cool place while you prepare the ice cream.

Dissolve the caster sugar in the water in a saucepan over a low heat. Bring to the boil and boil fiercely for 3 minutes. Remove from the heat and immediately add the broken chocolate. Dissolve the instant coffee in the water, add to the chocolate and stir until smooth. With an electric beater, whisk the eggs with the salt in a bowl until pale and frothy. Slowly add the hot chocolate syrup, whisking all the time at high speed. Continue to whisk until cool. Whisk the cream until thick and then fold it thoroughly into the cooled chocolate. Pour the mixture into the cake tin lined with sponge fingers and freeze for at least 6 hours or overnight.

Then sprinkle flaked or grated chocolate all over the top and push the iced charlotte up out of the cake tin. Take a long spatula and pass it between the bottom of the iced charlotte and the loose base of the cake tin and carefully push the charlotte on to a serving plate. Freeze again until ready to eat and serve straight from the freezer.

Serves 8

LEMON BANANA ICE CREAM CHARLOTTE

Here is one of those perfect mixtures of tastes – making my mouth water
as I write. Half-way up the River Nile in Egypt is a small island called
Banana Island where they grow so-called 'lemon bananas'. These look
like any normal banana with the same skin, colour and texture but they
are lemon-shaped, and the flesh tastes like a mixture of banana and lemon.
I dedicate this recipe to the memory of those wonderful fruit.

1 packet of trifle sponges
juice of 3 lemons
125 g (4 oz) granulated
sugar

the whites of 2 large eggs
(size 2)
½ teaspoon salt

175 g (6 oz) demerara
sugar
6 tablespoons water

4 medium-size bananas
300 ml (½ pint)
whipping cream

Cut the trifle sponges in half lengthways and lay them in a single layer in a large roasting pan or shallow dish, crumb side upwards. Make the juice of 2 lemons up to 150 ml (¼ pint) with water, pour into a saucepan and add the granulated sugar. Dissolve the sugar, stirring over a low heat, then bring to the boil and boil for 1 minute. Remove from the heat and spoon the hot syrup slowly over the sponges, letting each absorb some. Leave on one side.

Whisk the egg whites and salt in the bowl of an electric mixer until they form soft peaks. Dissolve the sugar in the water, stirring over a low heat, then bring to the boil and boil briskly, without stirring, for 3 minutes. Immediately pour this syrup in a thin stream onto the egg whites, whisking all the time at high speed. Continue whisking until it has cooled and the whites are stiff. Purée the bananas with the juice of the remaining lemon, either in a food processor or by pushing the mixture through a sieve. Fold the purée into the egg whites, using a metal spoon. Then whisk the cream until thick but not stiff, and fold into the mixture. Now lightly press the soaked side of the sponges against the sides of a deep 20 cm (8-inch) loose-based cake tin. Break up the remaining sponges roughly and press over the base of the tin. Spoon the ice cream mixture into the sponge-lined tin and freeze for several hours or overnight. To turn out, rub the outside of the tin with a hot cloth and then loosen the edges carefully with a spatula. Put the cake tin on a jar or tin and push it down carefully. Slip the spatula under the base of the charlotte and push out onto a serving plate. Put it back in the freezer until ready to eat.
Serves 6–8

CRANBERRY CASKET FILLED WITH GOLD

Here is a truly spectacular finale to a festive meal. The pudding looks like
a fantasy; a bright scarlet, crumpled flower with ragged petals, holding in
its open bud something creamy, yellow and tempting. The scarlet case is,
in fact, a cranberry sorbet and it is filled with a mango, lemon and rum ice
cream. You can make this well ahead and eat it straight from the freezer.

Pictured on the back cover.

*275 g (9 oz) fresh
cranberries
150 g (5 oz) granulated
sugar
juice of 2 oranges*

*2 large egg whites
(size 1–2)
250 g (8 oz) demerara
sugar*

*150 ml (1/4 pint) lemon
juice
300 ml (1/2 pint) whipping
cream*

*2 ripe mangoes
3–4 tablespoons rum*

Put the cranberries into a saucepan with the granulated sugar and the orange juice. Bring to the boil, stirring to dissolve the sugar, and then cover and simmer for about 8 minutes until the cranberries are mushy. Now whizz this cranberry mixture to a purée in a food processor and leave it to cool.

When the purée is cold line a deep bowl (at least 1.75-litre/3-pint capacity) with non-stick baking parchment, folding it so that it fits the shape of the bowl. The edges of the paper should come up above the edge of the bowl; they will be uneven but this doesn't matter. Spoon the cooled cranberry purée into the paper-lined bowl and, using a wide knife or spatula, smear it up the sides of the bowl, leaving an uneven edge. Put the bowl in the freezer for an hour or more. If you have too much mixture for your bowl, it's nice to make a second casket in a smaller bowl, which you can put in the centre of the large one.

Make the mango ice cream. Whisk the egg whites until they stand in soft peaks. Put the demerara sugar into a deepish pouring saucepan with the lemon juice.

Dissolve the sugar with the lemon juice, stirring over a low heat. When the sugar has dissolved bring it to the boil and let it bubble fiercely, without stirring, for 3 minutes. Pour the bubbling liquid in a thin stream on to the egg whites, whisking all the time at high speed. Continue whisking until the mixture is thick.

In another bowl, whisk the cream until thick but not too stiff. Fold the cream into the mixture with a metal spoon. Cut the mangoes in half (do this on a board in the sink as it can be messy) and cut and scrape as much flesh as you can off the stone and skin. Put the flesh in a food processor with the rum and whizz it to purée. Fold the purée gently but thoroughly into the cream and egg-white mixture. Take the cranberry bowl from the freezer, pour the mango mixture into it and freeze again overnight.

Lift the frozen casket out of the metal bowl with the edge of the paper. Gently peel off all the paper and put the casket on a serving plate. Put it back in the freezer until you are ready to serve it.

Serves 8

CRANBERRY AND CHOCOLATE SURPRISE BOMBE

This combination of cranberries and dark chocolate with a centre of
lemon syllabub is quite simply scrumptious. Because of the syllabub it is a
pudding which shouldn't be made more than a day in advance but it is
not time-consuming to prepare and really is an exciting treat with which
to end a festive meal.

*275 g (9 oz) fresh
cranberries
150 g (5 oz) caster sugar
5 tablespoons water*

*2 tablespoons dark rum
1 lemon*

*300 ml (½ pint) double
cream*

*50 g (2 oz) icing sugar,
sifted
150 g (5 oz) plain chocolate*

Put all but three or four of the cranberries into a saucepan with the caster sugar and 3 tablespoons of water. Stir over a medium heat until the sugar has dissolved. Then cover the pan and let it simmer for 6 – 8 minutes until all the berries have popped and the consistency is mushy and very thick. Remove from the heat and stir in the rum. Leave the mixture to become completely cold. Then spoon it into a 1.2-litre (2-pint) pudding basin and spread it up the sides to line it thickly and as evenly as possible.

Finely grate the lemon rind and squeeze out the juice of half the lemon. Whisk the cream until it is beginning to thicken. Then whisk in the sifted icing sugar and continue whisking until the cream holds soft peaks: it should not be too stiff. Very gradually stir in the lemon juice with a metal spoon; then stir in the grated rind. Spoon this syllabub into the centre of the cranberry-lined basin and refrigerate for at least 6 hours.

Break the chocolate up into small pieces and put it with 2 tablespoons of water in a bowl set over a saucepan of very hot, but not boiling, water. Stir now and then until melted and smooth. Then remove from the heat and allow to cool for 10 –15 minutes. Take the cranberry basin out of the fridge, dip it into a sink of very hot water for a minute or two and then turn out, giving a firm shake, on to a serving plate. Slowly spoon the melted chocolate over the mound of cranberries as evenly as you can. Top the mound with the reserved cranberries and refrigerate it again until you are ready to eat.

Serves 6 – 8

WHITE LIE BOMBE

It is difficult to explain the name of this wonderful ice cream. It is simply what we all decided to call it the first time I made it – I think I reassured a guilty guest on a diet with the transparent lie that as the ice cream contains yogurt it isn't nearly so fattening. This is in fact a yogurt and cream bombe (you will need an aluminium bombe mould), smoothly white and speckled with pieces of crunchy, caramelised walnuts. The sauce is a purée of prunes with lemon juice and brandy.
Pictured on the front cover.

For the bombe:
125 g (4 oz) walnut pieces
250 g (8 oz) caster sugar
2 large egg whites
(size 1–2)

a generous pinch of salt
6 tablespoons water
5 rounded tablespoons thick set yogurt
300 ml (1/2 pint) whipping cream

For the sauce:
125 g (4 oz) Ready to Eat soft pitted prunes, cut up roughly

50 g (2 oz) molasses or muscovado sugar
3 tablespoons lemon juice
300 ml (1/2 pint) water
3 tablespoons brandy

Put the walnut pieces into a sieve and run the tap over them so that all the nuts get wet. Shake the sieve to get rid of excess water. Then put the damp nuts into a bowl, add 50 g (2 oz) of the caster sugar and stir around so that all the nuts become coated with sugar. Put a dry frying-pan over high heat. When the pan is very hot, tip in the nuts, and stir for about 1–2 minutes until they are caramelised and dark brown all over. Turn the nuts out on to a board, spreading them out so that they don't all stick together.

Now put the egg whites into the bowl of an electric mixer, add a generous pinch of salt and whisk until the egg whites stand in soft peaks. Put the rest of the caster sugar into a saucepan with the water and stir over a medium heat until the sugar has dissolved. Then increase the heat and boil fiercely for 3 minutes. Pour immediately in a thin stream onto the whisked egg whites, whisking all the time at high speed. Continue whisking until the mixture has cooled and thickened. Then whisk in the yogurt.

In another bowl, whisk the cream until it holds soft peaks. Fold the cream into the egg white and yogurt mixture. Put 4 – 6 caramelised walnut pieces on one side for a garnish later, and tip the rest on to the ice cream mixture, folding them in roughly and quickly. Then pour into a 1.5-litre (2½-pint) aluminium bombe mould and freeze for several hours or overnight.

Meanwhile make the prune and brandy sauce. Put the prunes into a saucepan with the molasses or muscovado sugar, the lemon juice and the water. Stir over a medium heat to dissolve the sugar. Then cover the pan and simmer gently for about 20 minutes until the prunes are very soft. Remove from the heat and add the brandy. Then put into a food processor and whizz thoroughly until as smooth as possible. Pour into a serving bowl and leave to cool.

When you want to turn out the ice cream, dip the mould briefly in a sink of very hot water and turn on to a serving plate, giving a good shake against the plate. You may find you have to dip the mould in water several times before it will turn out, and the ice cream on the outside of the bombe may be uneven, as it has melted a little – this actually adds to its dramatic appearance. Place the reserved walnut pieces on to the bombe and put back in the freezer until needed. Serve with the prune sauce.
Serves 8

FRESH ORANGE ICE CREAM CAKE

This is sumptuous party ice cream made with fresh oranges, eggs and
cream. The eggs are separated so that the cake has stripes of tangy orange
and a white meringue mixture which incorporates crumbled sponge
fingers. Beautiful and extremely popular.

3 medium–large oranges
375 g (12 oz) granulated
sugar

2 large eggs (size 1–2),
separated
300 ml (½ pint) whipping
cream

6 tablespoons water
juice of 1 lemon
1 packet of sponge fingers

a few strips of angelica
slices of orange, to garnish
(optional)

Grate the rind of 2 oranges. Then squeeze out the
juice and pour into a measuring jug – it should be
about 150 ml (¼ pint) (if it is not, make up with more
orange or lemon juice). Put the orange rind and juice
and 175 g (6 oz) of the sugar into a pouring saucepan.
Put the egg yolks into the mixing bowl of an electric
whisk. Put the pan of orange juice and sugar over a
low heat and stir until the sugar is dissolved. Then
increase the heat and boil fiercely, without stirring,
for 3 minutes. Pour immediately on to the egg yolks
in a thin stream, whisking all the time at high speed.
Continue whisking until the mixture is thick and pale
orange in colour. In another bowl whisk the cream
until thick and then whisk in the orange and egg yolk
mixture. Put in the fridge.

Whisk the egg whites in a bowl until they stand
in soft peaks then put the remaining 175 g (6 oz) sugar
in a pouring saucepan with the water. As before, stir
to dissolve the sugar over a low heat and then boil
fiercely without stirring for 3 minutes. Pour the syrup
in a thin stream on to the whisked egg whites, whisking all the time at high speed. Continue whisking

until the mixture is thick and white. Gradually whisk
in the lemon juice. Crush the sponge fingers roughly
under a rolling pin and stir in.

To assemble the cake, peel the remaining orange
and, using a sharp knife, cut it into the thinnest
possible segments, removing any pips and as much
pith as possible. Arrange together with the angelica
strips in a circular pattern on the bottom of a deep
19–20 cm (7½ –8-inch) diameter cake tin. Then
spoon in the two ice cream mixtures to form a sandwich, starting with a layer of half the orange mixture,
followed by all the egg white mixture and ending
with the remaining orange mixture. Freeze thoroughly, overnight if possible. To turn the cake out,
rub the tin all over with a cloth dipped in very hot
water until it will slip out of the tin on to a serving
plate or cake stand. (If you are using a loose-based tin,
just rub the sides and press the cake out; then rub the
remaining base and carefully remove.) Put the cake
back in the freezer until ready to serve, garnished with
more slices of orange if you wish.

Serves 8–10

Fresh Orange Ice Cream Cake; Iced Lemon Soufflé in a Chocolate Case (page 158)

SHIVER ME TIMBERS

This wonderful treat for a special occasion is a beautiful swirl of rum and chocolate ice cream on an almond chocolate sponge which is soaked in orange juice and rum. I have a friend who is astonishingly disciplined about never eating sweet or creamy foods. For years I have tried to tempt her with my puddings. At the sight of this one her will finally broke: she had not one but two large helpings!
Pictured on pages 146/7.

For the cake and syrup:
butter for greasing
3 medium to large eggs
(size 2–3)
125 g (4 oz) icing sugar,
sifted
25 g (1 oz) cocoa
5 tablespoons strong coffee

finely grated rind of 1 and
juice of 2 oranges
a pinch of salt
125 g (4 oz) ground
almonds
125 g (4 oz) granulated
sugar
3 tablespoons dark rum

For the ice cream:
125 g (4 oz) plain
chocolate, broken into
small pieces
6 tablespoons dark rum
the whites of 2 eggs

½ teaspoon salt
150 g (5 oz) granulated
sugar
5 tablespoons water
300 ml (½ pint) whipping
cream

Butter the bottom of an 18.5–20 cm (7½–8-inch) loose-based cake tin. To make the cake, first separate the 3 eggs into 2 large bowls. Whisk the egg yolks with 75 g (3 oz) icing sugar until pale. In a small bowl, stir the cocoa to a paste with the grated orange rind. Preheat the oven to Gas Mark 4/180°C/350°F. Whisk the egg whites with a pinch of salt until they form soft peaks. Then thoroughly whisk in the remaining 25 g (1 oz) icing sugar. Fold the egg whites into the egg yolk and chocolate mixture alternately with the ground almonds. Pour the mixture into the cake tin and bake in the centre of the oven for 30–35 minutes until spongy to touch in the centre. Remove from the oven.

Now make the syrup. If necessary, make the orange juice up to 125 ml (4 fl oz) with water. Strain into a saucepan and add the granulated sugar. Dissolve the sugar in the liquid, stirring over a low heat, then bring to a brisk boil for 3 minutes without stirring. Remove from the heat and stir in the rum. Prick the cake all over, right through, with a fork. Spoon the syrup slowly all over the cake, then leave it to cool and to absorb the excess syrup. (It's a good idea to put the cake tin on a piece of kitchen paper towelling, as a little syrup might seep out.) When the cake is cool, start to make the ice cream.

Put the plain chocolate in the top of a double boiler or in a pudding basin with 4 tablespoons of the rum. Put over hot but not simmering water and stir until the chocolate is melted and smooth. Remove from the hot water and leave on one side. Put the egg whites and the salt into the bowl of an electric whisk. Whisk until they form soft peaks. Put the granulated sugar in a saucepan with the water. Dissolve the sugar, stirring over a low heat, then bring to the boil and boil fiercely, without stirring, for 3 minutes. Pour at once in a thin stream onto the egg whites, whisking all the time at high speed. Continue whisking until cool and thick. Whisk in the remaining 2 tablespoons rum. Then, in another bowl, whisk the cream until stiff and fold it thoroughly into the egg whites with a metal spoon. The chocolate should still be soft enough to be dropped from the spoon; if it is too stiff put it back over hot water for a minute to soften a little. Drop spoonfuls of the chocolate onto the cream mixture but don't stir it in. When you have used all but about a tablespoon of the chocolate, turn the mixture into the cake tin with a wide spatula, piling it up in the middle, and dribble the remaining chocolate on top. Freeze for several hours or overnight. To turn out, rub the sides of the tin with a hot cloth, then put the tin on a jar or tin and push the sides of the cake tin down carefully. Slide a spatula underneath the cake and push it onto a serving plate. Freeze again until ready to eat.
Serves 8–10

CHOCOLATE AND FRESH ORANGE BOMBE

Home-made ice cream is everybody's favourite and it seems to turn any
occasion into a celebration. I have made countless ice cream recipes over
the years, but to me this is simply the most mouthwatering of them all.
The chocolate is light, smooth and wonderfully chocolaty, while the
creamy orange centre has a lovely fresh tang. It is one of those puddings
which literally provokes gasps of pleasure at the first taste.
Pictured on pages 146/7.

For the chocolate ice cream:
4 large egg whites
(size 1–2)
½ teaspoon salt
175 g (6 oz) demerara
sugar
8 tablespoons water
250 g (8 oz) plain
chocolate, broken up
300 ml (½ pint) double or
whipping cream

For the orange ice cream:
4 egg yolks
rind of 1 orange, grated
finely
150 g (5 oz) caster sugar
125 ml (4 fl oz) orange
juice
150 ml (¼ pint) double or
whipping cream

Put the egg whites in a bowl of an electric mixer and
the yolks in a small bowl on one side, covered. Add
the salt to the egg whites and whisk until they stand
in soft peaks. Put the demerara sugar into a saucepan
with the water. Stir over a low heat until the sugar has
dissolved. Then increase the heat to high and boil
fiercely for 3 minutes exactly. Now pour gradually on
to the egg whites, whisking all the time at high speed.
Continue whisking until the mixture has cooled a
little.

Put the chocolate in the top of a double saucepan
or into a bowl set over a saucepan of hot, but not
boiling water. Stir until melted, and then pour gradually on to the egg white mixture, whisking all the
time. Allow to cool slightly. Put the cream into
another bowl and whisk until it holds soft peaks. Fold
the cream into the chocolate mixture and then pour
into a 1.2–1.5 litre (1–2½-pint) aluminium bombe
mould. Freeze for 6 –7 hours.

Now make the orange ice cream. Put the egg
yolks in the bowl of an electric mixer and whisk until
pale. Whisk in the grated orange rind. Put the caster
sugar and the orange juice in a saucepan and stir over
a gentle heat until the sugar has dissolved. Then
increase the heat and boil fiercely for 2 minutes. Pour
immediately on to the egg yolks whisking all the time
at high speed. Continue whisking until the mixture
has cooled and thickened a little. Whisk the cream
until it holds soft peaks, and fold into the orange and
egg yolk mixture.

Take the chocolate ice cream from the freezer,
and hollow out the centre using a metal spoon, putting the bits of ice cream in a bowl on one side. Spoon
the egg yolk and orange mixture into the cavity.
Soften the chocolate ice cream which you have
scooped out by stirring it around. Then spoon the
softened chocolate ice cream on top of the orange
mixture and spread it out to the sides. Freeze for at
least 6 –7 hours. To turn out, dip the mould briefly
into a sink of hot water just until it turns out if you
hold a serving plate up to it and give it a good shake.
When it comes out of the mould the ice cream may
have a rippled appearance. I like this, but you can
always smooth it with a spatula if you don't. Put the
bombe back in the freezer until ready to serve.
Serves 8–10

ICED LEMON SOUFFLÉ IN A CHOCOLATE CASE

The appearance of this party piece always provokes gasps of wonder. The
thin and jagged casing of dark chocolate, looking like the bark of some
exotic tree, encases a pale and light lemon soufflé. The combination of
flavour and texture could hardly be more mouthwatering.
Pictured on page 155.

oil for greasing
175 g (6 oz) plain
chocolate, plus extra for
decoration

3 tablespoons water
15 g (½ oz) butter
finely grated rind and juice
of 2 large lemons

175 g (6 oz) caster sugar
4 large eggs (size 1–2),
separated

15 g (½ oz) gelatine
300 ml (½ pint) double
cream

Oil a 19–20 cm (7½ –8-inch) loose-based cake tin
well and line the base with a disc of oiled greaseproof
paper. Break up the chocolate and melt with 1 tablespoon of the water in a double saucepan or a bowl set
over a pan of hot water. When melted stir in the
butter. Spoon the chocolate on to the base of the cake
tin and spread evenly with a spatula all over the
bottom and up the sides of the tin, leaving a rough
and uneven edge. Leave to become firm while you
make the soufflé.

Add the grated lemon rind and the caster sugar to
the egg yolks and whisk until the mixture is pale and
thick. Squeeze the lemon juice into a saucepan and
add the remaining 2 tablespoons water. Sprinkle in
the gelatine and dissolve in the liquid over a gentle
heat but don't let it boil. Pour the hot liquid slowly
on to the egg yolk mixture, whisking all the time.
Continue to whisk until cooled a bit and just beginning to thicken. Whisk the cream until thick but not

stiff and fold into the lemon mixture. Then whisk the
egg whites until they stand in soft peaks and fold in
with a metal spoon. Pour into the chocolate-lined tin
– the edge of the chocolate should be a little above
the top of the soufflé. Freeze for at least 2 hours.

To unmould, rub the sides of the frozen tin with
a hot cloth and then, using a small and very sharp
knife, cut down between the chocolate sides and the
tin until it is loosened enough all round to push up.
(I find the easiest way is to put the tin on top of a jam
jar and then push down.) Separate the chocolate base
from the base of the tin with a knife if necessary and
then carefully peel off the greaseproof paper. Put on
a serving dish and refreeze until about 1 hour before
you eat; then decorate the soufflé top with chocolate
shavings and move the soufflé to the main part of the
fridge, as it is most delicious eaten very cold, but not
quite frozen.
Serves 8

MANGO MERINGUE ICE WITH PINEAPPLE

This is an impressive sorbet. The rich flavour of the mango makes it taste
more like a cream ice, while the pineapple pieces are sharp and refreshing.
It has a beautiful golden yellow colour which will enhance any meal.

whites of 3 large eggs
(size 1–2)
250 g (8 oz) granulated
sugar

150 ml (¼ pint) water
2 ripe mangoes

juice of 2 fresh limes or
small lemons
1 small pineapple

50 g (2 oz) glacé cherries,
cut into quarters

In the bowl of an electric mixer, whisk the egg whites
until they stand in soft peaks. Dissolve the sugar in the
water over a low heat and then boil fiercely, over a

high heat without stirring, for 3 minutes. Pour immediately in a thin stream on to the egg whites, whisking
all the time at high speed. Continue whisking until

the mixture stands in stiff peaks.

Cut open the mangoes, pulling off the peel and scooping out the flesh into a food processor or liquidiser. Add the juice of the limes or lemons and whizz until smooth. Whisk this purée into the egg mixture.

Cut the peel from the pineapple and chop the soft flesh in small chunks. Reserving a handful, spoon the chunks roughly into the mango mixture. Pour in a serving bowl and lightly drop the reserved pineapple and chopped glacé cherries over the top (they should almost, but not quite, sink in). Freeze for approximately 3 – 6 hours, depending on your freezer, before serving.

Serves 8

BANANA AND MINT MERINGUE ICE CREAM CAKE

Layers of rich banana with a lemony tang alternate with crisp meringue to make this delicious party pudding. It is very convenient, as it can be made the day before, or even earlier if you like.

200 g (7 oz) icing sugar
3 large eggs (size 1–2), separated

2–3 drops of peppermint essence
250 g (8 oz) bananas
juice of 1/2 lemon

a pinch of salt
175 g (6 oz) demerara sugar
6 tablespoons water

300 ml (1/2 pint) double cream
shavings of plain chocolate, to decorate

Sift the icing sugar into a bowl. Whisk the egg whites in a large bowl until they stand in soft peaks and then whisk in the sifted icing sugar, a little at a time. Put the bowl over a large pan half-filled with gently simmering water and continue whisking for about 5 minutes until the meringue mixture is very stiff. Whisk in the peppermint essence. Heat the oven to Gas Mark 2/150°C/300°F. Put a large sheet of greaseproof paper on to a baking sheet and spread the meringue mixture over it about 2.5 cm (1 inch) thick. Put the baking sheet on to the bottom shelf of the oven and cook until the meringue is firm and dry – at least 1 1/2 hours. Allow to cool.

Now start to make the ice cream. Purée the bananas with the lemon juice until smooth. Whisk the egg yolks, with the salt added, until pale and thickly creamy. Dissolve the sugar in the water in a pouring saucepan over a low heat. Then boil fiercely for 3 minutes and pour immediately in a thin stream on to the egg yolks, whisking all the time at a high speed. Continue whisking for at least 5 minutes until it is pale and thick, then whisk in the banana purée. In another large bowl whisk the cream until thick but not stiff. Pour the banana and egg yolk mixture into the cream and fold in thoroughly with a metal spoon.

Now turn the cooked meringue upside down. Peel off the greaseproof paper and then break up the meringue, just roughly. In a deep 20 cm (8-inch) cake tin make layers of the ice cream mixture and the broken meringue, starting and ending with a layer of ice cream. Freeze. When well frozen turn the ice cream cake out on to a serving plate by rubbing the outside of the tin with a hot cloth until it slips out. Sprinkle shavings of plain chocolate on the top and refreeze until ready to eat.

Serves 10

WONDER BOMBE

A rather different kind of Bombe Surprise: this is not an ice cream but it is just as delicious and impressive in appearance. Sponges dipped in a luscious coating of dark chocolate and brandy hide a glossy, gooey centre of apricots. It is a dish whose appearance should cause a sensation at a dinner party and yet it is not difficult to make.

250 g (8 oz) dried apricots
75 g (3 oz) soft brown sugar
300 ml (½ pint) plus 5
tablespoons water

juice of 1 lemon
12 (1½ packets) trifle
sponges

oil for greasing
300 g (10 oz) plain
chocolate, broken into small
pieces

5 tablespoons brandy
a little icing sugar

Put the apricots in a bowl, pour some boiling water over them and leave them to soak for at least 2 hours. Then drain the apricots, and put in a saucepan with the brown sugar and 300 ml (½ pint) water. Bring to the boil, cover the pan and simmer gently for 15–20 minutes or until the apricots are mushy and have almost completely absorbed the liquid. Remove from the heat, stir in the lemon juice and leave to cool completely.

Cut the trifle sponges in half lengthways. Lightly oil a 1.5 litre (2½-pint) pudding basin. Put the chocolate with the 5 tablespoons of water in the top of a double boiler, or in a bowl set over a saucepan of very hot water. Stir until melted and smooth. Stir in the brandy a spoonful at a time. Dip the cut sponges into the hot chocolate and press them against the sides of the pudding basin, overlapping them slightly to line it completely with no gaps. Spoon in the cold apricot mixture. Cover the top of the basin with the remaining sponges dipped in chocolate, enclosing the apricots completely. Chill for several hours or overnight, in the fridge. To turn out, dip the pudding basin in a sink of very hot water for about a minute, loosen the top edges carefully with a spatula and turn the bombe onto a serving dish. Put it back in the fridge until ready to serve. At the last moment, sprinkle a little icing sugar through a sieve onto the top of the bombe.
Serves 10–12

BLACK CHERRY MOUSSE CAKE

Seductively soft, this 'half-cake, half-mousse' has a light, lemony flavour and is topped with black cherries and spread with cream around the sides. Late in the summer you could use strawberries or raspberries in the topping instead of black cherries.
Pictured on pages 146/7.

For the cake:
oil for greasing
3 large eggs (size 1–2),
separated
150 g (5 oz) caster sugar

grated rind and juice of
1 lemon
25 g (1 oz) cornflour
25 g (1 oz) self-raising flour
¼ teaspoon cream of tartar

a good pinch of salt

For the topping:
250 g (8 oz) fresh black
cherries (or strawberries or
raspberries)

3 tablespoons black cherry
(or strawberry) jam
1 tablespoon lemon juice
150 ml (5 fl oz) double or
whipping cream

Preheat the oven to Gas Mark 4/180°C/350°F. Lightly grease an 18 –20 cm (7– 8 inch) cake tin, line with a disc of greased greaseproof paper and dust with flour. Whisk the egg yolks with the caster sugar until very pale. Whisk in the rind and juice of the lemon. Sift the cornflour and flour on to the mixture and stir in. In another bowl, whisk the egg whites with the cream of tartar and salt until they stand in soft peaks and then, using a metal spoon, fold gently but thoroughly into the yolk mixture. Pour into the tin and bake in the centre of the oven for 35–40 minutes until well risen. Then cool the cake in the tin – it will sink a bit, but that is normal.

Loosen the sides of the cake with a knife and turn out on to a serving plate. Not more than 2–3 hours before you eat, make the topping. Cut the cherries in half and remove the stones. Put the cherry halves flesh side down on top of the cake. Put the cherry jam into a saucepan with the lemon juice, bring slowly to the boil, stirring, and bubble for a minute. (If using strawberries, cut them in half and place them flesh side down on top of the cake. If using raspberries, leave them whole. Replace the cherry jam with strawberry jam and cook with the lemon juice as directed above.) Remove from the heat and cool for a few minutes until thick enough to spoon all over the fresh fruit. Whisk the cream until stiff and spread the sides of the cake with it in rough flicks. Chill in the fridge until ready to eat.

Serves 6

MY DARLING CLEMENTINE

Clementines are sweet and seedless and the skin becomes tender when stewed. The mixture of apricot with the slightly marmalade-like taste of the clementines is lovely.

250 g (8 oz) dried apricots
250 –300 g (8 –10 oz) small clementines
275 g (9 oz) caster sugar
600 ml (1 pint) water
15 g (½ oz) gelatine
175 g (6 oz) butter
3 large eggs (size 1–2)
150 g (5 oz) self-raising flour
25 g (1 oz) cornflour
1 level teaspoon baking powder
2–3 tablespoons warm milk

Rinse the dried apricots and soak them in water for at least 3 hours. Drain them and put in a saucepan. Cut the clementines, unpeeled, into six and add to the apricots. Add 125 g (4 oz) of the caster sugar, and the water. Cover the pan, bring to the boil and simmer for 15 –20 minutes. Remove the lid and continue to cook until the apricots are mushy. Remove from the heat and, using a spoon, lift out the clementine pieces into a 1.75 litre (3-pint) capacity wide and fairly deep flan or cake tin (not one with a loose base). Arrange the clementines skin downwards in two circles on the base of the tin. Then sprinkle the gelatine over the apricots and put back over a medium heat. Stir round for a minute or two until it dissolves. Spoon the mixture over the clementine segments.

Preheat the oven to Gas Mark 4/180°C/350°F. Cream the butter with the remaining 150 g (5 oz) caster sugar in a bowl until fluffy. Whisk in the eggs thoroughly one by one (don't worry if the mixture curdles a bit). Sift the two flours and baking powder and stir them lightly into the bowl with a metal spoon. Stir in the milk to give a soft consistency. Spoon the cake mixture evenly over the apricots. Cook in the centre of the oven for 45 –50 minutes until the middle is firm to touch. Put on one side to cool and then chill for several hours. To turn out, loosen the edges with a round-bladed knife, then dip the tin briefly in hot water and turn out onto a serving plate, giving a shake. Chill until ready to eat.

Serves 8

ANNIVERSARY GÂTEAU

I made this for a wedding anniversary which we had both forgotten. My husband rang in the afternoon and since we had friends for dinner anyway I concocted this to make the occasion more festive. It is not really a cake but two layers of puff pastry sandwiched with a cream mousse and fresh fruit. We were married in midwinter and so I originally used kiwifruit, but I have since made the pudding during the summer using strawberries and raspberries.

400 g (13 oz) packet of puff pastry
4 large eggs (size 1–2)
25 g (1 oz) caster sugar
300 ml (½ pint) double or single cream
15 g (½ oz) gelatine
finely grated rind of 1 lemon
1 teaspoon vanilla essence
500 – 750 g (1–1½ lb) fresh strawberries (halved) or raspberries or 6–8 kiwifruit, peeled and sliced in thin rounds
4 tablespoons redcurrant jelly (for strawberries or raspberries) or lime jelly (for kiwifruit)
2 teaspoons lemon juice

Cut the pastry in half and shape into two balls. Roll out into two roughly shaped circles approximately 15 cm (10 inches) in diameter. (If you want a perfect circle you can put a large plate on the pastry and cut round it.) Place the two circles on a dampened baking sheet, prick all over with a fork and chill in the fridge for 15 minutes. Heat the oven to Gas Mark 7/220°C/425°F and cook the pastry circles, one at a time, just above the centre of the oven for 12–15 minutes until golden. Cool them on a wire rack.

To make the filling, separate the eggs, putting the yolks in a pudding basin or in the top of a double boiler and the whites in a large bowl. Whisk the caster sugar into the egg yolks. In a saucepan, bring the cream almost to the boil and then pour on to the egg yolks, whisking all the time. Put the pudding basin over a saucepan half-full of simmering water and stir constantly until the custard thickens – about 8–10 minutes. Dissolve the gelatine according to the instructions on the packet and then stir the liquid thoroughly into the custard, together with the lemon rind and the vanilla essence. Leave the custard to cool, stirring now and then, until almost cold and just beginning to set round the edge. (It must still be soft enough to fold into the egg whites – if you have left it too long dip the bowl in hot water for a little while.) Then whisk the custard until smooth again. Whisk the egg whites until they stand in soft peaks. Then spoon the custard on to them and fold in roughly, with a metal spoon. Place one of the pastry circles (the larger if there is any difference) on a serving plate. Spoon the custard mousse on to the circle and leave to set. Put on half the fruit and lay the second circle on top.

Not more than an hour before serving if possible, melt the jelly in a saucepan with the lemon juice. Brush the top of the pastry circle with some of the jelly glaze and then arrange the remaining fruit neatly in a circular pattern on it and brush with the remaining glaze. Leave the gâteau in a fairly cool place, but not in the fridge. To serve cut in slices.

Serves 10

Anniversary Gâteau

PRUNE AND WALNUT LEMON SYRUP CAKE

This is an upside-down cake, perfect for a hungry crowd at a weekend
lunch. It is gooey, nutty and tangy with a fresh lemon syrup which is
absorbed into the cake.

250 g (8 oz) pitted prunes
75 g (3 oz) soft dark brown
sugar
300 ml (½ pint) water
juice of 2 lemons plus 2
tablespoons

50 g (2 oz) unsalted butter
2 large eggs (size 1–2)
75 g (3 oz) caster sugar
4 tablespoons milk
175 g (6 oz) self-raising
flour, sifted

50 g (2 oz) candied peel
50 g (2 oz) walnuts,
chopped
175 g (6 oz) granulated
sugar

For the icing:
50 g (2 oz) icing sugar
a pinch of salt
a thin slice of lemon, halved

Put the prunes in a saucepan with the brown sugar and the water. Bring to the boil, cover the pan and simmer for about 20 minutes until the juice is syrupy. Stir in 1 tablespoon of lemon juice and spoon the mixture into a deep 17.5cm (7-inch) cake tin (not one with a loose base). Melt the butter in a small saucepan and put on one side. Separate the eggs into two bowls. Preheat the oven to Gas Mark 5/190°C/375°F.

Add the caster sugar and the milk to the egg yolks and whisk until very pale. Using a metal spoon, gently stir the flour into the yolk mixture, followed by the warm, melted butter. Add a good pinch of salt to the egg whites and beat until they stand in soft peaks. Stir them gently but thoroughly into the cake batter. Lastly, mix the candied peel and walnuts together and stir them gently into the mixture. Spoon into the cake tin on top of the prunes, making it higher round the sides, with a depression in the middle: there should be only enough batter to just cover the prunes in the middle. Cook in the centre of the oven for 45–55

minutes until well risen. When a knife inserted in the centre comes out dry the cake is cooked. Prick the cake all over right through with a skewer. Dissolve the granulated sugar with the juice of the 2 lemons in a saucepan over a gentle heat, bring to the boil, and boil vigorously for 2 minutes. Slowly spoon the hot syrup over the cake, letting the cake absorb it. Leave the cake in the tin for about 15 –20 minutes until all the syrup is absorbed. Then loosen the sides right to the bottom of the tin with a round-bladed knife, and turn the cake out onto a serving plate. You may need to give the tin a good shake as the prune mixture can stick a bit. Spoon out any left in the tin onto the cake and leave until cold.

Finally, put the icing sugar and salt in a bowl and thoroughly mix in the remaining tablespoon of lemon juice. Spoon the icing onto the centre of the prunes and let it dribble unevenly over the cake. Put two thin half-slices of lemon in the centre, and leave to set.

Serves 8

SOFT AND DARK CHOCOLATE CAKE

Time and time again, for special occasions, I make a variation of a dark and intensely chocolate cake. It always seems the best treat of all, and if you want it as a pudding it is perfect with a vanilla or sharp lemon ice cream, or simply with cream. The advantage of this cake is that it keeps well, so can be made in advance for a party. I nearly always cover the cake with smooth chocolate, so that I can write appropriate messages in glacé icing or decorate it with a few little fresh flowers from the garden.

To do fine writing, simply mix up a little icing sugar and a very little warm water to a thickish paste in a bowl, then snip the smallest possible corner off a polythene bag, spoon the icing sugar into the bag and squeeze it through the tiny hole to write or draw on the cake.

For the cake:
butter for greasing
250 g (8 oz) dark
chocolate, broken up

8 large eggs (size 1–2)
250 g (8 oz) caster sugar
50 g (2 oz) self-raising
flour, plus extra for dusting

½ teaspoon salt
3–4 tablespoons fresh sweet
orange marmalade or apricot
jam

For the topping:
175 g (6 oz) dark chocolate
25 g (1 oz) unsalted butter
2 tablespoons cream

First, make the cake. Butter 2 deepish 23 cm (9-inch) sandwich tins and line with discs of buttered grease-proof paper. Dust with flour. Put the chocolate into the top of a double boiler, or a bowl set over a pan of hot but not boiling water. Stir until the chocolate has melted, and then remove from the heat.

Put 2 whole eggs and 6 egg yolks into a large bowl and the egg whites into another bowl. Add the sugar to the eggs and egg yolks and whisk well until pale. Then whisk in the melted chocolate. Sift in the flour on to the mixture and stir in.

Heat the oven to Gas Mark 4/180°C/350°F. Now add the salt to the egg whites and whisk until they stand in soft peaks. Using a large metal spoon, fold the egg whites into the chocolate mixture a bit at a time, and then pour the mixture equally between the two tins. Bake in the centre of the oven for 20 –25 minutes until well risen and firm to a light touch in the centre.

Remove from the oven and leave to cool in the tins – the cakes will sink slightly, which is normal. When the cakes are cold, loosen the sides carefully with a knife and turn one cake out on to a serving plate, upside-down, the way it turns out. Spread a layer of fresh orange marmalade or jam on the cake and turn out the second cake on top of it, again upside down for the flattest top.

Now make the topping. Put the chocolate into the top of a double boiler, or a bowl set over a pan of hot but not boiling water. Stir until melted, then stir in the butter until also melted. Lastly add the cream. Remove the bowl from the hot water, and after a few minutes spoon the chocolate mixture slowly on top of the cake, spreading it out smoothly with a spatula to the edge of the cake and letting it dribble unevenly over the sides. If decorating with flowers, place them on the cake when the chocolate is still soft. Do any writing when it has set. Leave the cake at room temperature while the icing is setting.

Serves 14–16

WALNUT MOUSSE GÂTEAU

This luxurious nutty cake, layered with a rum-laced walnut mousse and
then coated with dark chocolate, is the perfect indulgence for a party. It is
a good idea for a buffet, where you could serve it with a contrasting
fresh fruit salad.

For the cake:
butter for greasing
175 g (6 oz) icing sugar
125 g (4 oz) ground
almonds
3 eggs
25 g (1 oz) plain flour,
sifted

4 egg whites
a pinch of salt

For the walnut mousse:
4 egg yolks
125 g (4 oz) caster sugar
4 tablespoons water

150 g (5 oz) unsalted
butter, at room temperature
3 tablespoons dark rum
125 g (4 oz) walnuts,
chopped finely
150 ml (5 fl oz) carton of
double or whipping cream,
whipped lightly

For the chocolate coating:
175 g (6 oz) plain
chocolate, broken into
small pieces
1 tablespoon clear honey
2 tablespoons water
25 g (1 oz) unsalted butter
walnut halves, to decorate

Preheat the oven to Gas Mark 6/200°C/400°F. Butter the sides of two 20 cm (8-inch) sandwich tins and
line the bases with discs of non-stick baking paper.
Put 125 g (4 oz) of the icing sugar, the ground
almonds and 3 whole eggs into a bowl and whisk
together until pale. Stir in the sifted flour gently.
Whisk the four egg whites with the salt until they
stand in soft peaks. Whisk in the remaining 50 g (2 oz)
icing sugar and then fold the whites into the almond
mixture with a metal spoon. Divide the mixture
between the two cake tins. Cook in the centre of the
oven for 15–20 minutes until the middle of the cakes
are springy to a light touch. They will sink a bit as
they cool.

To make the walnut mousse, first put the egg
yolks into the bowl of an electric mixer. Put the caster
sugar with the water in a saucepan and dissolve the
sugar, stirring over a low heat. Then boil vigorously
for 3 minutes, without stirring, and immediately pour
in a thin stream on to the egg yolks, whisking all the
time at high speed. Then whisk in the butter, adding
small pieces at a time, and continue whisking until

cool. Gradually whisk in the rum, stir in the chopped
walnuts and lastly, fold in the whipped cream.

Turn out the cooked cakes and cut each one
carefully in half with a sharp knife, so you have four
layers. Put one layer on a serving plate, spread with a
third of the walnut mousse and repeat with the other
layers.

To make the chocolate coating, put the chocolate
into the top of a double boiler or into a bowl which
you set over a pan of water. Add the honey and 1
tablespoon of the water and melt over a pan of hot
but not boiling water. Then stir in the butter until
melted and lastly the second tablespoon of water.
Remove from the heat and allow to thicken for a few
minutes. Lift up the sides of the cake gently and put
4 strips of greaseproof paper under the cake to protect
the plate while coating with the chocolate. Spoon the
chocolate on to the top of the cake and spread it
evenly all over. Then coat the sides with chocolate
that has run over the top. Remove the paper and
decorate with walnut halves.

Serves 12

Walnut Mousse Gâteau; Cheesecake Crécy (page 176); Orange and Strawberry Passion Torte (page 168)

ORANGE AND STRAWBERRY PASSION TORTE

However much you have eaten you will still have room for a little of this
delicate almond cake. It is sandwiched with a thick layer of jelly, fresh
orange pieces and strawberries, and is light and refreshing.
Pictured on page 167.

butter for greasing
3 eggs, separated
125 g (4 oz) icing sugar
sifted, plus a little extra

450 ml (³/4 pint) plus 3
tablespoons orange and
passion-fruit juice (or
unsweetened orange juice)

finely grated rind of 1
orange
125 g (4 oz) ground
almonds

4 seedless oranges
15 g (¹/2 oz) gelatine
250 g (8 oz) small
strawberries

Preheat the oven to Gas Mark 4/180°C/350°F. Butter the sides of a deep 18.5–20 cm (7¹/2–8 inch) cake
tin and line the base with a disc of non-stick baking
powder. Whisk the egg yolks with 75 g (3 oz) of the
icing sugar until pale. Whisk in 3 tablespoons of
orange and passion-fruit juice or unsweetened orange
juice followed by the grated orange rind. Whisk the
egg whites until they form soft peaks. Sift in the
remaining 25 g (1 oz) icing sugar and whisk again.
Fold the whisked egg whites and ground almonds
alternately into the yolk mixture. Pour into the prepared cake tin and cook in the centre of the oven for
30–35 minutes until springy to a light touch in the
centre.

Meanwhile cut the oranges across into thin slices,
cut off all the skin and pith and cut up into small
pieces. Pour 450 ml (³/4 pint) of the fruit juice into a
saucepan. Heat gently, sprinkle on the gelatine and
remove from the heat. Stir well until the gelatine has
dissolved. Then pour into a bowl and add the orange
pieces. Leave to cool but do not allow to set. Cut the
strawberries in half and stir them into the jelly, then
chill it in the fridge until set.

Leave the cooked cake in the tin for a few
minutes, then loosen the sides with a knife and turn
out onto a rack to cool. Just before serving, cut the
cake in half carefully, using a sharp knife. Put one half
on a serving plate. Stir the jelly until all broken up and
pile it evenly over the first half of the cake. Place the
second half of the cake on top. Lastly, sprinkle icing
sugar through a sieve all over the top. Serve with the
jelly very cold to contrast with the slightly-warm
cake.
Serves 6

INTENSE CHOCOLATE CAKE WITH REDCURRANTS

The popping sharpness of the redcurrant top goes wonderfully with this
soft, intensely chocolaty cake. It is a pudding which no one resists. The
cake is best made the day before with the topping put on a few hours
before you eat. I serve it either with cream or whipped cream
mixed with yogurt.
Pictured on the back cover.

butter for greasing
250 g (8 oz) plain
chocolate
2 tablespoons water

2 large eggs (size 1–2),
separated
75 g (3 oz) soft dark brown
sugar

1 tablespoon plain flour,
plus extra for dusting
2 teaspoons natural yogurt

125–175 g (4–6 oz) fresh
redcurrants
icing sugar
salt

Butter a 15 –18 cm (6–7-inch) cake tin, line the base
with a disc of buttered greasproof paper and dust with
flour. Break up three-quarters of the chocolate and
put into the top of a double saucepan, or into a bowl
set over barely simmering water. Add the water to the
chocolate and stir until melted and smooth. Remove

from the heat. Put the egg yolks in a mixing bowl and add the sugar and the melted chocolate. Whisk very thoroughly together. Then stir in the flour.

Heat the oven to Gas Mark 4/180°C/350°F. Whisk the egg whites with a good pinch of salt until they stand in soft peaks. Fold the egg whites into the chocolate mixture a little at a time, using a metal spoon, then pour the mixture into the prepared cake tin. Cook the cake in the centre of the oven for 25–30 minutes until a small knife inserted in the middle comes out clean.

Remove from the oven and leave in the tin for about 5 minutes (the cake will sink slightly – this is normal). Then loosen the edges carefully with a knife and turn the cake out onto a rack to cool, removing the greaseproof paper and turning the cake the right way up.

When the cake is cold, melt the remaining chocolate in a double saucepan over hot water, stirring in the yogurt when melted. Spread this chocolate on top of the cake and then push the redcurrants off their stalks with a fork and put them on top of the chocolate. Leave in a cool place but not the fridge. Shortly before serving, sprinkle a very little icing sugar through a sieve on top of the redcurrants.
Serves 4–6

EASTER RING

This delectable lemon ring is made with ground almonds instead of flour and with a little ground rice added to give it a subtle crunchiness. It is moist and light and absorbs the sharp lemon syrup. It can make a perfect Easter dessert when transformed into a nest with chocolate flake, eggs and chicks in the centre.

For the ring:
butter for greasing
flour for dusting
4 eggs, separated

175 g (6 oz) icing sugar, sifted
75 g (6 oz) ground almonds
25 g (1 oz) ground rice
3 tablespoons warm water

For the lemon syrup:
250 g (8 oz) granulated sugar
150 ml (1/4 pint) water

juice of two lemons
whipped cream, to decorate (optional)

Butter a 21–23 cm (8½–9 inch) ring mould tin and dust with flour. Put the egg yolks into a mixing bowl and stir in the sifted icing sugar. Whisk until light and fluffy. Whisk in the ground almonds, the ground rice and the warm water. Preheat the oven to Gas Mark 4/180°C/350°F. Then whisk the egg whites until they stand in soft peaks. Fold the yolk and almond mixture gently into the egg whites with a metal spoon, a half at a time. Pour the mixture into the ring mould and cook in the centre of the oven for 30 – 40 minutes until firm to a light touch in the centre. Allow to cool in the tin. Then ease both sides of the ring carefully away with a palette knife and turn out on to a serving plate – it should turn out perfectly if you give the tin several sharp taps.

To make the lemon syrup, put the granulated sugar into a saucepan and stir in the water and lemon juice. Dissolve the sugar over a low heat and then boil fiercely, without stirring, for 2 minutes. Spoon the hot syrup slowly over the cold ring, leaving time for the cake to absorb the syrup as you do so. Leave until quite cold. Fill the centre with whipped cream if desired and, for an Easter dessert, decorate as a nest.
Serves 6–8

CANARY CAKE

Many years ago, my parents bought a fisherman's cottage on the remote
southern coast of an unknown Canary island. There was no hotel and we
were the only foreigners there. I often think of Maria, who cooked for us.
One year she made a particularly good pudding-cake for my birthday
using local ingredients – almonds, oranges and bananas. A good
accompaniment to this, if you are using it as a pudding, is a bowl of good
vanilla ice cream.

For the cake:
butter for greasing
4 large eggs (size 1–2),
separated
75 g (3 oz) caster sugar

finely grated rind of 2 large
oranges
125 g (4 oz) ground
almonds
2 tablespoons hot water

a pinch of salt

For the syrup and banana
topping:
juice of 2 large oranges

juice of ½ lemon
75 g (3 oz) demerara sugar
1 teaspoon ground cinnamon
2–3 firm bananas

Preheat the oven to Gas Mark 4/180°C/350°F. Butter a 20 cm (8-inch) cake tin and line it with a disc of
buttered greaseproof paper. Put the yolks of the eggs
into a mixing bowl with the caster sugar and the
grated orange rinds and whisk until they are pale and
fluffy. Then whisk in the ground almonds a little at a
time, followed by the hot water to soften the mixture.
In another bowl, whisk the egg whites with the salt
until they stand in soft peaks and then fold them
gently into the yolk mixture with a metal spoon.
Spoon into the prepared tin and bake the cake in the
centre of the oven for 45–50 minutes until it is
browned and is resistant to a very light touch in the
centre.

Meanwhile, make the syrup. Strain the orange

and lemon juice through a sieve into a saucepan and
add the demerara sugar and cinnamon. Dissolve the
sugar in the juices, stirring it over a low heat. Then
increase the heat, boil the syrup briskly for 5 minutes,
remove it from the heat, and leave it on one side to
cool.

When the cake is ready, leave it in the tin for 10
minutes or so; don't worry if it sinks slightly. Loosen
the sides carefully with a knife and turn it out on to a
serving plate. Peel the bananas, slice them thinly and
arrange the slices over the top of the cake. Immediately spoon the cooled syrup all over the bananas.
Keep the cake at room temperature until you want to
serve it.

Serves 6–8

Canary Cake; Spain's Favourite Pudding (page 185)

INDULGENT LAYER CAKE

A perfect party cake, equally suitable as a dessert or as the grand finale to a
birthday celebration. The layers of light, lemony cake are spread with
black cherry jam and then sandwiched together with generous layers of a
lemon cream mousse speckled with dark chocolate.
Almost impossible to resist.

For the cake:
grated rind and juice of
1 large lemon
5 large eggs (size 1–2),
separated

175 g (6 oz) icing sugar
75 g (3 oz) plain flour,
plus extra for dusting
50 g (2 oz) cornflour
½ teaspoon baking powder

For the filling:
15 g (½ oz) gelatine
strained juice of 1 lemon
25 g (1 oz) caster sugar
600 ml (1 pint) whipping
cream

75 g (3 oz) plain chocolate,
grated coarsely
375 g (12 oz) jar of
black cherry conserve

Line the base of a greased, deep, 20 cm (8-inch) cake tin with a disc of greased greaseproof paper and dust with flour. Put the grated lemon rind and juice in a large bowl with the egg yolks and stir together. Sift in the icing sugar and stir again. Then whisk or beat until pale.

Preheat the oven to Gas Mark 4/180°C/350°F. Whisk the egg whites until they stand in soft peaks. Then, using a metal spoon, fold in the egg yolk mixture, a quarter at a time. Sift the flour, cornflour and baking powder together and then sift again into the bowl of egg mixture. Carefully but thoroughly fold with a metal spoon. Pour into the prepared tin and cook in the centre of the oven for 35–40 minutes until the cake is well risen and firm to a light touch in the centre. Cool for a little in the tin. Then loosen the edges with a knife and turn on to a cake rack covered with a folded clean teacloth. When the cake is completely cold cut carefully, using a long sharp knife,

into three or, if possible, four thin layers.

To make the filling, dissolve the gelatine according to the packet instructions. Put the strained lemon juice into a saucepan with the caster sugar and stir over a gentle heat until the sugar is dissolved. Then stir in the dissolved gelatine and remove the pan from the heat. Whip the cream until soft but not stiff. Pour the lemon and gelatine liquid into the cream and fold in. Stir in all but a tablespoon of the grated plain chocolate.

Put the bottom layer of the cake on a serving plate and spread it with black cherry conserve and then with a generous layer of the cream mixture. Continue in this way with the remaining layers, topping the cake with a thick, roughly flicked coating of the cream mixture. Finally, sprinkle with the reserved tablespoon of grated chocolate. Leave in a cool place, but not in the fridge, until ready to eat.

Serves 10–14

EASTER DAFFODIL CAKE

You could have this pretty marbled white and yellow cake either as a pudding to follow the Easter bird or as a teatime treat. The featherlight cake is sandwiched with fresh lemon curd made with the egg yolks and then iced all over with whipped cream. You can decorate it with chocolate nests, eggs, chicks or what you will – the heads of small daffodils look lovely.

For the cake:
65 g (2½ oz) self-raising flour
25 g (1 oz) cornflour
175 g (6 oz) icing sugar

whites of 6 large eggs (size 1–2)
½ teaspoon salt
¾ teaspoon cream of tartar
a few drops of yellow food colour

For the filling and icing:
yolks of 5 eggs
75 g (3 oz) caster sugar
grated rind and juice of 2 lemons

300 ml (½ pint) double or whipping cream

Line two greased, fairly deep, 20 –21 cm (8 – 8½-inch) sandwich tins with discs of greaseproof paper. Sift the flour and cornflour twice into a bowl. Sift the icing sugar into another bowl. Put the egg whites in another large bowl and whisk until just frothy. Then whisk in the salt and cream of tartar and continue whisking until the mixture holds peaks. Heat the oven to Gas Mark 4/180°C/350°F. Using a metal spoon, fold the sifted sugar into the beaten egg whites, a little at a time. Then gently fold in the sifted flours, also a little at a time.

Divide the mixture in half and stir some drops of yellow colouring into one half until you have a light lemon yellow. Spoon some of each batter alternately into the cake tins until all is used. Lightly level the top in each tin but mix the colours as little as possible. Cook in the centre of the oven for 25–35 minutes until well risen and firm to a light touch in the centre. Leave the cakes to cool completely in the tins. Then loosen the edges with a knife and turn out, carefully peeling off the greaseproof paper.

While the cakes are cooking you can make the filling. Put the egg yolks in a double boiler or in a bowl set over a pan of water. Stir in the sugar and grate in the lemon rind. Then stir the lemon juice gradually into the yolks. Cook over gently simmering water, stirring all the time with a wooden spoon, until the mixture is thick enough to coat the back of the spoon. Leave to get quite cold.

To assemble the cake, put it on a serving plate and sandwich with the lemon curd. Then whisk the cream until stiff and spread all over the top and sides with a knife. Decorate and chill in the fridge.
Serves about 10

LEMON, HONEY AND ALMOND CAKE WITH CREAMY LEMON PARFAIT

Here I have put two recipes together, because they merge so wonderfully and make a pudding which suits a dinner party as much as a Sunday lunch. The light almond cake is literally drenched with honey and lemon, producing a sharp sweetness which is one of my favourite tastes. The ice cream echoes the cake with a perfect contrast of creaminess and tangy lemon.

Lemon, honey and almond cake:
125 g (4 oz) butter, plus extra for greasing
150 g (5 oz) caster sugar
3 large eggs (size 1–2), whisked lightly
75 g (3 oz) ground almonds finely grated rind and juice of 2 lemons
40 g (1½ oz) self-raising flour, plus extra for dusting
2 rounded tablespoons honey

Butter a fairly deep 18 cm (7-inch) sandwich tin (I use a heart-shaped tin which makes the cake look really pretty) and line the bottom with a piece of buttered greaseproof paper. Dust the lined tin with flour. Cream the butter and sugar in a bowl until light and fluffy. Add the whisked eggs and ground almonds alternately and whisk well. Whisk in the grated lemon rind. Then fold in the flour with a metal spoon. Turn the mixture into the cake tin and smooth the top.

Heat the oven to Gas Mark 4/180°C/350°F. Bake the cake in the centre of the oven for 50 minutes to an hour, until springy to a light touch in the centre. Remove from the oven but leave the cake in the tin.

Pierce holes through the cake all over with a thin skewer. Strain the lemon juice into a saucepan, add the honey and dissolve over a medium heat. Then boil up fiercely for a minute or two.

Spoon the syrup slowly all over the cake, letting the cake absorb it. Leave in the tin until cold. Then loosen the sides carefully with a knife, turn the cake out gently on to a cloth, remove the greaseproof paper and then turn the cake right side up on to a serving plate. Before serving, I put a flower or two or evergreen leaves, according to the season, on top of the cake and then sprinkle a film of icing sugar all over the cake through a sieve.

Creamy lemon parfait:
2 large egg whites (size 1–2)
½ teaspoon salt
6 tablespoons lemon juice
175 g (6 oz) caster sugar
300 ml (½ pint) double cream

Whisk the egg whites with the salt until they stand in soft peaks. Put the lemon juice and sugar into a saucepan and dissolve over a low heat. Then turn up the heat and boil fiercely for 3 minutes. Pour the syrup immediately on to the egg whites in a thin stream, whisking all the time with an electric whisk.

Continue whisking until meringue-like and cool. In another bowl, whisk the cream until thick but not stiff and fold it into the egg white mixture. Turn into a glass serving bowl and freeze for several hours or overnight.
Serves 6

FRESH APRICOT CHEESECAKE RING

The imported fresh apricots we buy in England, which often seem almost tasteless, can acquire a wonderful flavour when cooked. At the beginning of the season, fresh apricots are often so hard that cooking them is in any case a necessity, so try them in this excellent cheesecake with its fudgy, walnut crust.

For the cheesecake:
oil for greasing
6 tablespoons apricot jam
375 g (12 oz) hard apricots
250 g (8 oz) curd cheese
250 g (8 oz) cream cheese
125 g (4 oz) caster sugar
1 teaspoon vanilla essence
2 large eggs (size 1–2)

For the crust:
125 g (4 oz) walnuts, chopped very finely
50 g (2 oz) butter
50 g (2 oz) soft dark brown sugar

Preheat the oven to Gas Mark 4/180°C/350°F. Lightly oil a 23 cm (9-inch) ring tin. Spread the apricot jam over the bottom of the tin. Cut the apricots in half, remove the stones and slice thinly. Arrange the slices in overlapping layers over the apricot jam in the tin. Put the curd cheese and cream cheese into a bowl and whisk until soft. Whisk in the caster sugar and vanilla essence until smooth. Whisk in the eggs thoroughly, one at a time. Then slowly pour the cheesecake mixture into the tin on top of the apricots. Bake just below the centre of the oven for 30 minutes.

Put the very finely chopped walnuts into a bowl. In a small saucepan, very gently melt the butter with the brown sugar, stir until smooth, but do not allow to boil. Pour into the bowl with the walnuts and mix well with a spoon. Then spoon the mixture lightly and evenly over the top of the cheesecake and leave in the tin to chill.

To turn out, carefully loosen the inner and outer rims of the tin by running around them with a wide knife; then dip just the bottom of the tin into a sink of very hot water to loosen the jam base. Put a serving plate on top of the tin and then turn over and gently shake the cheesecake ring out on to it, spooning over any apricot jam which might get left behind. Chill well in the fridge again before serving.
Serves 6–8

CHEESECAKE CRÉCY

A cheescake made with carrots doesn't sound very appealing, but anyone
who has had the pleasure of tasting carrot cake will be well disposed
towards it. Carrots have a subtly sweet taste, just right for the cheesecake,
and also give it a marvellous colour.
Pictured on page 167.

For the cheesecake:
375 g (12 oz) carrots
125 g (4 oz) plain
wholemeal flour
50 g (2 oz) soft pale
brown sugar

2 teaspoons cinnamon
50 g (2 oz) butter
500 g (1 lb) cream cheese
125 g (4 oz) caster sugar
2 eggs

the yolks of two eggs
25 g (1 oz) cornflour, sifted
½ teaspoon salt
oil for greasing

For the glaze:
50 –125 g (2–4 oz) carrots
juice of 1 large lemon
50 g (2 oz) caster sugar
2 teaspoons gelatine

Preheat the oven to Gas Mark 4/180°C/350°F. Boil
the carrots until soft. Meanwhile, put the flour,
brown sugar and cinnamon into a bowl and mix
together. Melt the butter in a pan and then pour it
into the flour mixture and mix it thoroughly with a
spoon. Turn the mixture into a loose-based 19 cm
(7½-inch) cake tin and press down firmly over the
bottom with a metal spoon, then refrigerate.

When the carrots are cooked, drain and rinse
under cold water to cool. Put them into a food
processor or liquidiser with the cream cheese, caster
sugar, eggs and egg yolks, and whizz until smooth.
(Alternatively, purée the carrots through a sieve and
then mix with the other ingredients.) Quickly whisk
in the sifted cornflour and the salt. Oil the sides of the
cake tin. Pour the cheesecake mixture on to the
chilled pastry base. Cook in the centre of the oven for
50 – 60 minutes – it will have risen slightly, but the
centre will seem rather uncooked. Leave to cool in
the tin and then chill in the fridge. When chilled, push
the cheesecake up out of the tin and, using a wide
spatula, ease it off the base on to a serving plate.

To make the glaze, coarsely grate the carrots
lengthways to make long strands and place in a saucepan. Make the lemon juice up to 300 ml (½ pint) with
water and strain into the saucepan. Add the caster
sugar and bring to the boil gently. Simmer for 5 – 8
minutes. Remove from the heat and sprinkle in the
gelatine. Then return to the heat and stir for another
minute until the gelatine has dissolved. Remove the
carrot shreds with a slotted spoon, leaving the juice in
the pan, and place over the cheesecake. When the
juices have cooled slightly and are not too liquid,
spoon them over the top and sides. Chill again in the
fridge until ready to eat.
Serves 8

ATHENIAN JELLY

This is not a jelly for a children's tea party. It is made from the three ingredients which epitomise a journey through Greece or Turkey: yogurt, honey and ouzo, the potent, aniseed-flavoured drink which turns white when you add water to it. Here they combine subtly to make a translucent white jelly which everyone seems to love. If you can't get ouzo the French Pernod or Ricard or the Turkish raki are all similar.

240 g (8 oz) carton of Greek yogurt
2 good tablespoons clear honey

1½ tablespoons ouzo
250 ml (8 fl oz) double or whipping cream

15 g (½ oz) gelatine
50 ml (2 fl oz) very hot water

ground cinnamon and thin slices of lime or lemon, to garnish

Empty the yogurt into a bowl. Whisk in the honey followed by the ouzo. In another mixing bowl, whisk the cream until thick but not stiff. Sprinkle the gelatine into the hot water and stir until dissolved. Thoroughly whisk the dissolved gelatine into the yogurt mixture and then immediately fold this into the whipped cream with a metal spoon. Turn the whole mixture into a 600 ml (1-pint) metal jelly mould and chill in the fridge until set. To turn out, rub the mould with a hot cloth and turn out onto a serving plate. Sprinkle the top with a little cinnamon and garnish the plate with a few slices of lime or lemon. Keep in the fridge until ready to serve.
Serves 6

NURI BEY'S FRESH LEMON JELLY

This is not jelly as we know it; it can't be turned out of a mould and it certainly doesn't wobble. Instead it is smooth and opaque with a strong, sharp lemon flavour which makes it perfectly refreshing after a rich meal.

150 g (5 oz) granulated sugar
2–3 large sprigs of lemon balm or mint

rind of 2 lemons, peeled off in strips

1 litre (1¾ pints) water
75 g (3 oz) cornflour

juice of 6 lemons
walnut halves, to decorate

Put the sugar, the lemon balm or mint leaves and the lemon peel into the water and boil them up together for 8–10 minutes. Remove the peel and leaves with a slotted spoon. Blend the cornflour with a little cold water to a smooth paste and then stir it into the hot lemon peel water. Bring the water to the boil, stirring all the time, and bubble it for a minute or two until thick. Stir in the juice of 3 lemons and boil for another 2 minutes; then leave it until cold and solid.

Add the juice of the other 3 lemons and whizz everything up in a food processor until smooth, or rub it through a sieve. Pour the jelly into a glass or china bowl and chill it well in the fridge overnight. Then decorate the top with walnut halves, and serve with creamed smetana or cream.
Serves 6–8

A PUDDING FOR PARVATI

Would this be fit for the Hindu goddess Parvati? I hope so. It has
characteristics drawn from the many different types of Indian sweetmeats,
being milky, scented and intriguingly textured, but not so intensely sweet.
I am afraid that I have a very sweet tooth and I always return fatter, rather
than thinner, after a visit to India. I do think that a little sharpness
combines with sweetness to make an even better taste, though,
which is why I often add lemon juice to eastern-style puddings.

2 tablespoons caster sugar
75 g (3 oz) flaked almonds
1 teaspoon ground cardamom

125 g (4 oz) semolina
6 tablespoons powdered milk

900 ml (1½ pints) milk
175 g (6 oz) demerara
sugar

125 g (4 oz) carrots, grated
juice of 1 lemon, strained
1 tablespoon rose-water

Sprinkle the caster sugar evenly over the bottom of a 1.2 litre (2-pint) capacity shallow mould or flan dish. Then sprinkle 50 g (2 oz) of the flaked almonds over the sugar. Heat a heavy-based saucepan over a medium heat, add the ground cardamom and stir for a moment or two to roast it. Remove the pan from the heat and after a minute or two add the semolina and powdered milk. Pour in 150 ml (¼ pint) milk and stir to mix smoothly. Then add the demerara sugar and gradually stir in the remaining 750 ml (1¼ pints) of milk. Now add the grated carrots. Put the pan back over a medium heat and bring to the boil, stirring all the time. Lower the heat and bubble, stirring con-

stantly, for 10–12 minutes, until very thick. Then remove from the heat and gradually stir in the lemon juice and rose-water. Mix in the remaining 25 g (1 oz) flaked almonds and carefully pour the mixture into the prepared mould or flan dish. Leave to cool and then chill until thoroughly cold in the fridge for several hours.

To turn out, loosen the edges with your fingers and then turn on to a serving plate, giving a good shake. Now put the cake under a medium grill until it is darkly speckled on top. Chill again in the fridge before serving it cut into pieces.
Serves 8

PASSION-FRUIT THRILL

Pictured on pages 6/7.

8 passion-fruit
unsweetened orange juice

juice of 2 lemons
175 g (6 oz) caster sugar

2 sachets or 25 g (1 oz)
gelatine

500 g (1 lb) carton of 8%
fat fromage frais

Using a sharp knife, cut open the passion-fruit one at a time and scoop out the contents into a sieve over a measuring jug. Rub as much juice as possible – this will take a little time and thorough rubbing – into the jug, leaving the seeds in the sieve. Then bring the juices up to 250 ml (8 fl oz) with unsweetened orange juice, and pour into a small saucepan. Strain the lemon juice into the saucepan. Add the caster sugar to the juices and put the saucepan over a gentle heat, stirring until the sugar has dissolved.

Then sprinkle in the gelatine and continue stirring over a gentle heat until the gelatine has dissolved

completely – this may take several minutes. Turn the fromage frais into a bowl. When the gelatine has dissolved, add the juices gradually to the fromage frais, stirring all the time. Then stir in about half the black pips from the sieve and pour into a 1.2–1.5 litre (2–2½ pint) aluminium mould.

Refrigerate for several hours. To unmould, loosen the edges gently with your fingers and then dip the mould briefly in a sink of hot water until the pudding turns out when you give it a good shake against a serving plate.
Serves 6–8

Sweet Rice Balls in Scented Cream (page 221); A Pudding for Parvati

PAGODA JELLY

I have still to travel in China, but excellent Chinese food can be found all
over the world so that it is impossible not to be influenced by it. It was
when I was first married and lived in New York that I realised how much
more there was to Chinese food than the occasional glutinous chop suey
I had tasted as a child. The only thing which always disappoints me is the
lack of variety of sweets to end the meal. Banana and apple fritters can be
delicious and lychees are one fruit which are very good canned, but I
always feel that restaurants chefs should do something more imaginative
with them than so obviously emptying a can into a bowl. Since the
following recipe is made with milk products which the Chinese do not
use, no Chinese restaurant is likely to take it up. But for those of us who
can mix our cuisines it is a delicate, white, jellied mousse which has a
creamy orangey yogurt base and is dotted with succulent, scented lychees.

425 (14 oz) can of lychees   *juice of 1 lemon*   *8 teaspoons gelatine*   *240 g (8 oz) of Greek*
juice of 3 oranges   *50 g (2 oz) caster sugar*   *300 ml (1/2 pint) creamed*   *yogurt*
                                                    smetana or soured cream

Drain the juices from the lychees into a saucepan and
leave the lychees on one side. Add the orange and
lemon juice and the caster sugar to the saucepan. Heat
the juices, sprinkle the gelatine and stir over a gentle
heat until it is dissolved. Then pour into a mixing
bowl and leave until cold and just beginning to set.

Stir the mixture round and then stir in the
creamed smetana or soured cream and the yogurt.

Add the reserved lychees and pour into a 1.2 litre
(2-pint) metal bombe or jelly mould. Chill in the
fridge for several hours or overnight until firmly set.

Dip the mould momentarily in a sink of very hot
water and turn it out with a shake on to a serving plate
(a dark coloured plate looks most effective with the
white jelly).
Serves 6–8

WINTER RASPBERRIES

In the middle of winter this luscious dessert is a luxurious echo of
summer. It is so easy to make that it almost feels like cheating, and it can
be made well ahead for a party. Serve it with light, thin biscuits.

1 packet of raspberry or   *2 tablespoons caster sugar*   *300 ml (1/2 pint) double*   *500 g (1 lb) frozen,*
strawberry jelly   *150 ml (5 fl oz) carton of*   *or whipping cream*   *unsweetened raspberries*
300 ml (1/2 pint) boiling   *soured cream*   *1 tablespoon lemon juice*   *chopped nuts or flaked*
water   *chocolate, to decorate*

Break up the jelly into a bowl. Pour over the boiling
water and stir until dissolved. Stir in the caster sugar,
add the soured cream and whisk until smooth. Whisk
the double cream until thick but not stiff and then
whisk gently into the jelly mixture. Whisk in the
lemon juice, a little at a time. Empty in the frozen

raspberries straight from the freezer and separate with
a fork until there is no piece bigger than a single fruit
left. (Stirring the raspberries in while they are still
frozen helps to set the mixture as you do it and so
prevents the fruit from sinking to the bottom of the
cream.)

Pour the mixture into a pretty serving bowl or individual glasses and put at once in the bottom of the fridge for 2–3 hours, or longer if possible. Decorate the top of the mousse with chopped nuts or flaked chocolate.
Serves 8

ALMOND DREAMS WITH LYCHEES

Wonderfully refreshing after a rich meal, this is an easy-to-make Chinese dessert. Almond Dreams are translucent white, softly jellied squares with a delicate flavour of almond. They look strange and beautiful in a bowl, topped with scented lychees under a glossy syrup. (If you dislike the flavour of almond omit the essence and add 1 tablespoon strong rose water to the liquid before cooling.)

2 x 15 g (½ oz) sachet of gelatine
600 ml (1 pint) plus 4 tablespoons water

450 ml (¾ pint) milk
3 tablespoons sugar
½ teaspoon almond essence

2 x 275 g (9 oz) can of lychees

For the syrup:
125 g (4 oz) sugar
1 tablespoon lemon juice

Lightly oil a cake tin or roasting pan about 23 cm x 23 cm (9 inches x 9 inches) large. Put the gelatine into a bowl with 4 tablespoons water and put the bowl over a saucepan of very hot water. Stir until dissolved.

In another saucepan heat 600 ml (1 pint) water with the milk, the sugar and the almond essence. Stir until the sugar is dissolved, and then stir in the dissolved gelatine. Pour into the cake tin, leave to cool and then chill in the fridge until set.

Meanwhile strain the juice from the tins of lychees into a saucepan and add the sugar and lemon juice. Put over the heat, stir until the sugar is dissolved, then bring to the boil and boil fiercely without stirring for 5 minutes.

When the almond mixture is set loosen the edges with a sharp knife and cut the jelly into 2.5 cm (1-inch) squares. Turn out carefully into a pretty glass bowl, arranging some of the squares up the sides of the bowl to make a depression in the middle. Shortly before serving spoon the lychees into the middle and spoon over the syrup. Chill until ready to serve.
Serves 6

LEMON SPICE AND STRAWBERRY DELIGHT

This is a delicious dessert. Underneath a topping of fresh strawberries (or you can use raspberries) there is a light, mousse-like lemon layer over a tangy custard. Try to make it in a glass ovenproof dish so that you can see the three layers. When soft fruit is out of season you can simply serve it on its own or sprinkle grated chocolate on top, whilst on cold days it is wonderful served hot with a chocolate sauce or cream.

50 g (2 oz) butter, plus extra for greasing
250 g (8 oz) caster sugar
juice and grated rind of 2 small lemons
4 eggs, separated
50 g (2 oz) self-raising flour
1/4 whole nutmeg grated, or 1/4 teaspoon ground nutmeg
250 ml (8 fl oz) milk
1/2 teaspoon cream of tartar
375 g (12 oz) small fresh strawberries
icing sugar

Butter a 1.5 –1.75 litre (2½–3 pint) ovenproof dish. Put a roasting pan half full of water in the centre of the oven and preheat to Gas Mark 4/180°C/350°F.

Cream the butter until soft, add the caster sugar and beat until fluffy. Beat in the lemon juice and rind and then the egg yolks. Sift the flour and nutmeg together and stir in. Gradually stir in the milk and beat or whisk the mixture thoroughly until very smooth.

Add the cream of tartar to the egg whites and whisk until standing in soft peaks. Fold gently into the lemon mixture with a metal spoon.

Pour into the dish, put this into the pan of water in the oven and bake for 35–40 minutes, until golden brown on top. Leave to cool and then arrange the strawberries on top. Serve with cream if you like. **Serves 6**

BANANA AND WHITE CHOCOLATE MOUSSE

You might think that a mixture of banana and white chocolate would taste cloying. In fact this light mousse, which has added lemon juice, honey and yogurt, melts in the mouth and some people find it so irresistible that they ask for third and fourth helpings. Children, who always seem to like bananas, really love it. I once made the mousse, which is enough for six to eight people, and left it in the fridge when I went out. On my return, two of my children had almost finished the whole mousse between them!

3 medium to large eggs (size 2–3), separated
150 ml (1/4 pint) milk
175 g (3 oz) white chocolate, grated
15 g (1/2 oz) gelatine
3 tablespoons water
4 medium-size bananas, preferably slightly under-ripe ones
juice of 1 lemon
1 tablespoon clear honey
1 rounded tablespoon natural yogurt
toasted nuts and slices of banana dipped in lemon juice to garnish

Put the egg yolks in the top of a double boiler or a bowl set over a pan of water. Add the milk and whisk together to amalgamate. Then put over a gentle heat and stir for about 4 minutes until thickened and creamy. Stir in the grated white chocolate. Dissolve the gelatine in the water over a gentle heat and then stir into the egg yolk mixture. Next peel and break up the bananas, put them into a food processor with the lemon juice and honey, and whizz until completely smooth. Whizz the egg yolk mixture into this banana purée, adding the yogurt, and turn into a mixing bowl.

Add a generous pinch of salt to the egg whites and whisk until they form soft peaks. Using a metal spoon, fold the egg whites into the banana mixture and pour into a 900 ml –1.2 litre (1½ –2 pint) metal jelly mould. Chill in the fridge until set. Then rub the outside of the mould with a hot cloth, pull back the edges of the mousse with your fingers to loosen and turn out onto a serving plate. Decorate the mousse with toasted nuts and banana slices, rubbed with lemon juice to keep them pale. Refrigerate again until ready to serve.

Serves 6–8

CHOCOLATE RUM MARQUISE

I feel sure that few people could resist this luxurious chocolate delicacy. It is a great favourite in our family, as it was inspired by a dish which the patron of a small hotel in France urged us to have one particularly memorable summer. When frozen, it makes a heavenly ice cream.
Pictured on the back cover.

25 sponge fingers
75 g (3 oz) granulated sugar
6 tablespoons dark rum

2 tablespoons water
125 g (4 oz) bitter chocolate
1 tablespoon top of the milk

15 g (½ oz) gelatine
2 tablespoons hot water
3 medium to large eggs
(size 2–3), separated

25 g (1 oz) caster sugar
175 ml (6 fl oz) double
cream

Put the sponge fingers in one layer in a shallow dish or tin. Dissolve the granulated sugar in the rum and water over a low heat. Allow to bubble for just a second or two but do not increase the heat. Then spoon the hot syrup over the sponge fingers. Leave them for 30 minutes or more to absorb the syrup, turning once. Line the bottom of a 1 kg (2 lb) loaf tin with a piece of greaseproof paper. Cover the bottom and sides of the loaf tin with the sponge fingers, cutting them off neatly at the top of the tin and using the bits to fill in any gaps. Melt the chocolate gently with the top of the milk. Dissolve the gelatine in the hot water and stir into the melted chocolate. Whisk the egg yolks with the caster sugar until pale and thick. Whisk in the chocolate while still warm. Whisk the cream until thick but not too stiff and fold gently into the chocolate and cream mixture. Whisk the egg whites till they form soft peaks and fold in. Spoon into the sponge-lined tin, smooth the top and chill for several hours.

Slip a knife carefully down the sides to loosen, and turn out onto a serving dish. Keep it in the fridge until ready to eat, then cut across into fairly thick slices.

Serves 6–8

PASSION-FRUIT AND HONEY SOUFFLÉ

3 rounded tablespoons clear or set honey

juice of 2 large lemons
11 g (1/3 oz) sachet or 3 teaspoons gelatine

4 large eggs (size 1–2)
6 passion-fruit

a pinch of salt

Put the honey in a small saucepan with the lemon juice and heat it gently. When the honey has melted, sprinkle in the gelatine and stir over the lowest heat (you mustn't let the mixture boil) until the gelatine has dissolved. Remove the pan from the heat and put it on one side. Separate the eggs, putting the whites in a large bowl and the yolks in the top of a double saucepan or a bowl. Using a wooden spoon, whisk the honey and lemon mixture briskly into the egg yolks and put over the saucepan base or a pan of barely simmering water. Continue stirring all the time for 5 minutes until the mixture has thickened slightly; then remove the pan from the heat and put a small sieve over it. Cut open five of the six passion-fruit and scoop the flesh into the sieve with a teaspoon. Rub

the flesh through the sieve with a small spoon until you have got as much juice and flesh as possible out of the seeds. Stir into the honey and egg mixture. Then spoon in the remaining passion-fruit, with its seeds, and stir thoroughly. Pour into a mixing bowl and allow to cool slightly.

Now add the salt to the egg whites and whisk until they hold soft peaks. Gently but thoroughly fold them into the egg yolk mixture with a metal spoon. Pour the mixture into a serving bowl or individual dishes. Scatter some of the sieved-out passion-fruit seeds on top and refrigerate until set, about 2 hours.

Note: it is easier to measure the honey accurately if you warm the measuring spoon.
Serves 6–7

NEW YEAR'S RESOLUTION

Here is a luscious dessert, with a wonderfully delicate flavour and texture.
As it can be made a day or two in advance it gives you more time for a
long lie-in after the previous night's celebrations.

3 large eggs (size 1–2), separated

125 g (4 oz) caster sugar, plus a little extra for decoration

300 g (11 oz) can of lychees
juice of 1 fresh lime (or small lemon)

4 teaspoons gelatine
4 kiwifruit
300 ml (1/2 pint) double cream

Put the yolks of the eggs (setting aside the whites in a large bowl) in the top of a double saucepan, or in a bowl set over a pan of gently simmering water. Add the caster sugar, the juice from the lychees and the lime or lemon juice. Sprinkle in the gelatine and whisk all together thoroughly. Stir for 10 minutes until slightly thickened and then put the bowl in a sink of cold water to cool the mixture.

Meanwhile, peel the kiwifruit. Cut two of them into largish chunks and the remaining two into thin circles. When the juice and yolk mixture is almost

cold whisk the cream until thick but not stiff and then whisk it into the mixture. Stir in the lychees and the chunks of kiwifruit. Whisk the reserved egg whites until they stand in soft peaks and fold gently into the mixture with a metal spoon. Pour into a serving bowl, preferably a glass one, and arrange the slices of kiwifruit in an overlapping circular pattern on the top. Chill well in the fridge until set. Just before serving, sprinkle a little more caster sugar over the kiwifruit. Serve with cream if you wish.
Serves 6 – 8

SPAIN'S FAVOURITE PUDDING

'Flan' means simply crème caramel or caramel custard, and for some odd reason it seems to be an unofficial national pudding in Spain. Made well from fresh eggs and creamy milk it can be exquisite, and I make it in this recipe with a fresh orange-flavoured caramel, and lemon-tinged custard. If you are planning to make a batch of meringues later, add a third egg yolk to the pudding for luxurious creaminess. I have never known a pudding slip down quite so swiftly.

Pictured on page 171.

125 g (4 oz) granulated sugar
150 ml (¼ pint) fresh orange juice

finely grated rind and juice of 1 lemon

3 large eggs (size 1–2)
2 egg yolks

50 g (2 oz) caster sugar
600 ml (1 pint) milk

Preheat the oven to Gas Mark 3/160°C/325°F, placing a deep roasting pan of hot water in the centre. Put the granulated sugar into a saucepan and strain in the orange and lemon juices. Dissolve the sugar in the juices, stirring it over a low heat. Then increase the heat, bring the syrup to the boil and boil it fiercely, still stirring now and then, until the syrup has thickened and turned a rich golden colour; this usually takes about 5 minutes. Remove the pan from the heat at the first hint of brown and pour the syrup into a 1.2-litre (2-pint) ovenproof soufflé dish, or into individual moulds.

Put the eggs and egg yolks in a bowl with the caster sugar and whisk them together thoroughly; then whisk in the reserved lemon rind. Warm the milk in a saucepan and whisk the warm milk lightly into the eggs. Then pour the milk mixture gently on to the caramel and put the dish or moulds into the roasting pan of water. Cook for 1–1¼ hours, when the custard should be just set and firm to touch in the centre. It shouldn't be solid but should wobble a little.

Remove the dish or moulds from the oven and let them cool; then cover them with cling film and refrigerate until you are ready to eat them. Just before eating, turn out on to a serving dish or dishes.

Serves 4

ORANGE AND ALMOND TART

This tart can be made well in advance, frozen, and then re-heated
before serving.

For the pastry:
250 g (8 oz) plain flour
3 tablespoons caster sugar
150 g (5 oz) butter, plus
extra for greasing

1 tablespoon water

For the filling:
1 medium-size,
thin-skinned orange

½ small thin-skinned
lemon
4 tablespoons double cream
1 large egg (size 1–2)
75 g (3 oz) caster sugar

½ teaspoon ground cloves
50 g (2 oz) ground almonds
50 –75 g (2–3 oz) whole
blanched almonds
icing sugar

Lightly butter a 24 cm (9½-inch), loose-based, aluminium, fluted flan tin. To make the pastry, sift the flour into a bowl. Stir in the caster sugar. Gently melt the butter with the water in a saucepan. Then pour it slowly into the flour mixing it in thoroughly with a wooden spoon to form a dough. Now take up pieces of the warm dough and press as evenly as possible over the base and up the sides of the flan tin. Refrigerate while you prepare the flan filling.

Cut the orange into quarters and pick out any pips. Cut the half lemon in half and again extract any pips. Put the orange and lemon pieces into a food processor with the cream, the egg, the caster sugar and the ground cloves. Whizz thoroughly to a mush.

Then briefly whizz in the ground almonds. Heat the oven to Gas Mark 4/180°C/350°F. Spread the fairly thick filling mixture evenly into the chilled pastry case. Carefully lay lines of blanched almonds fanning out from the centre of the tart in a fairly close 'star-burst' pattern. Bake in the centre of the oven for 35 – 40 minutes until browned and evenly risen, turning the tart round once or twice so that the pastry edges brown evenly.

Leave the tart in the tin for 8–10 minutes; then push it out and slide it carefully off the base of the tin on to a serving plate. Serve warm with cream or brandy butter. Sift some icing sugar over the top.
Serves 8

LYCHEE LIME RING

I like this pudding best served warm but it can be eaten cold if more
convenient. I usually mix a 150 ml (5 fl oz) carton of double cream with
the reserved lychee juices and use this as
a sauce to serve with the ring.

oil for greasing
425 g (14 oz) can of
lychees

2 small limes or 1 lemon
75 g (3 oz) unsalted butter
3 eggs, separated

3 tablespoons lime
marmalade
75 g (3 oz) caster sugar

125 g (4 oz) self-raising
flour, sifted
a pinch of salt

Oil a 1.2–1.5 (2–2½-pint) ring mould tin. Strain the juice from the lychees and leave it on one side. Cut the drained lychees in half and spread them over the bottom of the ring mould. Grate the lime or lemon rind and squeeze the juice and put both on one side. Gently melt the butter in a small pan and remove from the heat. Preheat the oven to Gas Mark 4/180°C/350°F. Put the egg yolks into a bowl with the lime marmalade and caster sugar and whisk thoroughly until pale and thick. Whisk in the melted

butter. Gradually whisk in the lime juice. Stir in the reserved, grated lime rind and the sifted flour with a metal spoon. Add a pinch of salt to the egg whites and whisk until you have soft peaks. Fold gently but thoroughly into the egg-yolk mixture and then spoon into the ring mould. Cook in the centre of the oven for 35– 40 minutes. Now loosen the outer and inner edges of the mould with a knife and turn out onto a serving plate.
Serves 6–8

Orange and Almond Tart

PROVENCAL PRUNE TART

One summer, we spent a perfect holiday on a farmhouse set amongst the
theatrical-looking rocky Alpilles in Provence. It was my annual break
from cooking, so we tried out all the surrounding family restaurants. On
our last night, however, we treated ourselves to a less modest
establishment and finished the meal with a wonderful Tarte aux Pruneaux
which was simply a few prunes scattered between thin, crisp layers of the
flakiest pastry. I tried to imitate it when we got home and found that I
achieved a rather amazing result very easily by using
ready-made puff pastry.
Pictured on page 191.

*250 g (8 oz) packet puff
pastry, fresh or frozen and
thawed*

flour for rolling

*15 g (1/2 oz) soft butter or
margarine, plus extra for
greasing*

*2 1/2 teaspoons caster sugar
125 g (4 oz) soft pitted
prunes*

Cut the pastry in half and form the halves into balls.
Roll them out thinly on a floured surface into two
roughly circular shapes about 25–28 cm (10 –11
inches) in diameter. Smear one circle all over with the
butter or margarine and sprinkle it evenly with 2
tablespoons of caster sugar, through a sieve. Cut the
soft prunes in half crossways and flatten them slightly
with your fingers. Arrange them on the butter and
sugar, spaced apart and leaving about 2 cm (3/4 inch)
around the edge. Lay the second circle of pastry on
top and roll over the edges all round to seal them.
Place carefully on a large, buttered, flat tin plate or
baking sheet. Rest the tart in the fridge for 30 minutes

or more, and, meanwhile, preheat the oven to Gas
Mark 7/220°C/425°F.

Brush the top of the tart lightly with cold water
and sprinkle the remaining caster sugar evenly all over
it through a sieve. Bake the tart towards the top of the
oven for 15–20 minutes until it is blackened on top.

Note: a good substitute for the French *crème fraîche*
to serve with this tart is 150 ml (5 fl oz) carton of
double cream, whipped until it is thick but not stiff,
with 4 tablespoons of natural yogurt then folded into
it. Another alternative would be natural fromage
frais.
Serves 6

FILO APPLE PIE

This is a bit like apple strudel, only formed into a crispy round pie. It can
be made ahead and then re-heated. The apples are buttery and spicy, with
a tang of orange and lemon peel. It is an ideal pudding for an autumn or
winter dinner or lunch party. Serve it with cream.

*1 kg (2 lb) cooking apples
175 g (6 oz) unsalted
butter
2 teaspoons ground
cinnamon*

*125 g (4 oz) demerara sugar
rind of 1 lemon and 2
oranges, grated coarsely*

*125 g (4 oz) sultanas
40 g (1 1/2 oz) walnuts,
chopped*

*40 g (1 1/2 oz) hazelnuts,
chopped
1 packet of filo pastry
icing sugar*

Peel half of the apples and slice finely, discarding the
core. Melt one-third of the butter in a large frying
pan. Add the apple slices and stir around over a

medium heat for about 4 –5 minutes until the slices
are just softening but not falling to bits. Then stir in 1
teaspoon of the cinnamon until it coats the slices and

turn the apples and the butter into a mixing bowl.

Now peel and slice the remaining apples, melt another one-third of the butter in the pan, add the apple slices and cook as before, adding the remaining teaspoon of cinnamon. Turn into the bowl with the other apples and butter and stir in the demerara sugar, the grated lemon and orange rinds, the sultanas and the nuts. Leave to cool.

When cool – they don't have to be completely cold – melt the remaining butter in a saucepan. Brush a large, ovenproof plate or pizza pan, 28–30 cm (11–12 inches) in diameter, with butter. Lay on a sheet of filo pastry, leaving it overlapping the edges of the plate, brush with butter, and then lay on another sheet the other way across. Then spread on a thin layer of the apple mixture, including a little of the buttery juices. Top this with another 2 layers of filo pastry, brushed with butter in between each. Follow with another layer of apples, and so on in layers, until you finish the apple mixture – none of this has to be done at all neatly.

Next, bring the overlapping pastry in over the apple mixture, pressing the pastry down and brushing it with butter. Put the remaining pastry in buttered layers on top, pressing it in under the sides of the pie. Brush the top with the rest of the butter.

Heat the oven to Gas Mark 4/180°C/350°F. Cook the pie just above the centre shelf for 45–50 minutes until it is a rich golden brown. Just before serving, sprinkle a little icing sugar through a fine sieve on top of the pie.

Serves 10

APPLE, CRANBERRY AND RICH CHOCOLATE PUDDING

This layered pudding is wonderful for a winter party. The intense dark chocolate top is surprisingly light, and the apples and cranberries beneath contrast with a fresh sharpness. I think it is best eaten hot, but if you like, you can eat it cold, sprinkling the top with a little icing sugar through a sieve.

juice of 2 lemons
750 g (1½ lb) dessert apples
125 g (4 oz) demerara sugar

ground cinnamon, to sprinkle
250 g (8 oz) fresh cranberries

300 g (10 oz) plain chocolate, broken up
4 medium – large eggs (size 2–3), separated

125 g (4 oz) caster sugar
2 tablespoons warm water
2 generous pinches of salt

Squeeze the lemon juice into a small jug. Wash the apples but leave unpeeled. Cut them in half and then cut into thin half-moon slices, discarding the cores. Put a layer of apple slices on the bottom of a 2.5 – 2.75-litres (4½–5 pint) ovenproof dish – heatproof glass looks best, as you can see the layers.

Sprinkle the apples with a little lemon juice, then with a little of the demerara sugar, then with a light sprinkling of ground cinnamon and finally with some of the cranberries, arranging them at the edge here and there as well as in the centre. Now start with a layer of apples again and continue on these layers until all the ingredients are used up. Cover the dish with foil, piercing two holes on top to allow steam to escape.

Heat the oven to Gas Mark 4/180°C/350°F. Put the dish in the centre of the oven for 1 hour until the apples are soft. Towards the end of the cooking time, start preparing the chocolate top. Put the chocolate in the top of a double boiler, or a bowl set over a saucepan of hot but not boiling water. Stir until the chocolate has melted, and put on one side.

Put the yolks of the eggs in one large mixing bowl and the egg whites in another. Add the caster sugar to the egg yolks and whisk until pale. Now whisk in the melted chocolate followed by the warm water. Add the salt to the egg whites and whisk until they hold soft peaks. Using a metal spoon fold the whisked whites into the chocolate mixture a little at a time. Then pour on top of the cooked apples, and return to the centre of the oven for 15–20 minutes until the chocolate has risen and is beginning to crack. Eat hot if possible, with cream.

Serves 8–10

TARTE A L'ORANGE

Few things could be more pleasant during the summer than sitting on a
terrace in Provence in the dappled shade of an old fig tree, ending a
perfect lunch with a slice of Tarte à L'Orange. This peaceful memory is
what prompted me to repeat the tarte as I remembered it. Tarte au Citron
had long been a favourite and I had never imagined that a tart made from
oranges could be quite so good. But both tarts, with their crisp biscuit-like
pastry case, light and creamy centre and tangy slices of fruit on top,
seemed to me to be equally good.

For the pastry:
250 g (8 oz) plain flour,
plus extra for rolling
50 g (2 oz) caster sugar
½ teaspoon salt

125 g (4 oz) unsalted
butter, plus extra for
greasing
1 large egg (size 1–2),
whisked

For the filling:
5 oranges
a little milk
2 egg yolks

1 large egg (size 1–2)
75 g (3 oz) plus 1
tablespoon caster sugar
salt

To make the pastry, sift the flour, the caster sugar and
the salt into a bowl. Cut the butter into small pieces
and rub it into the flour with your fingertips until the
mixture is the texture of breadcrumbs. Then stir in
the whisked egg with a fork. Press the mixture with
your hands until it sticks together in a piece; then cut
it into four and press it together again with your
hands. Repeat this three more times, and then press
the dough into a ball, cover it with cling film and leave
it to rest in the fridge for an hour or more. Then
preheat the oven to Gas Mark 8/230°C/450°F.

Butter a 24–25 cm (9½–10-inch) loose-based,
fluted, aluminium flan tin. Take the pastry from the
fridge and knead it briefly before rolling it out on a
floured surface into a piece big enough to line the flan
tin; if the pastry breaks up, just press it together again.
Roll the piece of pastry back over the rolling pin and
lift it on to the flan tin. Fold the edges back in to make
a double thickness of pastry round the sides, pushing
it a little above the top of the flan tin, and evening up
the edges with pieces of pastry if necessary. Prick the
base lightly all over with a fork. Lay a sheet of foil over
the pastry and put a layer of dried beans or rice all over
the base. Make sure that the foil comes up over the
edges of the pastry to stop them getting too brown
during the cooking. Bake the pastry case blind in the
centre of the oven for 25 minutes, turning the flan
round once during the cooking.

Meanwhile, prepare the filling. Finely grate the
zest of 1 orange and put it into a pouring saucepan.
Put the juice of 2 oranges into a measuring jug and
make it up to 150 ml (¼ pint) with milk. Pour this
on to the grated zest. In a mixing bowl, lightly whisk
the egg yolks and the whole egg with the 75 g (3 oz)
caster sugar and a little salt. Bring the orange juice and
milk to the boil, let it bubble for a minute and then
pour the boiling liquid on to the eggs in a steady
stream, whisking all the time.

When the pastry case is ready, turn the oven
down to Gas Mark 4/180°C/350°F and pour the egg
and orange mixture into the cooked pastry case. Put
it back in the oven for 15–20 minutes, until just set.
With a sharp knife slice the remaining 3 unpeeled
oranges across in the thinnest possible slices, removing any pips. Blanch the slices in a saucepan of boiling
water for 1 minute, and then drain and pat them dry
with kitchen paper. Arrange the orange slices on top
of the tart, bringing them right over the edges of the
pastry. Heat the grill to its highest heat. Sprinkle the
tablespoon of caster sugar evenly over the oranges and
put the tart briefly under the grill quite near the heat,
until the oranges have browned in patches. Push the
tart out of the flan tin and slide it carefully off the base
on to a serving plate. Eat it hot or cold, but not chilled,
to get the best flavour.

Serves 6

Tarte à l'Orange; Provençal Prune Tart (page 188)

CHOCOLATE LOVERS' TART

At a buffet party I have always noticed that if there are several different puddings on the table, anything chocolaty will disappear first. This is the darkest, most intensely chocolaty of tarts, but it is so rich and intense you should cut it in thin slices. For a summer party, a bowl of raspberries makes a good accompaniment.

For the pastry:
butter for greasing
125 g (4 oz) plain flour
50 g (2 oz) cocoa powder
75 g (3 oz) icing sugar
½ teaspoon salt

75 g (3 oz) unsalted butter
1 tablespoon water

For the filling:
165–175 g (5½–6 oz)
plain chocolate, broken up

3 medium–large eggs
(size 2–3), separated
125 g (4 oz) soft, light
brown sugar
4 tablespoons warm water
½ teaspoon salt

300 ml (½ pint) creamed
smetana, or Greek yogurt
a little grated or curled
chocolate (optional), to
decorate

Butter a 28 cm (11-inch) diameter fluted metal flan tin with a loose base. To make the case, sift the flour, cocoa powder, icing sugar and salt into a mixing bowl. Stir to mix well. Melt the butter gently in a small saucepan with the water. Then pour gradually into the flour and cocoa mixture, stirring with a wooden spoon, and then kneading briefly to form a dough.

Put the dough into the flan tin and press pieces of it out firmly, until both the base and the sides of the tin are evenly lined. Prick all over with a fork and refrigerate for half an hour or more. Heat the oven to Gas Mark 6/200°C/400°F. Cook on the centre shelf for 10 minutes. Remove from the oven, turn down the heat to Gas Mark 4/180°C/350°F and leave the tart on one side while you prepare the filling.

Put the chocolate in a bowl over hot but not boiling water until it is melted, stirring now and then. Put the yolks of the eggs in the bowl of an electric mixer and the whites in another large bowl. Add the brown sugar to the yolks and whisk thoroughly until light and fluffy. Then whisk in the melted chocolate followed by the warm water.

Add the salt to the egg whites and whisk until they form soft peaks. Fold the egg white gently but throughly into the chocolate with a metal spoon. Then pour the mixture into the lined flan tin and cook on the centre shelf of the oven for 12–15 minutes just until it has evenly risen and looks dry all over the top – don't prod it with your fingers as it has a very delicate crust. Leave in the tin until cold or almost cold.

Then push it up out of the loose-based tin, pass a spatula gently underneath all round to loosen, and then push carefully on to a large serving plate. Shortly before serving, spread the smetana or yogurt evenly over the top of the flan right to the edges of the crust. If you like, put a little grated chocolate in the centre of the flan to decorate.

Serves 12–14

THE MOUSE'S PICNIC

The odd title for this unusual pear tart came about because the first time I produced it my brother thought the pears looked like a circle of little mice nibbling away. They certainly did when he gave them currant eyes and string tails! Even without such elaboration it is an attractive and delicious tart – a rich, crisp base iced with dark chocolate, with a centre of creamed smetana around which the pears sit. Smetana is cultured milk with a wonderful flavour, rich but refreshing, and it is surprisingly inexpensive. However, if you can't get it you can use Greek yogurt or whole milk natural yogurt instead.

1 kg (2 lb) firm, fairly small pears
250 g (8 oz) self-raising flour
125 g (4 oz) icing sugar
½ teaspoon salt
150 g (5 oz) unsalted butter
4 tablespoons water
50 g (2 oz) caster sugar
75 g (3 oz) plain chocolate, broken into pieces
clear honey, for glazing
300 ml (½ pint) creamed smetana
demerara sugar

Preheat the oven to Gas Mark 4/180°C/350°F. Peel the pears and cut off the stalks. Cut in half lengthways and cut out the core with a sharp knife. Put the pears in a single layer on a roasting pan and pour in about 900 ml (1½ pints) water. Cover the pan with foil and cook the pears in the centre of the oven for about 50 minutes until they are tender when you insert a knife.

Meanwhile, sift the flour, icing sugar and salt into a bowl. Gently melt the butter with 1 tablespoon of the water in a saucepan and then pour gradually into the flour, mixing it in with a wooden spoon. Press the mixture together and then press it fairly thinly all over a large, well-buttered ovenproof plate (either round, 27–30 cm /11–12 inches in diameter or oval, 32–35 cm /13–14 inches in length). It doesn't matter if the edges are uneven. Prick the pastry all over with a fork and leave on one side until the pears are cooked.

When the pears are done, allow to cool, then drain and dry them with an absorbent cloth. Turn the oven up to Gas Mark 6/200°C/400°F and cook the pastry in the centre for 15–20 minutes until brown. Now dissolve the caster sugar in 2 tablespoons of the water in a saucepan over a gentle heat. Bring to the boil and boil fiercely for 1 minute. Remove from the heat, let the bubbles subside, allow to cool for 1–2 minutes and stir in another tablespoon of the water. Then add the broken chocolate, return to a low heat and stir until smooth. Spread the chocolate all over the pastry right to the edge. Now arrange the pears neatly all round the outer edge of the pastry and leave until the chocolate is cold. Not long before serving, brush the pears thinly with clear honey, spoon the smetana into the centre of the tart and sprinkle demerara sugar lightly over the smetana and the pears. Serve at room temperature.

Serves 8–10

DAMSON DREAM

I love intensely flavoured, sharp fruits like damsons, blackcurrants and dried apricots. But damson stones are a nuisance, so it is a good idea to rub the cooked fruit through a sieve to make a purée. This two-layered pudding has a damson base and a topping like a very light lemon sponge. It can be eaten hot or cold, with cream, according to your mood or the type of meal. It makes an ideal dessert for an informal party. As the pudding has two distinct layers, it looks more exciting if it is cooked in an ovenproof glass dish.

1 kg (2 lb) damsons
250 g (8 oz) demerara sugar

4 tablespoons unsweetened orange juice
5 large eggs (size 1–2), separated

175 g (6 oz) caster sugar finely grated rind and juice of 1 lemon

125 g (4 oz) plain flour, sifted
½ teaspoon salt

Wash the damsons and put into a saucepan. Add the demerara sugar and the orange juice. Cover the pan, bring to the boil, stir, and then simmer for about 20 minutes, or until the damsons are completely mushy. Pour the damsons and juices through a large sieve until as much of the flesh as possible has been sieved through.

Stir until smooth, and then pour into a fairly wide ovenproof dish, only about a quarter of which will be filled by the mixture. Leave to cool. Then heat the oven to Gas Mark 4/180°C/350°F. Put the egg yolks into the bowl of an electric mixer and the egg whites in a large mixing bowl. Add the caster sugar to the yolks and whisk until very pale. Whisk in the grated lemon rind and gradually whisk in the lemon juice. Then stir in the sifted flour. Add the salt to the egg whites and whisk until they stand in soft peaks, then fold them a little at a time into the yolk mixture.

Pour gently and slowly on to the cooled damson purée. Cook in the centre of the oven for 45 minutes– 1 hour until the top is well browned. If eating cold, sprinkle a little icing sugar through a fine sieve on top of the pudding before serving.
Serves 6–8

Sunday Special (page 197); Damson Dream

PASSION-FRUIT AND FRESH LIME FLAN

Under the jelly lies a layer of cream and under this a secret light lemony
sponge; secret because the cream covers the sides of the finished flan so
that the three layers are not revealed until you cut into it.

For the cake:
butter for greasing
3 large eggs (size 1–2)
175 g (6 oz) caster sugar
¼ teaspoon salt

125 g (4 oz) self-raising
flour, plus extra for dusting
finely grated rind and juice
of 2 lemons

For the jelly:
5 passion-fruit
juice of 4 fresh limes
unsweetened orange juice
150 ml (¼ pint) water

75 g (3 oz) caster sugar
1 tablespoon honey
2 sachets (about 25 g/1 oz)
of gelatine
300 ml (½ pint)
whipping cream

To make the cake, generously butter the base and sides of a 25 cm (10-inch) diameter flan tin or dish (not one with a loose base) which is at least 4 cm (1½ inches) deep. Line the base with a disc of buttered greaseproof paper and then dust all over with flour. Put the eggs into a large bowl with 125 g (4 oz) of the caster sugar and place the bowl over a large saucepan of very hot but not boiling water. Whisk until pale, creamy, much increased in volume and thick enough to leave a trail on the surface when the whisk is lifted out. Remove the bowl from the heat and whisk again for 4–5 minutes. Whisk in the salt.

Heat the oven to Gas Mark 5/190°C/375°F. Sift half the flour on to the whisked egg mixture through a fine sieve and fold in very gently with a metal spoon. Then sift in the remaining flour and fold in again as lightly as possible. Lastly, sprinkle on the grated lemon rind and fold in gently but quickly. Pour the mixture into the prepared flan tin, smooth level and cook in the centre of the oven for 20–25 minutes until risen and springy to a very light touch in the centre. Remove from the oven and leave in the tin.

Strain the juice of the lemons into a saucepan and add the remaining 50 g (2 oz) caster sugar. Stir to dissolve the sugar over a low heat and then boil fiercely for about 2 minutes. Prick holes all over the cake with a skewer, piercing right through. Slowly spoon the lemon syrup all over the cake so that it is absorbed into it. Loosen the edges of the cake with a round-bladed knife and leave to cool in the tin.

Meanwhile start to prepare the jelly. Put a sieve over a bowl. Then cut the passion-fruit in half and scrape out the insides into a sieve. Rub thoroughly with a spoon until as much juice as possible has dripped through into the bowl. Then put the pips on a saucer and reserve. Pour the juice from the limes through the sieve into the bowl. Pour the juices into a measuring jug and bring up to 600 ml (1 pint) with orange juice (if this is fresh you must strain it). Turn out the cake and thoroughly wash and dry the flan tin or dish in which you cooked it. Pour the juices into a saucepan, warm them slightly, and put aside.

Now put the water into a small saucepan, add the caster sugar and honey and stir over a medium heat until the sugar and honey have dissolved. Sprinkle in the gelatine and stir until completely dissolved, but don't let the liquid boil. Then pour into the saucepan of juices, stirring all the time. Lastly, stir in a little more than half the reserved passion-fruit pips, and pour into the flan dish. Leave until cool then put in the fridge until really set – this sometimes takes several hours.

Turn the cake out on to a large serving plate and peel off the greaseproof paper. When the jelly is thoroughly set, whisk the cream until it holds fairly soft peaks. Spread not more than three-quarters of the cream thickly on top of the cake with a spatula. Dip the flan dish containing the set jelly in a sink of very hot water; a tin container will absorb the heat very quickly and loosen the jelly, whereas an earthenware flan dish can take longer.

Make sure the edges of the jelly are loose by pulling them back gently with your fingers. Carefully turn the jelly out on top of the cake and cream. Then spread the remaining cream round the sides of the cake, bringing it up to the top of the jelly in rough flicks. Refrigerate again until ready to serve.
Serves 12–14

SUNDAY SPECIAL

Cooking Sunday lunch for friends is something I always enjoy. It has none of the strains of a dinner party; the atmosphere is relaxed and children are often part of it. It is still important that the food should taste delicious, but it shouldn't be fussy, and you don't have to bother with a first course.

One vital element of a real Sunday lunch is a real pudding. This is a mouth-watering old-fashioned type of pudding; a rich vanilla custard with caramelised apples topped with a mass of beautiful meringue. The custard is made with vanilla pods instead of essence, which I think makes all the difference. I keep my vanilla pods in a jar of caster sugar which also becomes vanilla-flavoured, so I use this for vanilla custard and ice creams too.

To make your Sunday morning easier, you can make the pudding up to the apple stage the day before, leaving you only the meringue to whisk up and put in the oven to finish off.
Pictured on page 195.

450 ml (¾ pint) double cream	5 large eggs (size 1–2), separated	1 kg (2 lb) dessert apples	250 g (8 oz) caster sugar (for the meringue)
150 ml (¼ pint) full cream milk	2 teaspoons caster sugar (vanilla sugar if it is available)	25 g (1 oz) butter	a little salt
1–2 vanilla pods		25 g (1 oz) soft light brown sugar	

Pour the cream and milk into a large saucepan and stir. Add the vanilla pods, bring to the boil and simmer, stirring, for a moment or two. Then cover the pan and leave until cold, stirring occasionally to mix in any skin which forms. This cooling period allows the vanilla to be infused. When cold, take out the vanilla pods, wash them and leave to dry before storing away again for use another time.

Put the egg yolks into the bowl of an electric mixer and the egg whites in a covered bowl on one side. Add the 2 teaspoons of caster sugar to the egg yolks with a generous pinch of salt and whisk until pale. Bring the cream and milk to the boil and pour immediately on to the egg yolk and sugar mixture, whisking all the time. Pour into a large heavy-based saucepan, put over a medium heat and stir constantly for about 10 minutes without letting it quite boil, until you feel the mixture has thickened. Then pour the custard into a wide, ovenproof 1.5–1.75 litre (2½–3-pint) dish and put on one side.

Now peel the apples, cut out the core and slice into roughly 2.5 cm (1-inch) pieces. Melt the butter in a large, deep frying-pan over a high heat. Add the apple pieces and stir around for about 10 minutes until the apples feel soft when you stick a knife through them. Then add the brown sugar and stir for a minute or two until dissolved and toffeeish.

Remove from the heat and leave the apples in the pan for about 10 minutes. Then spoon the apples on to the custard and spoon over the sugar juices. When you are ready to cook the pudding, heat the oven to Gas Mark 5/190°C/375°F, put the egg whites in a large bowl, add a good pinch of salt and whisk until they form soft peaks. Add all but about 2 tablespoons of the 250 g (8 oz) caster sugar and whisk again until they hold peaks. Spoon the meringue on top of the pudding in rough flicks and sprinkle on the remaining sugar. Put the pudding just below the centre of the oven for 12–15 minutes. Serve warm or cold.
Serves 8

TROPICAL SPLENDOUR

The tropical element in this recipe is the guavas. They are one of my
favourite tropical fruits and have the advantage of canning well. Here,
guava halves stuffed and piled up with meringue swim in a tangy guava
juice custard. This is a useful recipe because it is simple to prepare, visually
effective and relatively inexpensive.

2 x 235 g (7 oz) can of   *juice of 1 lemon*   *the whites of 3 eggs*
guava halves   *the yolks of 4 eggs*   *175 g (6 oz) caster sugar*

Preheat the oven to Gas Mark 2/150°C/300°F.
Drain the juice from the guavas through a sieve into
a bowl. Using a teaspoon spoon the pips and any flesh
which is attached out of each guava half into the sieve
and put the guavas on one side. Rub the pips in the
sieve until the flesh has passed through the sieve into
the juice. Whisk the lemon juice into the guava juice
followed by the egg yolks. Pour into a large, shallow,
ovenproof dish. Gently place the scooped-out guava
halves in this sauce, hollow side up.

Whisk the egg whites until they hold soft peaks.
Then whisk in about half the sugar and continue
whisking until stiff. Fold in the remaining sugar gently
but evenly with a metal spoon. Using a teaspoon
spoon the meringue into the guava halves, until it is
all used up. Cook in the centre of the oven for 35–
45 minutes until the meringues are pale brown and
the juices are set around the edges. Serve either hot
or warm, as the sauce may separate as it cools.
Serves 8

HAZELNUT MERINGUE IN A CRUST

For the crust: *½ teaspoon salt*   *For the meringue:*   *25 g (1 oz) roasted*
butter for greasing   *75 g (3 oz) unsalted butter*   *the whites of 3 large eggs*   *hazelnuts, chopped*
175 g (6 oz) plain flour   *the yolks of 3 large eggs*   *(size 1–2)*   *15 g (½ oz) candied peel*
75 g (3 oz) icing sugar   *(size 1–2)*   *a pinch of salt*   *15 g (½ oz) cornflour*
                                                 175 g (6 oz) caster sugar   *1 teaspoon grated nutmeg*

Butter a 20 cm (8-inch) diameter deep cake tin with
a push up base. To make the crust, sift the flour, icing
sugar and salt into a bowl. Gently melt the butter in
a saucepan. Gradually pour the hot butter into the
flour, stirring it in with a wooden spoon. Then work
in the egg yolks one at a time. Put the dough into the
cake tin and press it lightly over the bottom and up
the sides of the tin (it doesn't matter if it has an uneven
edge at the top). Prick the bottom all over with a fork
and put the tin in the fridge for half an hour or more.
Then heat the oven to Gas Mark 6/200°C/400°F.
Whisk the egg whites with the salt until they form soft
peaks. Tip in half of the caster sugar and whisk again
until stiff. Then, using a metal spoon, gently fold in
the remaining sugar, the chopped nuts, the candied

peel and lastly the cornflour, sifted with the nutmeg.
Spoon the meringue into the lined cake tin. Scatter
a few extra chopped hazelnuts on top. (The meringue
won't fill the tin, don't worry about this as it rises a
lot.) Cook the meringue in the centre of the oven for
15 minutes, then turn the heat down to Gas Mark
3/160°C/200°F for another 50–60 minutes. It
should be light golden-brown in colour. Leave in the
tin for 10 –15 minutes. Then carefully loosen the
edges of the tin with a knife, put the cake tin on a jar
or tin and gently press it down. Either leave the
meringue on the base of the cake tin, or slide a spatula
underneath and edge it onto a serving plate. Serve
warm or cold with cream.
Serves 6–8

DREAM OF PUDDINGS WITH ELDERFLOWER MERINGUE

This is truly a dream of puddings. It is a rare treat as it can only be made at one time of year: in early summer when elderflowers are in bloom and fresh apricots are in the shops. I have long enjoyed the magical muscat flavour which elderflowers give to gooseberries and apricots, or to sweet cordials when they are used on their own. But when I tried putting the flowers into the soft meringue top of this mouth-watering three-layered pudding, the effect seemed better than anything before. As the pudding can be made ahead up to the apricot stage, and chilled, it is ideal for a dinner party. After you have made the meringue, eat it as soon as possible.

For the custard cream:
6 egg yolks
2 tablespoons honey
300 ml (½ pint) double cream)
150 ml (¼ pint) milk

For the apricots:
1 kg (2 lb) large, firm apricots, halved and stoned
2 tablespoons caster sugar

For the meringue:
6 egg whites
250 g (8 oz) caster sugar
3–4 large elderflower heads

To make the custard put the egg yolks in the top of a double boiler or pudding basin. Mix in the honey thoroughly, and then stir in the cream and milk. Put over just-simmering water, stirring with a wooden spoon all the time for 10–15 minutes until thickened and coating the back of the spoon.

Remove from the heat and stir to cool slightly, then pour gradually into the bottom of an ovenproof dish (ovenproof glass looks nice, as you will see the layers of the pudding) of approximately 2.25 litres (4 pints) capacity. Leave until cold, and then chill in the fridge until very thick.

Meanwhile, heat the oven to Gas Mark 6/200°C/400°F. Arrange the apricots cut-side down in a large roasting pan or baking sheet, and sprinkle the caster sugar over them. Put the pan towards the top of the oven for 20–30 minutes until the apricots feel soft when you insert a knife, and the sugar has begun to brown and caramelise. Then remove from the oven and leave to cool.

When the custard is chilled arrange the baked apricots on top, and spoon on any caramelised juices from the pan, heat the oven to Gas Mark 5/ 190°C/375°F.

To make the meringue, whisk the egg whites until stiff, then whisk in half the caster sugar. Fold in the remaining sugar with a little spoon and lastly, using a fork, push off the elderflowers from their stalks and fold into the meringue.

Spoon on top of the apricots and custard and put in the centre of the oven for 10 –14 minutes until the top has browned. Remove from the oven, leave to cool, and then chill in the fridge until ready to serve. **Serves 8–10**

STUFFED PANCAKE CLOUDS

If you want something special for Shrove Tuesday try this delectable and impressive dish, which consists of pancakes stuffed with tangy apricot and a light, soft meringue and then coated with rich egg custard sauce. I use the lacy thin Brittany crêpes which you can buy in packets – they are excellent and certainly save time. For a party this dish can be made well ahead and is unfailingly popular.

300 g (10 oz) dried apricots
175 g (6 oz) light brown sugar
300 ml (1/2 pint) water

10 large Brittany crêpes or very large home-made pancakes (about 33 cm/13-inch)

5 large eggs (size 1–2), separated
300 g (10 oz) icing sugar, sifted

25 g (1 oz) caster sugar
300 ml (1/2 pint) double cream
150 ml (1/4 pint) milk
vanilla essence

Soak the apricots in a bowl of cold water for several hours. Then drain them and put in a saucepan with the brown sugar, adding the water. Cover the pan, bring to the boil and simmer for 20–30 minutes until soft. Uncover the pan and boil fiercely for 2–3 minutes until the syrup is thick. Leave until cold.

Lay the pancakes out on a flat surface. Whisk the egg whites until stiff and then gradually whisk in half of the icing sugar. Fold in the remaining icing sugar with a metal spoon. Preheat the oven to Gas Mark 4/180°F/350°F. Spoon the apricot mixture on to one side of each pancake and then spoon the meringue mixture on top of the apricot. Turn the sides of the pancakes in and then, starting from the apricot and meringue end, roll up the pancakes loosely. Carefully transfer them to a very large, well buttered, shallow ovenproof dish. Cover the dish with foil and cook in the centre of the oven for 45 minutes.

Meanwhile, make the sauce. Beat the egg yolks together with the caster sugar. Put the cream and milk in a saucepan and bring almost to the boil. Gradually whisk this into the egg yolk mixture. Put the bowl over a large saucepan of simmering water and stir for about 10 minutes until the sauce has slightly thickened. Add a few drops of vanilla essence and leave to become quite cold.

When the pancakes are cooked remove from the oven and cool. Shortly before serving, whisk the cold sauce until smooth and pour over the pancake rolls.
Serves 10

STRAWBERRY AND PINEAPPLE SALAD WITH ORANGE CREAM

Pictured on pages 146/7.

*500 g (1 lb) strawberries
1 small pineapple*

*2–3 tablespoons caster sugar
juice of 1 lemon*

*300 ml (½ pint) double
cream*

*grated rind and juice of 1
small orange*

Cut the strawberries in half only if they are very large. Cut the skin off the pineapple and cut the flesh into smallish pieces. Mix with the strawberries in a glass bowl. Gently mix in the sugar and lemon juice.

Whisk the cream until thick but not too stiff and then gradually stir in the orange juice and the grated rind. Serve this cream in a separate bowl.
Serves 6–8

SWEET SUNDAY SALAD

*For the syrup:
175 g (6 oz) granulated
sugar*

*strained juice of 1 large
lemon brought up to
150 ml (¼ pint)
with water*

*1 tablespoon triple strength
rose or orange flower water
3–4 peaches or nectarines*

*1 small melon
a little extra lemon juice
500 g (1 lb) strawberries*

To make the syrup, put the sugar in a pan with the diluted lemon juice and dissolve over a low heat. Then bring to the boil and bubble fiercely for 4 minutes. Stir in the flower water and leave to cool.

Pour boiling water over the peaches in a bowl and leave for a minute or two until the skins peel off easily. Peel the melon with a potato peeler; slice it in half, remove the seeds and cut into very thin semi-circles.

Arrange neatly round the outer edge of a large round or oval dish. Sprinkle with the extra lemon juice. Then slice the peeled peaches or nectarines thinly and arrange to overlap the inner half of the melon slices. Finally hull and halve the strawberries and pile in the centre. Shortly before serving, spoon the cold syrup all over the fruit.
Serves 8

DRIED FRUIT COMPOTE WITH GINGER AND RUM

*2 x 250 g (8 oz) packets of
dried mixed fruit (apricots,
apples, etc. – cut
any extra-large fruits in half)*

*50 g (2 oz) crystallised
ginger, cut into small pieces*

*50 –125 g (2–4 oz)
demerara or granulated
sugar*

*juice of 2 lemons and
1 orange
2–3 tablespoons dark rum*

Soak the dried fruit overnight or for at least 6 hours. Drain it and put into a large saucepan with the ginger, sugar and fruit juice. Bring to the boil, then cover and

simmer gently for half an hour. Stir in the rum, transfer to a serving bowl and let cool. Serve with cream.
Serves 4–6

OUR FAVOURITE CHRISTMAS PUDDING

This is an old North Country recipe for a dark, moist full-flavoured
pudding. I make it every year and it seems to have just the right
mature, traditional flavour.

125 g (4 oz) self-raising
flour
½ teaspoon salt
1 teasoon mixed spice
1 teaspoon ground
cinnamon
½ – ¾ of a whole
nutmeg, grated

½ teaspoon ground cloves
250 g (8 oz) shredded suet
300 g (10 oz) fresh white
breadcrumbs
grated rind and juice of
1 lemon and 1 orange

250 g (8 oz) demerara
sugar
250 g (8 oz) grated carrots
250 g (8 oz) grated
cooking apples
375 g (12 oz) raisins
250 g (8 oz) currants

250 g (8 oz) sultanas
125 g (4 oz) mixed peel
50 g (2 oz) flaked almonds
2 tablespoons black treacle
½ large wine glass of
Cointreau or brandy
4 eggs (size 4), lightly
whisked

Sieve the flour, salt and spice into a large mixing bowl.
Add all the remaining dry ingredients. Mix together
thoroughly. Melt the treacle in a pan to make it a little
runny. Stir into it the lemon and orange juice and the
Cointreau or brandy and finally the eggs. Pour the
liquid into the pudding mixture and stir thoroughly.
Cover the bowl with a cloth and leave until the next
day. Butter two 1.2-litre (2-pint) pudding basins and
spoon in the mixture. Cover with a double layer of
buttered greaseproof paper and then either a cloth
tied on with string or foil tucked in round the rim.
Steam for 5 – 6 hours in pans of simmering water
which should be kept topped up two-thirds up the
sides of the basins. When cool, re-cover the basins and
store in a cool place. On Christmas Day steam for a
further 2–3 hours, making sure that the water level is
kept topped up.

Makes 2 puddings, each feeding 8–10 people

APPLES IN ORANGE AND CARDAMOM FUDGE SAUCE

From India to Scandinavia, spicy cardamom is often used to enhance
sweet things , and I think it makes all the difference in this easy apple dish.
It's the sort of pudding you can whip up at the last moment if you feel the
rest of the meal might be a bit sparse and needs a treat at the end.

150 ml (5 fl oz) carton of
double or whipping cream
4 tablespoons natural
yogurt

125 g (4 oz) unsalted butter
175 g (6 oz) soft pale
brown sugar

2 teaspoons ground
cardamom
½ teaspoon salt

150 ml (¼ pint) freshly
squeezed orange juice
1 kg (2 lb) dessert apples

First, whisk the cream until stiff and then fold in the
yogurt. Put in the fridge to chill. Gently melt the
butter in a large saucepan with the brown sugar,
stirring over a low heat. Add the cardamom and salt.
Strain in the orange juice and stir. Bring to the boil
and boil vigorously without stirring, for 3 minutes.
Remove from the heat. Peel the apples and cut into
medium-size slices. Add them to the fudge sauce and
replace over a high heat. Boil, stirring round a little
with a wooden spoon for 3–5 minutes until the apples
have just softened but are not yet breaking up. If you
are not going to eat the pudding quite soon keep the
apples in the saucepan and re-heat gently before the
meal. Then pour into a serving bowl. Just before
serving spoon over the chilled cream.

Serves 5–6

Our Favourite Christmas Pudding; Rum Butter (page 141)

LUSCIOUS LEMON RING

I have a particular passion for any sweet made with lemon and this
delicately textured ring is truly exquisite. It has a delicious shiny lemon
curd top and creamy honeycombed base, and it slips down the throat in
the most irresistible way. It is specially refreshing after a rich or heavy
meal, or as an accompaniment to a bowl of strawberries at a summer party.

*25 g (1 oz) self-raising
flour, sifted
250 g (8 oz) caster sugar
a pinch of salt*

*finely grated rind of 1 lemon
3 tablespoons lemon juice*

*3 large eggs (size 1–2),
separated
300 ml (½ pint) single
cream*

*chopped toasted nuts, to
garnish (optional)*

Mix together the sifted flour, caster sugar, and salt. Sift into a mixing bowl and stir in the lemon rind and juice. In another bowl whisk the egg yolks with an electric whisk until pale and creamy. Stir into the flour, sugar and lemon mixture. Then stir in the cream gradually.

Put a roasting pan full of warm water on the centre shelf of the oven and heat to Gas Mark 3/160°C/325°F. Then whisk the egg whites until they hold soft peaks and fold them gently into the yolk and lemon mixture, using a large metal spoon. Pour into a wetted 1.2-litre (2-pint) ring mould and set it in the pan of water in the oven. Cook for 1 hour. Let it cool (it will sink a bit as it cools) and when very cold, loosen the edges carefully and turn out, giving a shake, on to a serving plate. If you like, sprinkle a few nuts on top. Refrigerate until needed.
Serves 5–6

HONEYED GREENGAGES ON A CHOCOLATE AND WALNUT CRUST

When greengages are either not completely ripe or lacking in flavour,
cooking them is the answer. This is a luxurious pudding of syrupy fruit on
a rich dark chocolate base studded with walnuts. I think it is best served
with creamed smetana or Greek yogurt. It can be made at least
a day in advance.

*2 rounded tablespoons
honey*

*1 kg (2 lb) greengages,
halved and stoned*

*50 g (2 oz) caster sugar
200 g (7 oz) plain
chocolate, broken up*

*75 g (3 oz) unsalted butter
125 g (4 oz) walnuts,
chopped fairly small*

Spread the honey over the bottom of a 25 cm (10 inch) china flan dish. Arrange the greengages in a single layer skin-side downwards, close together on the honey. This will use about three-quarters of the fruit. Heat the oven to Gas Mark 4/180°C/350°F and put the greengages in the centre for 20–25 minutes until they are soft.

Meanwhile, put the remaining halved greengages into a saucepan with the caster sugar. Put the pan over a medium heat and stir to dissolve the sugar. Then bring up to the boil, stirring often, for about 10 minutes until the greengages are very soft.

When the greengages in the oven are soft, carefully pour as much of the juice as you can into the saucepan of stewed greengages, being careful not to disarrange the layer of greengages in the flan dish. Then put the stewed greengages into a food processor and whizz until smooth. Spread evenly over the greengages in the dish and leave until cold.

Then put the chocolate in the top of a double saucepan or into a bowl set over a pan of very hot, but not boiling water. Stir often until melted, then stir in the butter, cut into pieces, a bit at a time. When the butter has melted, stir in the chopped walnuts.

Remove the bowl from the hot water and leave for a few minutes until slightly cooled. Then spoon evenly over the cold greengage purée. Refrigerate for at least an hour. To turn out, loosen the edges, if necessary, with a knife and turn upside-down on to a serving plate giving a good shake. If it won't turn out, dip the bottom of the dish briefly into a sink of very hot water and then turn out. Refrigerate again until ready to eat. Cut into slices with a sharp knife.
Serves 8–10

BAKED APRICOTS FLOATING ON FRESH LIME SAUCE

When fresh apricots are in the shops, disappointingly few have enough flavour to eat raw. However, cook them for a few minutes and like magic that wonderful, strong apricot taste is suddenly there, combined with a light succulence which no dried apricots can have. With its combination of intense, tangy flavours and beautiful orange glow, this is an arresting pudding in all ways. As it is served cold it can be made a day or two ahead. Serve with plenty of double cream.

For the sauce:
4 fresh limes
unsweetened orange juice

2 rounded tablespoons
honey
40 g (1½ oz) caster sugar

2 rounded teaspoons
arrowroot

For the apricots:
500 g (1 lb) fresh ripe
apricots, halved and stoned
caster sugar

First make the sauce. Make up the juice of the limes to 300 ml (½ pint) with orange juice, and pour into a saucepan. Add the honey and caster sugar, put over a medium heat and stir until the honey and caster sugar are dissolved. Remove from the heat.

In a cup, stir the arrowroot with 1 tablespoon orange juice until smooth, and then pour it into the juices in the saucepan, stirring. Put the pan back over the heat and bring to the boil, stirring all the time. Continue to boil, stirring for 2–3 minutes until thickened. Then pass the sauce through a fine sieve on to a large shallow dish or plate – spreading the sauce out. Leave on one side to cool while you cook the apricots. Lay the apricot halves skin-side upwards on a large baking sheet. Heat the oven to Gas Mark 9/240°C/475°F. Brush each apricot skin with enough water to moisten the skin and sprinkle about 1–2 teaspoons caster sugar over each apricot.

Put them at the very top of the oven for about 10 minutes until they are soft. They will probably still have a little caster sugar undissolved on top of them, and some sugar syrup round them. Let them cool and then transfer the fruit with a slotted spatula to the cold sauce, laying the apricot halves gently on top of it. Spoon any syrup from the apricots on top. Leave in a coolish place until needed, but don't refrigerate. Serve with a jug of cream.
Serves 6

Part 6

CAKES, BISCUITS AND SWEETS

Balinese Carrot Cake (page 208);
Fruited Chocolate Christmas Cake (page 209);
Whole Lemon and Almond Cake Coated with Chocolate (page 210);
Lemon Ginger Shortbread (page 217);
Orange, Cranberry, Almond and Honey Cake (page 212)

BALINESE CARROT CAKE

In the hills of Bali in Indonesia, a small teahouse we visited made a carrot
cake with coconut spiced with cardamom and to me it is the best of all the
many variations I have tried. You can sandwich the cake with a layer of
sweetened cream cheese, but it is so moist that I prefer it plain.
Pictured on pages 206/7.

175 g (6 oz) caster sugar
2 rounded tablespoons clear
honey
250 ml (8 fl oz) sunflower
oil, plus extra for greasing

3 large eggs (size 1–2)
1 teaspoon ground
cardamom
½ teaspoon salt

175 g (6 oz) self-raising
wholemeal or 81% flour or
plain wholemeal flour plus
1½ teaspoons baking
powder

300 g (10 oz) carrots,
grated
125 g (4 oz) unsweetened
desiccated coconut
125 g (4 oz) walnuts,
chopped roughly

Preheat the oven to Gas Mark 4/180°C/350°F.
Grease an 18–20 cm (7–8-inch) cake tin (not one
with a loose base) and line it with a disc of greaseproof
paper. Put the caster sugar and the honey into a
mixing bowl. Add the sunflower oil and whisk until
well mixed. Whisk in the eggs one at a time until
amalgamated, and then continue whisking until the
mixture is pale and frothy. Mix the ground cardamom
and salt into the flour and then whisk the flour into
the egg mixture a little at a time until thoroughly
mixed. Stir in the grated carrots, the coconut and the
chopped walnuts and pour the mixture into the prepared cake tin. Cook in the centre of the oven for
1½ –1¾ hours until a small, sharp knife stuck into
the centre comes out clean. If the top of the cake
begins to look too brown before it is cooked, lay a
piece of greaseproof paper or foil loosely on it.
Serves 8

HONEYED APRICOT AND BRANDY CAKE

250 g (8 oz) dried apricots
125 g (4 oz) seedless raisins
125 ml (4 fl oz) brandy

125 ml (4 fl oz)
unsweetened fresh orange
juice
175 g (6 oz) self-raising
flour, plus extra for dusting

2 teaspoons baking powder
175 g (6 oz) softened
butter, plus extra for
greasing

4 rounded tablespoons honey
4 medium–large eggs
(size 2-3), separated
1 teaspoon caraway seeds
icing sugar

Chop up the dried apricots and put them in a saucepan with the raisins. Pour in the brandy and orange
juice. Cover the pan and bring to the boil over a
medium heat. Stir well, and then remove from the
heat and leave on one side for at least an hour.

Thoroughly butter and flour a 21–25 cm (8½ –9
inch) diameter, deep, loose-based cake tin. Sift the
flour and baking powder into a bowl. Heat the oven
to Gas Mark 4/180°C/350°F. Cream the butter with
the honey until light and fluffy. Whisk the egg yolks
one at a time, whisking hard after each addition.
Then, using a metal spoon, stir in half of the flour
followed by the apricot and raisin mixture and the
caraway seeds. Then stir in the rest of the flour. Lastly,
whisk the egg whites until they stand in soft peaks and
fold them gently into the cake mixture a bit at a time,
using a large metal spoon. Spoon into the prepared
tin and spread level.

Cook just below the centre of the oven for 60–70
minutes until a small knife comes out clean. Remove
from the oven, leave in the tin for 10 minutes or more,
and then push the cake out of the tin and manoeuvre
it with a spatula on to a cooling rack. Before serving
sprinkle a fairly thick layer of icing sugar through a
sieve over the top of the cake.
Serves 8-10

FRUITED CHOCOLATE CHRISTMAS CAKE

This is a real fruit cake but it is also a real chocolate cake. It is densely packed with dried pineapple, prunes, peel, raisins, crystallised ginger and walnuts: a mixture which combines irresistibly with the rich chocolate flavour. I make the cake two or three weeks before Christmas then glaze it with apricot jam and ice it with lemony royal icing only two or three days before eating it, so that the icing is still slightly soft.

Pictured on pages 206/7.

175 g (6 oz) dried pineapple pieces
175 g (6 oz) dark cooking chocolate
125 g (4 oz) unsalted butter, plus extra for greasing

150 g (5 oz) soft dark brown sugar
4 large eggs (size 1–2), beaten
150 g (5 oz) self-raising flour
2 tablespoons cocoa

75 g (3 oz) ground almonds
5 tablespoons brandy or rum
2 teaspoons ground cinnamon
125 g (4 oz) soft pitted prunes, chopped roughly

125 g (4 oz) crystallised ginger, chopped roughly
125 g (4 oz) walnuts, chopped roughly
125 g (4 oz) candied peel
125 g (4 oz) raisins coarsely grated rind of 2 lemons

Put the dried pineapple into a bowl, pour over plenty of boiling water and leave for 15–30 minutes and then drain. Line the base of a deep, 23 cm (9-inch), round cake tin with a piece of well buttered grease-proof paper. Line the sides with a wide strip of buttered paper which comes up above the edges.

Melt the chocolate in a bowl over hot water. Cream the butter and the brown sugar in a mixing bowl, add the melted chocolate and whisk thoroughly until smooth, paler in colour and fluffy. Add the beaten eggs a little at a time, whisking well after each addition. Then sift the flour and cocoa into the bowl and fold them in with a large metal spoon. Fold in the ground almonds, the brandy and the cinnamon. Then fold in the chopped prunes, ginger, walnuts, the candied peel, the raisins and the grated lemon rind. Lastly stir in the soaked pineaple pieces.

Spoon the mixture into the lined cake tin and level the top. Heat the oven to Gas Mark 3/160°C/325°F and bake the cake in the centre for 1 hour; then turn down to Gas Mark 1/140°C/275°F for 1¼–1½ hours until a knife stuck in the centre comes out clean. Leave the cake in the tin for 10–15 minutes and then take it out of the tin and leave it on a rack to cool. When cold, wrap well in several layers of cling film and store in a cool place until you are ready to ice it.

Serves about 16

WHOLE LEMON AND ALMOND CAKE COATED WITH CHOCOLATE

Literally whole lemons, boiled and puréed, are used to give this cake
a distinctive flavour and tang. I got the idea from a recipe of Claudia
Roden's. Although my recipe produces a very moist cake it is not so
much a pudding as hers and with the dark chocolate glaze it is best for a
special tea. I usually decorate the cake by putting a simple fresh rosebud
from the garden on it before the chocolate sets. If it is a personal
celebration for someone I write a message in white glacé icing
on the chocolate when it has set.
Pictured on pages 206/7.

For the cake:
2 small-medium lemons
75 g (3 oz) butter, plus
extra for greasing

5 large eggs, (size 1–2)
250 g (8 oz) caster sugar
150 g (5 oz) ground
almonds

75 g (3 oz) self-raising
flour, plus extra for dusting
1 teaspoon baking powder

For the chocolate coating:
150 g (5 oz) plain
chocolate, broken into pieces
1 tablespoon water
25 g (1 oz) butter

To make the cake, put the whole lemons in a sauce-pan of water, bring to the boil, then cover and simmer gently for about 1½ hours. Meanwhile butter an 18 cm (7-inch) deep cake tin and line the base with a disc of buttered greaseproof paper. Dust the tin with flour. When the lemons are soft, cut them open and remove any pips. Put them into a food processor with the butter, cut into pieces. Whizz to a smooth purée.

Put the eggs into the bowl of an electric mixer and whisk until fluffy. Whisk in the caster sugar a little at a time, whisking thoroughly after each addition. Heat the oven to Gas Mark 4/180°C/350°F. Whisk the lemon and butter purée into the eggs and sugar. Then whisk in the ground almonds. Lastly, sift the flour and baking powder into the bowl and stir into the mixture with a metal spoon. Turn into the pre-pared cake tin and spread level.

Cook on the centre shelf of the oven for 1¼ hours until a small knife inserted in the middle of the cake comes out clean. If the top looks as if it is getting too brown, lay a piece of greaseproof paper over it. Remove the cake from the oven and leave in the tin for a few minutes. Loosen the edges with a knife if necessary and turn out on to a cooling rack, top-side upwards.

When the cake is cool, make the chocolate coating. Put the chocolate into a double saucepan or a bowl set over a saucepan of hot water which must be well below boiling heat. Add the water to the choco-late and stir until melted, then add the butter and continue stirring until melted and blended in. Remove from the hot water and leave for a minute or two to cool very slightly. Then, with the cake still on the cooling rack, pour the chocolate very slowly over the top and spread over the sides with a spatula. Leave the cake at room temperature while the choc-olate sets, as this gives it a shinier appearance.
Serves 8–10

UNCONVENTIONAL CELEBRATION CAKE

Here is a cake to have for Christmas, a birthday or even a wedding for those who are tired of the traditional fruit cake draped in marzipan which never seems to be finished. This is in fact a glorified carrot cake but packed with apricots and walnuts with a bite of crystallised ginger. It is moist and tangy and is always very popular. I make the cake two or three weeks in advance. As I like the icing to be firm on the outside but still fairly soft beneath, I only ice it three or four days before we plan to eat it. Glycerine for the icing is available from chemists. This cake looks pretty decorated with frosted violet forget-me-nots and angelica leaves.

300 g (10 oz) butter, plus extra for greasing
175 g (6 oz) soft, light brown sugar
5 eggs (size 2–3)
25 g (1 oz) ground almonds
juice and grated rind of 1 lemon

250 g (8 oz) self-raising flour, plus extra for dusting
1 teaspoon baking powder
½ level teaspoon salt
50 g (2 oz) crystallized ginger, peeled and chopped roughly
300 g (10 oz) dried apricots, chopped roughly

375 g (12 oz) carrots, grated coarsely
75 g (3 oz) candied peel
25 g (4 oz) walnut pieces
3 tablespoons unsweetened orange juice
5–6 tablespoons brandy

For the icing:
3 tablespoons apricot jam
3 egg whites
about 650 g (1 lb 5 oz) icing sugar
1 tablespoon lemon juice
2 teaspoons glycerine

To make the cake, butter a 23 cm (9-inch) diameter deep cake tin, line the base with a disc of buttered greaseproof paper and dust all over with flour. Whisk the butter until soft, add the soft brown sugar and whisk until fluffy.

In another bowl whisk the eggs until frothy. Add the whisked eggs to the butter and sugar a little at a time, whisking after each addition. Then whisk in the ground almonds followed by the lemon juice. Sift the flour with the baking powder and salt and fold it into the butter and sugar mixture with a metal spoon. Then, using a wooden spoon, thoroughly mix in the ginger, apricots and carrots, plus the candied peel and walnut pieces. Lastly, stir in the orange juice.

Heat the oven to Gas Mark 4/180°C/350°F. Spoon the cake mixture into the prepared tin and spread level. Bake in the centre of the oven for 30 minutes, then turn down the oven to Gas Mark 3/160°C/325°F for another 1¼–1½ hours until a knife stuck in the centre comes out clean.

Leave the cake in the tin and, using a skewer, pierce the cake carefully all over right through. Dribble the brandy all over the top, letting it be absorbed through the holes. Leave the cake in the tin until cold, then release the sides with a round bladed knife, turn the cake out and remove the greaseproof paper. Wrap the cake up well with cling film and foil and leave in a cool place until ready to ice.

To ice the cake unwrap it and put it on a cake stand or serving plate. Put the apricot jam into a saucepan and melt over a gentle heat. Brush the cake all over with the melted jam and leave until set. Then make the icing. Whisk the egg whites in a bowl until frothy. Then sift and stir in about a quarter of the icing sugar with a wooden spoon. Continue adding the sugar gradually, whisking well after each addition, until about three-quarters of the sugar has been added. Whisk in the lemon juice and continue whisking for a few minutes until the icing is smooth. Whisk in the remaining sugar just until the icing is thick enough to hold soft peaks. Finally, stir in the glycerine. Ice the cake thickly in rough flicks, starting on top and then doing the sides. Decorate to suit the occasion and leave in a cool place until you want to eat it.

Serves 16–18

ORANGE, CRANBERRY, ALMOND AND HONEY CAKE

For a special tea this cake has many qualities. Although it is made with
ground almonds and wholemeal flour it has a light texture. It is also
wonderfully moist and keeps well. The cranberries give the cake a tangy
freshness which blends with the buttery almond and orange flavour.
Finally, it looks beautiful – dark and tempting with a shining orange glaze.
Pictured on pages 206/7.

175 g (6 oz) butter, plus
extra for greasing
75 g (3 oz) soft brown
sugar
125 g (4 oz) honey

coarsely grated rind and
juice of 2 oranges
2 teaspoons baking powder

75 g (3 oz) self-raising
wholemeal flour, plus extra
for dusting
4 eggs
2 tablespoons milk

125 g (4 oz) ground
almonds
125 g (4 oz) fresh
cranberries
50 g (2 oz) caster sugar

Butter a deep 18 cm (7-inch) cake tin and line the
bottom with a disc of buttered greaseproof paper.
Dust the bottom and sides of the tin with a little
wholemeal flour. Put the butter, the brown sugar and
the honey into a bowl and beat or whisk until thoroughly blended and fluffy.

Whisk the orange rind into the mixture. In a bowl
mix the baking powder with the flour. Now whisk
the eggs into the cake mixture one at a time, whisking
thoroughly after each addition and whisking in a little
of the flour after each egg, too. Then whisk in the
milk, a tablespoon at a time and finally add any
remaining flour.

Preheat the oven to Gas Mark 4/180°C/350°F.
Stir the ground almonds into the cake mixture and
lastly stir in the cranberries. Spoon the mixture into
the prepared cake tin and spread level. Cook in the
centre of the oven for 55 – 65 minutes until a small
knife inserted in the centre of the cake comes out
clean. Leave the cake in the tin while you make the
orange glaze.

Squeeze the juice of the oranges and strain it into
a saucepan. Add the caster sugar. Put over a low heat
and stir to dissolve the sugar. Then increase the heat
and boil rapidly for 2–3 minutes until the juice has
turned to a thick syrup but hasn't begun to caramelise.
Remove from the heat and put on one side.

Now turn the cake out of the tin on to a cooling
rack, remove the greaseproof paper and then turn
carefully so that it is on the rack the right way up.
Slowly spoon and spread the syrup over the top of the
cake, making a thick shiny gloss with a few dribbles
beginning to trickle down the sides.
Serves 8–10

FRUIT AND RUM LOAF

This is festive but not too rich. It has a refreshing, tangy lemon flavour
and if you are really feeling self-indulgent the slices can be spread with
butter. You can make this loaf several days before you need it and
keep it in an airtight wrapping.

175 g (6 oz) candied peel
75 g (3 oz) glacé cherries,
quartered
75 g (3 oz) sultanas

50 g (2 oz) currants
6–8 tablespoons white rum
125 g (4 oz) unsalted
butter, plus extra for
greasing

125 g (4 oz) caster sugar
2 large eggs (size 1–2)
coarsely grated rind and
juice of 1 large lemon

250 g (8 oz) plain flour
2 teaspoons baking powder
icing sugar, to decorate

Grease and line the base of a 1 kg (2 lb) loaf tin with greaseproof paper. Put the dried fruit in a bowl and stir in the rum. Cover the bowl and leave for at least an hour, or overnight if possible, turning the fruit once or twice.

Cream the butter and sugar until light and fluffy. In another bowl whisk the eggs until pale and frothy. Beat the eggs a little at a time into the butter and sugar mixture. Beat in the grated lemon rind.

Heat the oven to Gas Mark 4/180°C/350°F. Sift the flour with the baking powder and stir into the butter and egg mixture with a metal spoon. Gradually stir in the lemon juice, followed by the soaked fruit and rum. Spoon the mixture into the prepared tin and smooth the top. Cook in the centre of the oven for 1½ hours, or until a thin knife inserted in the centre comes out clean. If the cake is beginning to look too brown while cooking put a piece of foil over the top. Cool in the tin, then turn out and wrap well in the cling film or foil until ready to eat. Before serving, sprinkle icing sugar through a sieve all over the top. **Serves 10–12**

DARK CHOCOLATE CAKE

This frosted moist chocolate cake is ideal for any occasion.

For the cranberry and orange filling:
125 ml (4 fl oz) fresh orange juice (about 2 oranges)
125 ml (4 fl oz) sugar
250 g (9 oz) fresh cranberries

For the cake:
125 g (4 oz) plain chocolate
3 tablespoons water
175 g (6 oz) butter or margarine
300 g (10 oz) soft dark brown sugar
1 teaspoon vanilla essence

3 large eggs (size 2) lightly whisked
175 ml (6 fl oz) milk, soured by adding the juice of ½ lemon
300 g (10 oz) plain flour
½ teaspoon baking powder
1½ level teaspoons bicarbonate of soda

For the frosting:
2 large egg whites (size 2)
375 g (12 oz) caster sugar
a good pinch of salt
juice of 1 lemon
1 tablespoon water
½ teaspoon cream of tartar

Make the filling first. Put the orange juice in a saucepan and stir in the sugar. Add the cranberries. Cover, bring to the boil and simmer for 5 minutes. Cool and chill well in the fridge before using.

Now line two greased 22–24 cm (8½ –9½-inch) sandwich tins with greased greaseproof paper. Break the chocolate into small pieces, then put with the 3 tablespoons of hot water in a bowl over a pan of very hot water, stirring occasionally until smooth. Remove from the heat and cool slightly. Preheat the oven to Gas Mark 4/180°C/350°F. Cream the fat with the sugar and vanilla essence until light and fluffy. Thoroughly beat in the eggs and melted chocolate. Add the soured milk alternately with the sifted flour, baking powder and bicarbonate of soda. Divide the mixture between the two tins and smooth with a knife. Bake towards the centre of the oven for 30–40 minutes until well risen and springy to touch in the centre. Leave in the tins for 10 minutes, then turn the cakes carefully out on to a wire tray to cool, and remove the greaseproof paper. When cold, sandwich together with the cranberry and orange filling.

To make the frosting, put all the ingredients together in a large deep bowl and whisk together. Put the bowl over a pan of very hot water and continue to whisk for about 10 minutes until the mixture is thick enough to stand in peaks and the sugar has dissolved. Spread at once thickly all over the cake with a wide knife, making rough flicks, decorate, leave in a cool place but not the fridge. You can, of course, make the cake in advance and freeze it. The icing is best done a day before you plan to eat the cake.
Serves 6 – 8

KIBRIZLI CAKE

Turkish cakes are often made with semolina, almonds and honey and
I devised this recipe to try and epitomise what the best of them can be
like. It has turned out particularly well. You can either eat it with tea or
coffee or as a pudding with yogurt.

For the cake:
butter for greasing
5 eggs
finely grated rind of 1 lemon
250 g (8 oz) caster sugar

125 g (4 oz) semolina
125 g (4 oz) ground
almonds
a pinch of baking powder
150 ml (¼ pint) water

¼ teaspoon salt
1 tablespoon sesame seeds

For the syrup:
175 g (6 oz) granulated
sugar

2 tablespoons clear or set
honey
just under 300 ml (½ pint)
water
juice of 1 lemon

Preheat the oven to Gas Mark 4/180°C/350°F.
Lightly butter a 20 cm (8-inch) deep cake tin (not one
with a loose base) and line it with a disc of greaseproof
paper. Break the egg whites into a large bowl and put
the yolks into another. Add the grated lemon rind to
the yolks, with the caster sugar. Whisk them until
they are very pale and then add the semolina, the
ground almonds, the baking powder and the water
and whisk until smooth. Add the salt to the egg whites
and whisk them until they stand in soft peaks. Then,
using a metal spoon, fold them gently into the yolk
mixture and pour it into the prepared cake tin.
Sprinkle the sesame seeds over the top and then bake
the cake in the centre of the oven for 40–45 minutes.

Meanwhile, make the syrup. Put the granulated
sugar and honey into a saucepan, with the water.
Dissolve over a low heat, and then increase the heat
and boil fiercely for 4–5 minutes. Remove from the
heat, pour in the lemon juice through a sieve and stir
it in. Put the pan in a sink of cold water to cool.

When the cake is ready, remove it from the oven
but leave it in its tin. Spoon the cold syrup gradually
and evenly over the hot cake, letting it soak in. Leave
the cake in the tin until cold and then loosen the sides
carefully with a knife and turn it out (you may have
to shake the tin). Turn the cake the right way up on
to a serving plate.
Serves 8–10

Kibrizli Cake; Walnut and Fruit Baklava (page 220)

CHOCOLATE CHIP AND HAZELNUT COOKIES

American cookies seem the rage in England now and you can buy them
'home-made', sometimes even still warm. They taste good but it is much
cheaper, and very simple, to rustle some up at home shortly before you
have guests to tea so that the house will smell wonderful when they arrive.
These cookies are soft and gooey in the middle and the demerara sugar
and nuts give them a crunchiness too.

125 g (4 oz) butter, plus
extra for greasing
125 g (4 oz) soft brown
sugar

a few drops of vanilla essence
50 g (2 oz) demerara sugar
1 egg

2 tablespoons unsweetened
orange juice
½ teaspoon salt
½ teaspoon bicarbonate of
soda

150 g (5 oz) self-raising
flour
50 g (2 oz) roasted
hazelnuts, chopped
75 g (3 oz) chocolate chips

Butter 2 large baking sheets. Heat the oven to Gas
Mark 4/180°C/350°F. Whisk the butter, the soft
brown sugar and the vanilla essence in a bowl until
fluffy. Then whisk in the demerara sugar and the egg
followed by the orange juice. Sift the salt and bicarbonate of soda with the flour, and whisk into the
mixture. Stir in the chopped hazelnuts and chocolate
chips.

Spoon piles of the mixture, roughly the size of a
large walnut, on to the baking sheets about 4–5 cm
(1½–2 inches) apart. Bake the cookies, one sheet at
a time, on the centre shelf of the oven for 14–16
minutes until the edges of the cookies are firm and
the centres slightly soft to a gentle touch. Leave the
cookies on the baking sheet for a few minutes and
then remove with a spatula and leave to cool on a
rack.
Makes 30–35

CHOCOLATE NUT CRESCENTS

125 g (4 oz) unsalted
butter
125 g (4 oz) caster sugar
25 g (1 oz) cocoa

2 tablespoons hot water
1 large egg (size 1–2),
whisked lightly
1 teaspoon vanilla essence

125 g (4 oz) ground
almonds
50 g (2 oz) plain flour,
sifted

25 g (1 oz) chopped toasted
hazelnuts
icing sugar, to decorate

Cream the butter with the caster sugar until light and
fluffy. Put the cocoa in a bowl with the hot water and
stir until smooth. Then beat into the creamed butter and sugar. Add the egg and the vanilla essence.
Finally, beat in the ground almonds, followed by
the flour, and stir in the chopped hazelnuts.

Heat the oven to Gas Mark 4/180°C/350°F. Cut
a 1 cm (½-inch) opening off one corner of a plastic
bag, spoon the biscuit mixture into the bag and
squeeze out in crescent shapes on to ungreased baking
sheets. Cook in the centre of the oven for 10 minutes.
Remove the biscuits carefully with a spatula and cool
on a wire rack. Store in an airtight container until
needed and dust generously with icing sugar through
a sieve before eating.
Makes about 40

ORANGE BUTTER SPICE BISCUITS

This American method of biscuit-making is so convenient. The roll of rich, soft dough will keep firm in the fridge for up to a fortnight. Just cut thin slices from it as you like, whenever you want a batch of freshly made biscuits. Within ten minutes you will be nibbling these crisp, light biscuits, which are a perfect accompaniment to ice cream and fruit fools. The quantities given here will make at least three batches of biscuits.

125 g (4 oz) butter
200 g (7 oz) caster sugar

1 large egg (size 2–3)
finely grated rind of
1 orange

250 g (8 oz) strong plain
flour

2 teaspoons mixed spice
½ teaspoon salt
2 teaspoons baking powder

Beat the butter and sugar until light and creamy. Thoroughly beat in the egg. Add the orange rind. Sift the flour with the spice, salt and baking powder and stir into the butter and egg mixture. Flour your hands and shape the dough into one long or two short rolls, about 2 inches (5 cm) thick. (If you find the dough too soft to shape, put it in the fridge until it is more manageable.) Wrap the roll in foil or cling-film and chill for at least 3 hours, more if possible.

To cook, heat the oven to Gas Mark 5/ 190°C/375°F, take the roll of dough from the fridge and, using a sharp knife, slice off about 10 –12 thin rounds and arrange on the baking sheet – well spaced out. Bake in the centre of the oven for 7–9 minutes, until a pale golden colour. Remove biscuits while hot with a palette knife and place on a cooling rack. Repeat with the rest of the dough when required.
Makes about 6 dozen biscuits

LEMON GINGER SHORTBREAD

You must hide this away in a tin or it will get eaten up too quickly! If you like you can use wholemeal flour which will give a nuttier taste and texture.
Pictured on pages 206/7.

250 g (8 oz) butter, plus
extra for greasing
125 g (4 oz) icing sugar

grated rind of 2 lemons
175 g (6 oz) plain flour

50 g (2 oz) cornflour
75 g (3 oz) ground rice

2 rounded teaspoons
ground ginger
caster sugar

Put the butter, the icing sugar and the grated lemon rind into a bowl and cream them together with a whisk. This doesn't need to be done very thoroughly. Mix the flour, cornflour, ground rice and ginger together in a bowl and then gradually whisk them into the creamed butter and sugar. Using floured hands gather up the dough, divide it in half and press it quickly into two buttered 20 cm (8-inch) sandwich tins. Prick all over with a fork. Heat the oven to Gas Mark 2/150°C/300°F. Bake the shortbread on the bottom shelf for 60 –70 minutes until it is a pale golden colour. Cut the shortbread into pieces in the tins while still hot. Sprinkle with caster sugar and leave until almost cold in the tin before carefully taking out with a spatula.
Makes about 16

MINCE PIES DE LUXE

Mince pies can be rather dry but here the mixture of the spicy mincemeat
with smooth cream cheese makes them a real luxury. To try and alleviate
any last-minute panic, I always make a large batch of mince pies
beforehand and put them in the freezer. I take them out and heat them up
as I need them and they taste perfect.

*250 g (8 oz) full cream
cheese*
50 g (2 oz) caster sugar

*500 g (1 lb) orange pastry
(below)*

*500 –625 g (1–1¼ lb)
mincemeat*

*a spot of milk
caster or icing sugar for
dusting*

First put the cream cheese and the 50 g (2 oz) caster
sugar into a bowl and beat until smooth. Preheat the
oven to Gas Mark 7/220°C/425°F. Knead the pastry
lightly and roll out rather more thickly than usual.
Using a 7 cm (3-inch) fluted pastry cutter, cut out 24
rounds, re-rolling the pastry as necessary, and line
greased patty tins with the rounds. Fill to about half
their depth with mincemeat. Then put a teaspoonful
of the beaten cream cheese mixture on top of the
mincemeat and smooth over. Roll out the remaining
pastry and with a smaller (5 cm /2¼-inch) fluted
cutter, cut out another 24 rounds. Moisten the underside of the rounds and place them on top of the filled
pies. Press the edges lightly together and make a small
slit in the top of each pie. Brush with cold milk and
bake in the centre of the oven for 15 –20 minutes
until light golden brown. The pastry is so deliciously
crumbly that it is best to let these mince pies cool
down before gently easing them from the tins with a
round- bladed knife.

Before serving either warm – which of course is
best – or cold, sprinkle them generously with caster
or icing sugar.
Makes 24

ORANGE PASTRY FOR MINCE PIES

This light, crumbly, rich pastry really complements
home-made mincemeat.

500 g (1 lb) plain flour
250 g (8 oz) butter

125 g (4 oz) lard

*grated rind of 1 large orange
orange juice*

Cut the fat into the flour and rub with your fingertips
until it resembles breadcrumbs. Stir in the grated rind.
With a knife, stir the orange juice into the pastry until
it just begins to stick together (if there isn't enough
juice add a spot of cold water). Gather into a ball, wrap
in foil or plastic and put into the fridge for half an hour
or more before using.
For 24 mince pies

Mince Pies De Luxe

WALNUT AND FRUIT BAKLAVA

Pictured on page 215.

For the syrup:
150 g (5 oz) granulated sugar
6 tablespoons water
1 tablespoon lemon juice
1 tablespoon rose-water or orange-flower water

For the pastry:
125 g (4 oz) unsalted butter, melted
250 g (8 oz) filo pastry
125 g (4 oz) walnuts, chopped coarsely
1 tablespoon soft light brown sugar
50 g (2 oz) sultanas
25 g (1 oz) currants

Make the syrup first. Dissolve the sugar in the water and lemon juice over a low heat. Bring it to the boil and boil fiercely for 2 minutes to thicken it slightly. Remove it from the heat and stir in the rose-water or orange-flower water. Allow to cool and then leave the syrup in the fridge. Preheat the oven to Gas Mark 3/160°C/325°F.

To make the baklava, brush a large, rather shallow, oblong dish or roasting tin, measuring about 30 x 45 cm (12 x 18 inches), with some of the melted butter. If your filo pastry is in very large sheets, cut them in half and keep the rest under a damp cloth until the moment you use them. Lay one sheet on the bottom of the dish, brush it with melted butter and continue in layers until you have used up a little under half the sheets, brushing with butter between each layer and then folding over the edges if necessary to fit the dish. Then evenly sprinkle over the chopped nuts, the brown sugar, the sultanas and the currants. Put on the remaining sheets of pastry, again brushing with butter between each and buttering the top piece as well. Then using a sharp knife cut diagonal lines about 2.5 cm (1 inch) apart across the pastry and then straight lines lengthways, making diamond shapes, without cutting right through.

Bake in the centre of the oven for 25 –30 minutes and then raise the heat to Gas Mark 7/220°C/425°F for another 8 –10 minutes, or until the baklava is a rich golden brown. Remove from the oven and pour the cold syrup all over the baklava and then leave it to cool. To serve, cut the pastries out of the tray.
Serves 6–8

ORANGE AND CURRANT PUFFS

250 g (8 oz) packet of puff pastry
finely grated rind of 1 large orange
25 g (1 oz) currants, chopped finely
25 g (1 oz) demerara sugar
½ teaspoon salt
25 g (1 oz) cold unsalted butter
caster sugar, for sprinkling

Roll out the puff pastry thinly to about 35 x 35 cm (14 x 14 inch) on a floured surface. Cut out circles with a 7 cm (3-inch) diameter fluted cutter, gathering up and re-rolling the pastry trimmings and ending up with an even number of circles. Put the grated orange rind into a bowl. Add the chopped currants and stir in the demerara sugar and salt. Spoon teaspoonfuls of the mixture on to the centre of half of the pastry circles. Cut the butter into the same number of pieces and put a piece on top of each pile of orange and currant mixture. Brush the edges of the filled circles with water. Place the remaining circles of pastry on top and press round the edges firmly to seal.

Heat the oven to Gas Mark 8/230°C/450°F. Lightly butter a large baking sheet and place the puffs on it. Brush the tops with water and sprinkle lightly with caster sugar. Bake just above the centre of the oven for 10 –15 minutes until puffed up and richly browned. Serve warm if possible.
Makes 10–12

SWEET RICE BALLS IN SCENTED CREAM

Some of the Indian sweets are too sweet even for my shamefully sweet tooth but a few of the concentrated milk sweetmeats, flavoured with cardamom and rose-water, are completely irresistible. Bengalis are the great sweetmeat makers and in Calcutta you see shops and stalls laden with an extraordinary variety. It's quite fun occasionally to make some at home. I treat them more like chocolates to eat after the meal than as a pudding, and they are a good accompaniment to fresh fruit.
Pictured on page 179.

For the rice balls:
600 ml (1 pint) milk
75 g (3 oz) milk powder
a few strands of saffron (optional)

75 g (3 oz) pudding rice
50 g (2 oz) soft light brown sugar
½ level teaspoon ground cardamom

15 g (½ oz) butter
25 g (1 oz) unsalted cashew nuts
25 g (1 oz) sultanas
about 25 g (1 oz) dessicated coconut

For the cream:
300 ml (½ pint) milk
50 g (2 oz) milk powder
2 teaspoons caster sugar
1 tablespoon rose-water

To make the rice balls, put the milk into a heavy saucepan and sprinkle in the milk powder. Stir to mix and add the saffron, if used. Add the rice and bring the milk to the boil, stirring all the time. Then simmer gently, stirring almost constantly, for about 15 minutes until very thick. Now stir in the brown sugar and the ground cardamom and remove the pan from the heat. Melt the butter in a frying pan over a medium heat. Add the cashew nuts and stir around for a moment or two just until the nuts are beginning to brown, add the sultanas and stir for a moment or two more until they are puffing up and browning. Stir the nuts and sultanas into the rice mixture and then turn everything into a bowl, cover it and leave until the mixture is completely cold, about 30 minutes.

Meanwhile, make the cream. Put the milk in a saucepan and add the milk powder and the caster sugar. Stir over a low heat, just to dissolve the milk powder and sugar and immediately remove from the heat. Stir in the rose-water and leave until cold. When the rice mixture is cold, roll it into walnut-sized balls in your hands and then roll these lightly in dessicated coconut. Arrange the balls in a fairly shallow serving dish – metal or glass looks best – and pour the scented cream all over them.

Serves 6–10

INDEX

Almond Dreams with Lychees 181
Anchovy-stuffed Mullet with Vegetable
    Stew 122
Anglo-chinese Pie 78
Anniversary Gâteau 162
apple 67, 188, 189, 197, 202
Apple, Cranberry and Rich Chocolate
    Pudding 189
Apples in Orange and Cardamom Fudge
    Sauce 202
Apricot and Clementine Sauce for Ham
    and Other Cold Meats 142
Apricot Ice Cream with Toasted
    Almonds 148
apricots
    dried 116, 117, 142, 148, 161, 166,
        200, 208
    fresh 69, 175, 199, 205
artichoke
    globe 74
    hearts 108
    jerusalem 103, 110
Athenian Jelly 177
aubergine 46, 134, 143
    first course 14, 17, 25, 138
    fish dishes 120, 124, 126
    meat dishes 66, 81, 84
avocado 22, 25, 31
Avocado Oranges 22
Avocado and Watercress Surprise 25

Baked Apricots Floating on Fresh Lime
    Sauce 205
Baked Aubergines with Fresh Mint
    Chutney 143
Baklava 220
Balinese Carrot Cake 208
banana 150, 159, 170, 182
Banana and Mint Meringue Ice Cream
    Cake 159
Banana and White Chocolate Mousse 182
Barbecue Meatballs with Surprise Centre
    61
beans
    broad 140
    butter 57
    haricot 57
    kidney 53, 57
    white kidney 102
Beef and Bean Hotpot 57
Beef and Mushroom Rissoles in Fresh
    Tomato Sauce 57
Bhatura Bread 145
Black Cherry Mousse Cake 160
Black Pearl Mushrooms 20

Bosporus Mussel Stew 124
Boxing Night Beef 61
Braised Beef in Walnut, Chilli and
    Chocolate Sauce 60
Brandy Sauce 141
Bread Sauce 142
broad beans 140
Brown Bread Sauce 142
Bulghur Flan with Pine Kernels 82
Burmese Fish Curry 124

cabbage
    green 119
    red 109, 117, 132
Canary Cake 170
carrots 20, 28, 133, 136
    in cakes 208
    in desserts 176, 178
celebration cake 211
celeriac 64
celery 21
Celery and Walnut Pies 21
Chapatis 145
cheese 40
    blue 62
    cottage 135
    cream 175, 218
    curd 62, 175
    full fat soft 134
    goat's 128, 133
    parmesan 144
Cheesecake Crécy 176
cherries, black 160
chick-peas 82, 127
chicken 94, 99, 101
    breast 18, 24, 36, 42, 43, 85, 93, 97, 98,
        99, 100
    joints 92, 96, 98, 100, 101
Chicken Baked in a Salt Crust with
    Rose-tinted Sauce 94
Chicken and Fish Casserole with Lemon
    98
Chicken and Mushroom Paprika 93
Chicken Noodles with Cashew Nuts in
    the Burmese Way 100
Chicken Roasted in Yogurt 93
Chicken and Smoked Oysters with
    Grilled Peppers in Saffron and Fresh
    Lime Sauce 98
Chicken Stuffed with Couscous 99
Chilled Almond and Garlic Soup 12
Chilled Aubergine and Raspberry Soup
    14
Chilled Brandy Sauce 141
Chinese Hedgehogs 41
Chinese Leaf and Broad Bean Salad 140
Chinese Salad Dressing 144
Chinoiserie of Rabbit with Jerusalem
    Slices 103

chocolate
    cake 165, 168, 172, 209, 210, 213
    dessert 158, 183, 189, 192, 204
    ice cream 148, 149, 156, 157
    savoury 60
    white 182
Chocolate Chip and Hazelnut Cookies
    216
Chocolate and Fresh Orange Bombe 157
Chocolate Lovers' Tart 192
Chocolate Nut Crescents 216
Chocolate Rum Marquise 183
Chocolate Swirl Ice Cream 148
Christina's Seafood Cradle 32
Christmas Cake 209, 211
Christmas Pudding 202
Chutney, Fresh Mint, with Coconut 143
Clear Chicken Ball and Watercress Soup
    36
clementines 142
coconut 143, 208
cod 33, 48, 118, 119, 124
    smoked 49, 98, 125
Cold Duck with Tuna Cream Sauce and
    Spring Onions 52
Cold Spiced Mushroom and Tomato
    Soup 12
courgettes 16, 25, 133
couscous 39, 99
crab 33
cranberries 151, 189, 212, 213
Cranberry Casket Filled with Gold 151
Cream of Potato and Saffron Soup with
    Courgettes 16
Creamy Aubergine Purée 17
Creamy Chicken Pasta 99
crème caramel 185
Crispy Chicken Joints with Piquant
    Sauce 96
Crunchy Stuffed Meatballs 39

Damson Dream 194
Dark Chocolate Cake 213
Dream of Damascus 85
Dream of Puddings with Elderflower
    Meringue 199
Dried Fruit Compote with Ginger and
    Rum 201
duck 52, 104, 106, 108, 109
    mallard 105
Duck with Gooseberry and Brazil Nut
    Stuffing 104
Duck Poached in Tea and Honey 106

Easter Daffodil Cake 173
Easter Ring 169
Eastern Promise 25
Egg and Vegetable Curry 46
Egyptian Pizza 37

elderflower 199
Exotic Ravioli 42

fennel 26, 49, 52, 73, 114, 126
Fillets of Plaice with Tropical Stuffing 48
Filo Apple Pie 188
Fish Baked in Cabbage Leaves 119
Fish Rolls with Spanish Sauce 49
Fish Sausages in a Golden Sauce with
  Spring Onions 118
French Dressing with Mustard and Garlic
  144
Fresh Apricot Cheesecake Ring 175
Fresh Mint Chutney with Coconut 143
Fresh Orange Ice Cream Cake 154
Fruit and Rum Loaf 212
Fruited Chocolate Christmas Cake 209
Fruited Galantine with Pigeon Breast 17

gammon 79
Ginger Pigeon with Honey, Apricots and
  Walnuts 117
Ginger Pork Steaks with Chinese
  Noodles 72
Glossy-top Avocado Gâteau 22
Glowing Ring 20
gnocchi 70
Golden Patties 28
Golden Purée with a Gratinée of Goat's
  Cheese 133
greengages 204
Grilled Aromatic Lamb Fillet with Fresh
  Coriander Yogurt 91
Grilled Chicken Strips, Indian-style 43
Grilled Duck Breast Slices with Parsnip
  and Wine Sauce 108
guava 198
Guinea Fowl Cooked in Artichoke Purée
  with Shallots and Lychees 110

haddock 48, 119
  smoked 49, 98
Harvester's Chicken 96
Hazelnut Meringue in a Crust 198
hazelnuts 104, 132, 198, 216
herring roes 53
honey 174, 204, 208, 212
Honeyed Apricot and Brandy Cake 208
Honeyed Greengages on a Chocolate and
  Walnut Crust 204

ice cream 148, 149, 150, 151, 153, 154,
  156, 157, 158, 159
Iced Chocolate Charlotte 149
Iced Lemon Soufflé in a Chocolate Case
  158
Indian-spiced Meatballs Stuffed with
  Curd Cheese 62

Indulgent Layer Cake 172
Intense Chocolate Cake with
  Redcurrants 168
Italian Green Sauce 144
Italian Moussaka 66

Jellied Cream of Spinach and Sorrel Soup
  16
jelly 177, 180, 181

Kate's Pie 60
Kibrizli Cake 214
kidney
  lamb's 39
  pig's 117
Kidney and Bacon Dumplings 39
kipper 50
kiwifruit 162, 184

Lamb and Aubergine Dome with Fresh
  Tomato Sauce 81
Lamb Cooked in Milk 90
Lamb Meatballs Poached in Tomato and
  Chick-pea Sauce 82
Lamb's Liver with Parsley and Buttered
  Leeks 88
lasagne 128
Leek and Parsnip Soup 36
leeks 26, 44, 88, 129, 132, 138, 140
Leeks in Two Dressings 140
Lemon Banana Ice Cream Charlotte 150
Lemon Ginger Shortbread 217
Lemon, Honey and Almond Cake with
  Creamy Lemon Parfait 174
Lemon Spice and Strawberry Delight 182
Levantine Lamb Pie 90
Little Mussel Pies 32
liver
  calf's 24
  lamb's 88
Luscious Lemon Ring 204
Lychee Lime Ring 186
lychees 180, 181, 184, 186

mango 24, 151, 158
Mango Chicken Salad 24
Mango Meringue Ice with Pineapple 158
Marinated Leg of Lamb with Porcini and
  Tomato Sauce 88
Marinated Scallop Salad 31
Marinated Shoulder of Lamb Stuffed
  with Swiss Chard, with a Tomato,
  Brandy and Cream Sauce 89
Marinated and Spiked Roast Leg of Pork
  79
Meat Loaf with Blue Cheese Filling 62
melon 201
Memsahib's Curried Chicken 92

Mince Pies de Luxe 218
Minced Lamb with Creamy Cheese
  Topping 86
Minced Pork with Apples and Spinach 67
Moghul Chicken 100
monkfish 120, 126
Monkfish Kebabs with Aubergine and
  Yogurt Sauce 120
Mouse's Picnic 193
moussaka 66
Mousseline for Captian Beale 50
mullet 122
mushrooms 12, 20, 57, 93, 109, 112,
  132, 138
  dried 88
  oyster 105
Mushrooms stuffed with Leek and
  Watercress Purée 138
mussels 32, 124
My Bubble and Squeak 74
My Darling Clementine 161
My Mother's Steak Tartare 38

New Year's Resolution 184
noodles 65, 72, 100
Nouvelle Terrine 18
Nuri Bey's Fresh Lemon Jelly 177

Onion, Brandy and Orange Sauce 141
Onion Tart with Olive Pastry 46
Orange and Almond Tart 186
Orange Butter Spice Biscuits 217
Orange, Cranberry, Almond and Honey
  Cake 212
Orange and Currant Puffs 220
Orange Pastry for Mince Pies 218
Orange and Strawberry Passion Torte 168
Orient Onions 137
Ossi Buchi with Green Lemon Sauce 63
Our Favourite Christmas Pudding 202
oysters, smoked 30, 38, 98

Pagoda Jelly 180
pancakes 200
parsnip, 36, 108, 132, 133, 136
Parsnip Timbales 136
passion-fruit 178, 184, 196
Passion-fruit and Fresh Lime Flan 196
Passion-fruit and Honey Soufflé 184
Passion-fruit Thrill 178
pasta 42, 52, 65, 70, 72, 99, 100, 128
peach 201
pear 24, 41, 193
Pear and Calf's Liver Flower 24
Pear and Pork Parcels 41
Peppers Par Excellence 138
Pera Palas Pie 84
Peruvian Potatoes 135

pheasant 114, 115
Pheasant Breast with Brandy Sauce 115
Pheasants with Fennel Sauce 114
Pheasants in Saffron Sauce 114
pigeon 17, 117
Pigeons with a Compote of Red
    Cabbage 117
Piglet pie 67
pineapple 158, 201
pizza 37
plaice 48, 49, 119
porcini 88
Pork, Onions and Mushrooms in Crispy
    Batter 43
Pork Rissoles Stuffed with Fennel 73
Pork Rolls Stuffed with Artichoke, with
    Mushroom and Mustard Sauce 74
Potatoes Roasted in their Skins with
    Olive Oil 135
Prawn Pasta 52
prawns 49, 52
Prize Pumpkin 97
Provençal Prune Tart 188
Prune and Walnut Lemon Syrup Cake
    164
Pudding for Parvati 178
pumpkin 97, 102, 128
Pumpkin and Goat's Cheese Lasagne
    with Yogurt and Cardamom 128

Quenelle-stuffed Pink Trout 125

rabbit 102, 103
Rabbit and Pumpkin with Mustard and
    White Kidney Beans 102
raspberries 14, 160, 162, 180
ravioli 42
Red cabbage, Parsnip and Hazelnut Salad
    132
Red Kidney Bean Salad with Streaky
    Pork 53
Red Mullet 122
redcurrants 168
Roast Barbary Duck Stuffed with Red
    Cabbage and Mushrooms 109
Roast Duck with Red Onions and
    Artichoke Hearts 108
Roast Pork with Apple and Walnut
    Stuffing 76
Roast Pork with Tomato and Tarragon
    Sauce 77
Roasted Mallards with Sweet Onion and
    Oyster Mushrooms 105
Roasted Monkfish with Aubergine and
    Cream Sauce 126
Rolled Pork and Potato Pie 68
Rolled and Stuffed Veal Escalopes 64
Roman Cobbler 70
Rum Butter 141

Saffron and Garlic Mashed Potatoes with
    Grated Courgettes 133
Saffron Sea Cakes 33
salmon
    fresh 121
    smoked 30
Salmon Fillets with a Special Cream
    Sauce 121
sardines 47
Scallop and Monkfish with Fennel in
    Saffron Yogurt Cream 126
scallops 31, 32, 126
Shiver Me Timbers 156
Smoked Fish and Fennel in Olive Oil 49
Smoked Oyster Surprises 30
Smoky Aubergine Purée with Pine
    Kernels 134
Soft and Dark Chocolate Cake 165
Soft Roe Salad 53
sorrel 16
Spain's Favourite Pudding 185
Spiced Duck with Prune and Hazelnut
    Stuffing 104
Spicy Beef and Guinness Pie 58
spinach 16, 63, 64, 67, 90, 127
Spinach Noodles with Veal and
    Sweetbread Sauce 65
Spinach Stuffed with Pork, Cheese and
    Mushrooms 70
Spring Lamb Pie 80
Springtime Eggs 28
Sprout Snow 134
sprouts 134
Squid Lequeitio 118
Star Leek Pie 129
Steamed Chicken Pudding with
    Chicory, Lemon and Ginger 101
Steamed Pork Pudding with Red Pepper
    and Green Peppercorns 68
Steamed Turkey Balls with Scarlet Sauce
    113
Straw Leeks with Spiced Mushrooms 132
strawberries 160, 162, 168, 182, 201
Strawberry and Pineapple Salad with
    Orange Cream 201
Stuffed Boned Shoulder of Venison with
    Creamy Onion Sauce 116
Stuffed Fillets of Plaice 119
Stuffed Pancake Clouds 200
Stuffed Pork Rissoles with Apricot and
    Onion Sauce 69
Stuffed Sardines 47
Stuffed Smoked Salmon Parcels 30
Stuffed Turkey Breasts in Chinese Pasties
    112
Sublime Scallops in their Shells 31
Summer Chicken 92
Sunday Special 197

Sweet Rice Balls in Scented Cream 221
Sweet Spiced Gammon 79
Sweet Sunday Salad 201
Sweet and Tender Lamb Cooked in Beer
    80
sweetbreads 65
Swiss chard 89

Tarte à l'Orange 190
Tea Leaf Eggs 29
Terrine of Broccoli 136
tomato 12, 40, 57, 113, 127
Tomatoes Stuffed with Pork and Cheese
    40
Tropical Splendour 198
trout 125
tuna 52, 63
turkey 17, 78, 93, 110, 111, 112, 113
Turkey Balls Kiev 110
Turkey in Puff Pastry 111
Turkey-stuffed Mushroom Puffs 112
Turkish Meatballs in Egg and Lemon
    Sauce 86
Turkish Pasties 44
Two Onion Soup 14

Unconventional Celebration Cake 211

Veal Roulade with Walnut and Tomato
    Sauce 64
Veal and Tuna Croquettes with Creamy
    Caper Sauce 63
Veal-stuffed Pork Rolls with Lemon and
    Parsley Sauce 76
Vegetable Consommé with Shredded
    Lettuce 13
Vegetables in a Light Crust 26
Vegetarian Indian 127
venison 116

Walnut and Fruit Baklava 220
Walnut Mousse Gâteau 166
Walnut Soup 13
watercress 25, 36, 138
Wellington Pies 38
White Lie Bombe 153
Whole Lemon and Almond Cake
    Coated with Chocolate 210
Whole Orange Pork and Mushroom
    Casserole 72
Winter Raspberries 180
Wonder Bombe 166
Wrapped Fish Quenelles with Saffron
    and Vermouth Sauce 48

Yellow Pepper Tart 45
Yogurt with Aubergine, Mint and
    Cumin 143